ALSO BY GEORGE M. TABER

*Judgment of Paris: California vs. France and the Historic
1976 Paris Tasting That Revolutionized Wine*

*To Cork or Not To Cork: Tradition, Romance, Science,
and the Battle for the Wine Bottle*

In Search of Bacchus: Wanderings in the Wonderful World of Wine Tourism

A TOAST

TO

BARGAIN WINES

———————◆———————

How Innovators, Iconoclasts, and Winemaking Revolutionaries
Are Changing the Way the World Drinks

GEORGE M. TABER

SCRIBNER

New York   London   Toronto   Sydney   New Delhi

SCRIBNER
A Division of Simon & Schuster, Inc.
1230 Avenue of the Americas
New York, NY 10020

First Scribner edition November 2011

SCRIBNER and design are registered trademarks of The Gale Group, Inc., used under license by Simon & Schuster, Inc., the publisher of this work.

For information about special discounts for bulk purchases, please contact Simon & Schuster Special Sales at 1-866-506-1949 or business@simonandschuster.com.

The Simon & Schuster Speakers Bureau can bring authors to your live event. For more information or to book an event, contact the Simon & Schuster Speakers Bureau at 1-866-248-3049 or visit our website at www.simonspeakers.com.

Manufactured in the United States of America

1   3   5   7   9   10   8   6   4   2

ISBN 978-1-4516-4436-4
ISBN 978-1-4391-9518-5 (pbk)
ISBN 978-1-4391-9520-8 (ebook)

Prière du Vigneron
Mon Dieu, donnez-moi
La santé pour longtemps,
De l'amour de temps en temps
Du boulot pas trop souvent,
Mais du Vin tous l'temps.

Prayer of the Wine Grower
My God, give me
Health for a long time,
Love from time to time
A job not too often
But wine all the time.

Contents

Introduction

Every time I open a bottle of wine, I thank my lucky stars that I am living in the golden age of wine. Whether shopping in a local wine store, seeking out the latest offerings on the Internet, or ordering a bottle in a restaurant, I have an incredible array of choices at a wide range of prices. There is a wine for every taste, from sweet to dry, and every wallet, from fat to lean.

Though people have been making wine for some nine thousand years, during most of that period, good wine was produced in a relatively small part of Western Europe, and many people thought that truly great wine came only out of France. Today, however, the wine business has a global reach, and no single country or company can control the market. Large-scale wine production spreads from Cape Horn, South Africa, and New Zealand's South Island to the north in Britain, where in recent years some interesting sparkling wines have been made. Even Canada is now famous for ice wines. As a result of all this competition, today the consumer is king.

In addition to widespread growth, there has been a dramatic increase in the quality of the wine being produced. A huge difference long existed between the top of the market, the famous French First Growths, and the daily wine drunk by the masses, which the French called *vin ordinaire*—and it was indeed very ordinary. The chasm, though, has dramatically narrowed in the last generation. British wine critic Jancis Robinson has noted: "The irony is that just as the difference in price between best and worst wines is greater than it has ever been, the difference in quality is narrower than ever before." Outstanding wines such as Richebourg from Burgundy remain wonderful, but now less expensive Pinot Noirs from Oregon or New Zealand are also very good. Enological knowledge today flows easily from one region

1

to another, and winemakers around the world have adopted best-practices procedures and invested heavily in the latest equipment. That is particularly true in Argentina, Chile, and South Africa.

Elliott Morss, a wine connoisseur and researcher, as well as a former Harvard professor and economist for the International Monetary Fund, in 2010 wrote, "There are people in the world who can actually tell the difference between a Romanée-Conti vintage 1990 and vintage 1991. Amazing! For the wine expert, a good part of the enjoyment in drinking wine is the ability to make such fine distinctions. But the vast majority of people who drink wine (myself included) have difficulty distinguishing between a wine rated 88 and 95 by WS [*Wine Spectator*]."

During the past few years, a group of young iconoclasts have begun challenging conventional wine wisdom with bold new ideas. They don't live within the fences that an earlier generation built. They are trashing the rules, breaking the molds, and creating new production models. The innovators that you will meet in these pages are raising fundamental questions about how consumers learn about wine, how people taste, how judges select winning wines, and above all how much consumers should pay. They are changing the wine market in ways never seen before, and the old *vin ordinaire* is becoming something *extraordinaire*. These iconoclasts are the driving force behind the movement that is making better wines available to the masses.

I'd like to dedicate this book to the numerous people who have approached me since the 2005 publication of my first wine book, *Judgment of Paris,* with a simple question: Could you recommend a good wine that costs less than $10?

It's not as difficult as one might imagine. James T. Lapsley, a professor of wine economics at the University of California–Davis, notes that California produces 60 percent of all the wine consumed in the United States, and half of that sells for less than $5 a bottle. In fact, good $10 bottles are available from all over the world. Critics and consultants, who recommend what wines people should drink, rarely talk or write about them. It's the greatest story never told.

PART ONE

A Global Business in Turmoil

In the past few decades and without much public attention, the wine business has gone through many seismic shifts. Countries that once ruled the market, such as France, are dramatically losing their share. At the same time, new producers in the United States, Australia, and Chile have dramatically increased the quality of their products and become major international players. There is also a large glut of good wine out there that is likely to be the dominant factor in the business for years to come. All those trends are good news for bargain hunters. Even Queen Elizabeth II, who serves five thousand bottles a year to guests, spends cautiously. Jancis Robinson, a member of the team that advises Her Majesty on wines, writes: "By far the majority of the wines we buy are . . . inexpensive New Zealand Sauvignon Blanc and the most basic red Bordeaux." A royal favorite is Italy's Rosso Piceno, which several wineries produce and usually sells for $8 to $10 in the United States.

CHAPTER ONE

Embarrassing Moments in Wine History

In 1863, Englishman Thomas George Shaw published a delightful book entitled *Wine, the Vine, and the Cellar* that painted an insider's picture of the British wine trade in the early and mid-nineteenth century. He recounts how, in the 1820s, as a young clerk and salesman for a London port and sherry house, he used to play a trick on the venerated wine tasters who worked alongside him at the docks, where wine arrived from the continent. He would pour two glasses from exactly the same wooden barrel, give them to two tasters, and ask which they thought was better. The men would sample each wine, then try it again and again until they invariably declared that although the two were similar, one glass had "rather more of this or that than the other" and was therefore definitely superior. Shaw wrote, "I kept my own counsel, but was convinced forty years ago, and the conviction remains to this day, that in wine-tasting and wine-talk there is an enormous amount of humbug."

As the French say, *plus ça change, plus c'est la même chose (the more things change, the more they remain the same)*. So-called wine experts still pour out their views on paper, on the Internet, and anywhere people will listen, and those opinions can determine whether a wine consumer will spend hundreds of dollars on a prized bottle for some special evening. And much of the tasting and talk, then and now, remains humbug.

Blind wine tastings, when people cannot see the brand of the wine they are drinking, are unfailingly honest. They can also be very humbling. When the identity of a wine is unknown, nothing stands between the person's taste buds and what's in the glass. The taster is forced to decide whether he or she likes the wine only on the basis of his or her senses. Does the wine taste like some wondrously exotic fruit or does it resemble nondescript sugar water?

Seeing a wine label dangerously prejudices anyone's opinion. As Jancis Robinson has written, "It is absolutely staggering how important a part the label plays in the business of tasting. If we know that a favorite region, producer, or vintage is coming up, we automatically start relishing it—giving it every benefit of the tasting doubt." Judges are only human and have their predilections, whether they will admit them or not. That's why there is no substitute for a blind tasting, where the taster knows little more than the color of the wine and perhaps the grape variety. Michael Broadbent, a famous British taster, admitted, "A sight of the label is worth fifty years' experience. A cynical truism, for what an impressionable lot we are! Even the most disciplined taster is biased by the mere glimpse of a label, even the shape of the bottle."

Thomas George Shaw's tastings at the London docks were not the last instances of people mistaking a wine when they didn't know its origin. In an oft-repeated anecdote, Britain's Harry Waugh, a leading wine expert from the 1940s to the 1960s, who traveled the world drinking great wines and writing books about them, was once asked if he had ever mistaken a red Bordeaux, which is made usually with Cabernet Sauvignon grapes, for a red Burgundy, which has only Pinot Noir. His quip answer: "Not since lunch."

I was lucky enough to be the only journalist present at one of the most famous cases of wine confusion, which took place in Paris in May 1976. It was an event that Anthony Dias Blue, the American food and wine critic, has called the "most important wine tasting of the [twentieth] century." The wines being sampled that day were some of the best Chardonnays from Burgundy, such as Bâtard-Montrachet Ramonet-Prudhon and Puligny-Montrachet Les Pucelles Domaine Leflaive, and leading Bordeaux reds, including Château Haut-Brion and Château Mouton Rothschild. The French wines were tasted blind alongside unknown California Chardonnays, including Chalone and David Bruce, as well as Cabernet Sauvignons, such as Mayacamas and Ridge Monte Bello. The judges included some of the world's most eminent wine experts: sommeliers at prestigious French restaurants, the editor of France's leading wine magazine, and famous winery owners. But during the tasting, those prestigious judges became totally confused and couldn't even accurately distinguish which wines were French and which were from California. At the end of the day, they selected a California Chardonnay (Chateau Montelena) and a California Cabernet Sauvignon (Stag's Leap Wine Cellars) as best in the white and red categories. The Californians were delighted, while the French judges were shocked and suffered the wrath of their compatriots, who condemned them for rendering such an outrageous decision.

Hardy Rodenstock, a German collector of old bottles of wine, was well known in the 1980s for uncovering wine treasures, although some of those finds later turned out to be fakes that left experts with red faces to match the red wines. Thomas Jefferson had supposedly purchased the most famous of the Rodenstock bottles in the 1780s, when he was the American minister to Paris. Rodenstock wouldn't reveal how he had uncovered the bottles, saying only that they had been recently discovered in a Paris building that was being demolished. The bottles even had Jefferson's initials on them. What more proof of authenticity did anyone need?

In December 1985, the billionaire media mogul Malcolm Forbes bought at auction one of the bottles, a 1787 Lafite, for $156,000, which remains the highest price ever paid for a single bottle of wine. Although there were some doubts about the authenticity of the Rodenstock bottles, some of the most famous names in the wine world, such as Robert M. Parker Jr. and Hugh Johnson, were enthusiastic about the wonderful wines. Broadbent, the world's foremost authority on historic wines, gave them his unofficial stamp of approval by running the auction of Rodenstock's bottles, implicitly vouching for them. The fight over the authenticity of the wines is still going on in court, but it is now generally believed that they were all fakes. Rodenstock insists the wines are authentic, but skeptics say he most likely put wine of unknown origin and quality into old bottles and passed them off as historic masterpieces. Benjamin Wallace recounted the story of this great wine hoax in *The Billionaire's Vinegar: The Mystery of the World's Most Expensive Bottle of Wine.*

On June 3, 1986, Rodenstock and several top wine experts were at Château Mouton to taste a 1787 bottle of Branne-Mouton, the prior name of the winery. Broadbent sampled it and described it as having a "rich, warm, whole meal, gingery smell." Going over the top, he said it smelled like "dunked ginger nuts." Rodenstock said it resembled "lovely coffee." Jancis Robinson was smitten, calling the wine "the most exciting liquid I ever expect to drink."

No one in the room voiced any doubts about the authenticity of the 1787 wine, and Broadbent provided the final judgment: "I thought it would be a bit acidic, a bit decayed, but there wasn't a trace. . . . The wine is genuine. No doubt about it."

It is now generally believed that Rodenstock had taken in all those experts, and the 1787 Branne-Mouton was a fake.

E. & J. Gallo is the largest wine company in the world. Its labs in Modesto, California, have been called the best private enology research center. Gallo wines might not rank among the world's finest, but no one says anything against the expertise and professionalism of the winery's staff.

In the aftermath of the 2005 hit movie *Sideways,* Pinot Noir, which the film celebrated, became the hot wine for American consumers. They couldn't get enough of it, and wineries scrambled to keep up with demand. Gallo's Red Bicyclette Pinot Noir, which proudly noted on its label that the wine was made with French grapes, cost about $7 and flew off shelves. Between January 2006 and March 2008, Gallo bought 135,334 hectoliters of Pinot Noir from Languedoc-Roussillon, enough for 18 million bottles of wine. Cost: €4 million ($5.2 million).

French wine inspectors, however, began suspecting that something was amiss. The whole region traditionally produced only about 50,000 hectoliters a year, but Gallo was buying nearly three times as much. Moreover, a wine merchant who played a key role in the Gallo purchases was paying just €58 ($87) per hectoliter for Pinot, while the official price was €97 ($145). The cost of other grape varieties at the time, though, was €45 ($68). Experts suspected that Gallo was getting a mix of Merlot or Syrah, although the three types of grape are entirely different. Pinot Noir is delicate and known for its elegance, while Merlot has a medium body and Syrah is big and powerful.

In February 2010, a French court convicted a dozen people of selling fake Pinot Noir wine. The companies received fines ranging from €3,000 ($4,000) to €180,000 ($250,000), and jail terms of between one month and six, which were all suspended. The court said those convicted had illegally pocketed €7 million ($9 million).

Gallo was never accused of being part of the scam, unless you consider it a crime to be unable to taste the difference between Pinot Noir and Merlot or Syrah. Gina Gallo, winemaker and granddaughter of the family, later said, "I haven't tasted the offending wine that often, and we're committed to the Languedoc, especially Limoux, as a source of Pinot. But I admit it was something of a disaster."

Why didn't the Gallo empire pick up on something in the eighteen million bottles of supposed Pinot Noir? How could all those experts not recognize the difference between Pinot Noir and Merlot or Syrah? In addition, why didn't one of the millions of Americans who drank the Red Bicyclette Pinot Noir lodge a complaint? A lawyer for one of the condemned French firms attempted to explain the scandal away by saying, "Not a single American consumer complained."

There have been many other occasions when people misjudged wines because they didn't have the comfort of knowing what had been poured into their glass. If the world's best experts sometimes mix up a rarefied Bordeaux First Growth with pedestrian plonk, how are average consumers supposed to tell them apart? That is not to say that any $5 bottle is just as good as a 2005 Domaine de la Romanée-Conti Montrachet that costs $4,000 a bottle. It isn't. Yet these incidents raise questions about the professional tasters and other experts who tell average consumers what wines they should drink. Clearly, wine consumers should not be buying a bottle simply because it is expensive or because some famous person says it's good. People should decide for themselves which wines to drink no matter the price or the pedigree. They may be pleasantly surprised by what they discover.

CHAPTER TWO

Booms, Busts, and Bargains

For the last forty years, the American wine business has been enduring cycles of good times and bad. Prices go up and winemakers are delighted, but consumers are annoyed. Prices go down and the public is happy, but producers complain. There are too many bottles for sale, or not enough. Those conflicting trends play an important role in the wines people drink and what they pay for them.

The person best suited to explain what has been going on and predict what is likely to happen is Jon Fredrikson, the keeper of Napa Valley's secrets. As the owner, along with his wife, Eileen, of Gomberg, Fredrikson & Associates, a market research and consulting service for the California wine business, he not only has the best information on the wine-market trends but has also worked with wineries at crucial points in their corporate histories.

Early each year, in good times and bad, Fredrikson puts together the definitive report on California wine sales during the previous twelve months. The study is based on insider information that wineries share with him. These are numbers they would not give to the press, public, or maybe even their families, but they provide them to Fredrikson because they know he will not reveal a company's individual results.

Fredrikson also acts as a confidential advisor to wineries as they develop corporate strategies, especially when they are looking to sell their businesses. For many years, Fredrikson was a member of the private board of advisors for the Winiarski family, owners of Napa's famed Stag's Leap Wine Cellars. He helped them work through issues of possible succession, and eventually helped develop the strategy to sell the winery in July 2007 for $185 million to a partnership of Italian wine legend Piero Antinori and Washington's Chateau Ste. Michelle Wine Estates.

Fredrikson and his wife live in sylvan splendor on bumpy Ware Road in Woodside, California, a retreat for such Silicon Valley legends as Steve Jobs, Gordon Moore, and Larry Ellison, as well as singer Joan Baez and actress Michelle Pfeiffer. The much-feared San Andreas Fault runs right through town. From their deck full of flowers, the Fredriksons look out at the redwoods, oaks, and firs of the Santa Cruz Mountains that separate them from the Pacific Ocean. Walls are decorated with old ads for California wines featuring Hollywood stars such as Orson Welles, Jane Russell, and Lucille Ball, as well as other artifacts of wine history.

In his nearly half century in the California wine business, Fredrikson has seen the good times and the bad: the periods when winemakers could hardly give away their bottles, and also the years of wine mania, when they were forced to allocate stock to consumers and restaurants. He knows about the icon wineries that sell their product for hundreds of dollars a bottle and get breathless attention from press and public, and also the wineries getting little, if any, notice selling inexpensive wines with perhaps high quality but low prestige. Fredrikson watches all of them equally. So when I wanted to get the inside story on what's been happening in the wine business, I drove down bumpy Ware Road.

As Fredrikson explained to me, the international wine business in recent years has been going through what Charles Dickens would have called the best of times and the worst of times. It is the best of times for wine consumers but the worst of times for many producers, especially for traditional European wineries.

French winemakers, who were once the unchallenged rulers of the global business, have been particularly hard hit in recent years. Local consumption of *vin ordinaire* has been plummeting since the 1960s because of a shift in their domestic market to beer and nonalcoholic drinks, and because of tough drunk-driving penalties. French wine has also fallen out of favor with many consumers abroad, especially Americans, because many of them have become too expensive and their style is not in sync with new-world drinkers. The most famous Bordeaux wines continue to sell well, but less prestigious French ones are suffering. Some four hundred premium Bordeaux wines are sold for high prices *en primeur*—before they are even bottled—but there are five thousand wineries in the region and many of them are struggling. The French share of shelf space in American wine shops has also shrunk dramatically in recent years, as merchants make room for wines from Australia, Chile, and Australia. "In one generation," said Bertrand Praz, purchasing manager of Grand Chais de France, a leading wine exporting company, "we lost twenty to thirty percent of the share of our principal markets."

At the same time, however, wine prices in the past few decades have been soaring. The production of the world's great vineyards has not increased that much, but demand has been driving up the cost of the most-sought-after labels. Prized vintages of the most famous wines now top $1,000 a bottle.

This has been due to the influx of new wine consumers, especially the nouveaux riches, first from the United States, then Japan, and more recently China and India. A handful of iconic products such as the First Growths of France and a few international stars like Australia's Grange, Spain's Vega Sicilia, Italy's Sassicaia, and California's Screaming Eagle sell out almost as soon as they reach the market. In May 1787, when Thomas Jefferson visited the famous Château Haut-Brion vineyard in Bordeaux, few people outside France, Holland, and England bought its wine. The vineyard is only slightly bigger than it was at the end of the seventeenth century, but the market for its wine now stretches from Bordeaux to Beijing. Wealthy wine drinkers are often slaves to conspicuous consumption, a theory that American sociologist and economist Thorstein Veblen developed in the early twentieth century. Some wealthy people, Veblen contended, have so much money that spending hundreds, or even thousands, of dollars for a bottle of wine means little to them. The prestige of drinking the wine or giving it as a gift is all that counts. Most of the world will unfortunately never taste the wines Jefferson drank. At the same time, however, we can enjoy many wines of excellent quality at low prices. Jefferson never had the broad selection that consumers now experience. It's not such a bad thing that wine prices have soared. Not everyone can afford to drive a Maserati, but that doesn't mean they have to walk.

People, of course, pay prices for a host of products that bear no relationship to their inherent values. A Rolex Oyster watch can cost more than $10,000, but it doesn't tell time that much better than a Timex selling for $25. At the peak of the tulip mania in Holland, in February 1637, a tulip bulb sold for ten times the annual salary of a skilled worker. A tulip bulb costing only a few pennies undoubtedly gave someone just as much pleasure when it bloomed.

Some, perhaps many, consumers pay more for wine in expectation that the costly wine must be better. Ernest Gallo, cofounder of California's E. & J. Gallo Winery, used to recount the lesson he learned in his early days in the wine business on sales trips to New York City in the 1930s. He would offer prospective clients two glasses of the same red wine and tell them that one cost five cents a bottle and the other ten cents a bottle. Gallo said that buyers almost invariably chose the ten-cent one.

Wineries have long been making claims about the superiority of their wines based on the outstanding land where their grapes were grown. Owners trying to get the best possible price for their product have to find something that makes their vineyards unique and thus worth the high prices. What's special about one wine that makes it different from what is being produced at the winery down the road? The sun is the same; the grapes are often alike; the two winemakers use the same equipment and technology. So why should one bottle cost hundreds of times more than another?

The answer may be found in the ground. Wineries create a cult around their unique soil, or *terroir*. The practice has been going on for a long time. The top wines of the Roman Empire in the first century came from the Latium and Campania areas south of Rome, and there was even then a pecking order of quality and price. Later the French established their First Growths on the basis of the price for which the wines sold, which in turn was determined by the vineyards. In the 1970s, Beaulieu Vineyard in Napa Valley demanded high prices for its wines when a creative promoter came up with the idea that they were better because of the "Rutherford dust" where the grapes grew. Thomas George Shaw would certainly have called that "humbug." But it's a marketing ploy that has paved the road to riches for many small wineries. And the smaller the vineyard, the better. Pomerol's Château Pétrus has only twelve acres of vineyards and produces about twenty-five thousand bottles a year. Wine enthusiasts around the world are willing to spend whatever it takes to buy just one bottle. That creates scarcity and drives up prices.

The story is dramatically different outside Europe. Spanish conquistadores planted vines in Chile and Argentina in the sixteenth century, and the Dutch started making wine in South Africa in 1659. Winemaking skills also spread to the United States and Australia. Those countries actually had more reliable climates for grape growing and planted vast areas, using all the latest technology. Europeans, though, viewed the newcomers with haughty disdain. André Simon, an Anglo-French wine expert and critic, wrote in 1919, "In the old world, winemaking is an art; in the new world it is an industry."

Prohibition, which lasted from 1919 to 1933, was devastating for American wine. Consumers in the dry years had switched to cocktails, and wine consumers were largely immigrants who often made their own. Roper Associates, a polling company, did a study showing that drinking wine was considered an "old world custom" for the elderly. The most popular wines were locally produced port, sherry, sauterne, burgundy, and muscatel that bore little resemblance to their European counterparts. Lingering state and city restrictions made it illegal to drink in many places. Alcohol became legal in Kansas only in 1948, Oklahoma in 1959, and Mississippi in 1966. In 1970, thirty-two states still had local prohibition laws.

Wine was drunk in the 1940s and 1950s largely in New York City and only a few isolated cities, such as San Francisco, Chicago, and Miami. The hot wines in the United States during the 1950s were Segesta, a red from Sicily, and Bucalossi, a Chianti in a wicker basket that sold for $8 a case. Mateus and Lancers, imports from Portugal, were just beginning to catch on. Domestic best sellers were Almaden, Paul Masson, and Gallo, plus Mogen David and Manischewitz kosher wines. But in the 1960s, business finally started to pick up. In December 1967, the first shipments of Italy's Riunite, a sparkling Lambrusco, arrived in New York City, and soon the brand was selling millions of cases a year.

The most important American wine company in those days was E. & J. Gallo, which was on its way to becoming the biggest in the world. Gallo had its headquarters in Modesto in California's Central Valley, the home of inexpensive bulk wine. Gallo, though, bought lots of premium Napa Valley grapes and blended them with lower-quality wine. Ernest Gallo in those days had a fairly straightforward approach in deciding which wines to make. "I'm not too particularly interested in how deep the color is and how pronounced the bouquet is and how high is the total acid and how low is the sugar," he once told an interviewer. "To me, is it something I enjoy drinking and want more? If so, then it's good. And if it's not, I don't think it's good, regardless."

Two of Gallo's early successes in table wines were Hearty Burgundy and Chablis, a generic red and a generic white that had no relation to the French wines made with those names. Hearty Burgundy was made with Petite Sirah and Zinfandel grapes, while the Chablis contained French Colombard and Chenin Blanc. The quality, though, was remarkably good, and the wine cost only about $1 for a standard bottle. In 1966, Britain's Hugh Johnson, one of the first international wine gurus, wrote in his book entitled simply *Wine*, "Most of the cheap Burgundies of California are simple, clean, dry red wines of at least as high a quality as *vin ordinaire* in France, and generally higher. In this field the enormous firm of Gallo produces admirable carafe wine for well under a dollar a bottle." In 1972, a *Los Angeles Times* wine critic called Hearty Burgundy "the best wine value in the country today." The price: $1.25. It seems that good inexpensive wine always finds a market.

On the first working day in January 1970, Jon Fredrikson entered that slowly awakening world of American wine, when he started a job with Joseph E. Seagram & Sons, a Canadian liquor company. Fredrikson had studied economics at Colby College in Maine, had a Fulbright Scholarship in Nicaragua, then earned an MBA at Columbia University before serving in the U.S. Navy during the Vietnam War. After leaving the military in 1969, he went to New York City and landed at Seagram. One of the first things he did was to sign up for the prestigious Grossman Beverage Program, which introduced him to wine. He later took Grossman's advanced wine course, where he sampled the best European vintages of the 1950s and 1960s. Fredrikson quickly became the wine guy on the financial side of Seagram, which took him to France for more tastings and eventually to Northern California.

A host of big corporations were then moving into America's wine country to profit from the expected boom that market studies done by Bank of America and Arthur D. Little, a consulting company, promised was about to take place. Wine sales were growing fast, and the reports showed per capita consumption going off the charts. In addition to Seagram, other big companies, such as Nestlé, Coca-Cola, and Pillsbury, began planting vineyards in order to increase production to meet the new demand. Seagram, for example, put in a vineyard in Monterey south of San Francisco. As a sign of the naïveté of the time, the company planted 96 percent red-wine grapes in an area better suited for white varieties.

Jon Fredrikson's responsibility increased at Seagram as the company's wine business expanded. While spending more and more time in Northern California, he was also developing a relationship with Eileen Costales, who worked for the upmarket retailer Joseph Magnum as director of operations. Eileen had grown up near Tranquillity, California, on the west side of the rich Central Valley, the daughter of a farmer who cultivated, among other products, Angus cattle and grapes. She left the farm for the University of California at Berkeley, where she got a degree in business administration. Soon the couple was talking about marriage, and Jon began looking for a dream place to live. His quest eventually ended at the end of Ware Road in Woodside. Jon and Eileen were married in June 1977, but it took more than two years to construct their house. They had two children by the time they finally moved, in November 1979.

By the mid-1980s, however, the bloom was off the boom for California's wine business. The big companies had made excessively optimistic assumptions about the growth of wine consumption and had planted vineyards or signed contracts to buy more grapes than they needed. Soon those corporations were rushing for the exits. Coca-Cola left in 1981, and Seagram brought most of its California staff back to New York City. Fredrikson, though, decided to remain in California and in 1982 resigned from the company. At the time, he didn't have another job in hand, but he was confident he could find something that would combine his analytical skills in finance and his inside knowledge of the California wine business. When Fredrikson began looking around, he almost immediately focused on Louis R. Gomberg Associates, a market-research company based in San Francisco that specialized in the wine trade. It seemed like a perfect fit.

White-bearded Lou Gomberg was a former lawyer and journalist who published *The Gomberg Report,* the definitive market-research publication on California wine trends. He also helped put together some of the biggest transactions among wineries, including the 1964 sale of the historic Inglenook Winery to United Vintners. Born in Minnesota in 1907, Gomberg had been around California wine since just after Prohibition ended. He knew everyone important in the California trade, and they all respected him. But by then he was in his late seventies, and Fredrikson thought he might be interested in slowing down or selling his business, which needed some technical updating to join the digital age. Gomberg was still writing his newsletters on an antique manual typewriter, crunching his numbers on an antediluvian mechanical calculator, and storing statistics in loose-leaf binders. When the young man approached the older one about a sale, Gomberg replied, "I'm not tired of working, so why should I retire?" But later he admitted to Fredrikson that he had been looking for someone "worthy" to take over the business. After a few meetings, Gomberg concluded that Fredrikson was that person and sold him the company in 1983. The founder stayed on for a few months, but Fredrikson was quickly running the business. Small companies have a way of sucking wives into the operation, and Eileen was soon working with Jon collecting data. Jon wrote the first computer program for the *Gomberg Report* while on a Mexican vacation. Soon after, he changed the name to the *Gomberg-Fredrikson Report*.

Fredrikson's timing could have been better. California's wine business was about to hit its most dire period since Prohibition. After growing steadily through the 1960s, 1970s, and early 1980s, per capita wine consumption in the United States began falling. From 1987 to 1995, it dropped from 2.43 gallons per resident to 1.77 gallons. As a result, there was a glut of unsold wine on the market, a situation made worse by that rush of planting in the 1970s.

Another antialcohol movement, which Maynard Amerine, an influential professor in the wine program at the University of California–Davis, called "neo-Prohibition," exacerbated the situation. Increased drunk-driving accidents and the belief that wine, beer, and liquor were stepping-stones to other drugs made everything worse. Mothers Against Drunk Driving was founded in 1980 and soon had a strong following. President Ronald Reagan's wife, Nancy, started a crusade preaching that people should "Just Say No" to both alcohol and drugs. She and Surgeon General C. Everett Koop lumped wine and marijuana together, calling them "gateway drugs" to narcotics, and the Center for Science in the Public Interest pushed the same agenda. Bottled water made its debut, and the drink of choice at business lunches became Perrier with lime.

In October 1975, John De Luca, the former deputy mayor of San

Francisco, took over as president of California's powerful Wine Institute, then largely controlled by Central Valley producers, who made inexpensive wines. Some of his board members, such as Robert Mondavi, argued for fighting the antialcohol campaign with a major public relations initiative that would include endorsements for wine drinking from newsman Walter Cronkite, the most trusted man in America, and Father Theodore Hesburgh, the esteemed president of the University of Notre Dame. De Luca, though, wanted to steer the organization toward a greater role in public policy discussions at both the state and the national level. De Luca eventually won the debate over strategy, and winery owners began making trips to Sacramento and Washington, D.C., to argue that scientific, publicly funded research showed that wine consumed in moderation was healthful. In 1982, a delegation of thirty people, mostly winery owners, went to Washington for a weeklong visit and had meetings with not only the gang of Californians that Ronald Reagan had gathered in the White House but also Republican and Democrat Congressional leaders. The highlight of the trip was a wine tasting in the U.S. State Department.

The 1982 harvest in California was particularly large, which created a huge oversupply at a time when sales were slipping. Out of the wine glut, though, came new inexpensive wines. Frank Schoonmaker, an East Coast–based importer and author of some of the earliest American wine books, had long been leading a lonely crusade to call wines by the type of grape that went into them, rather than by European names such as Rhine, Burgundy, or Chablis. In 1985, Glen Ellen, a Sonoma County winery, picked up Schoonmaker's suggestion for its 1983 vintage that was just being bottled and named new products by their grape variety: Chardonnay, Cabernet Sauvignon, or Merlot. The biggest word on the label after the Glen Ellen brand was the name of the grape. The wines sold in standard-size bottles at a suggested retail price of $5 for two bottles. The bottle also had a cork, rather than the screwcap that sealed the bottles of inexpensive jug wines. Glen Ellen's wines were a classy, attractive product at a great price.

Americans loved the simple concept, especially in Chardonnay form. Glen Ellen enjoyed a quick market hit and a small army of imitators followed its lead, offering similar products at the same price. Whereas in the 1970s, Americans in restaurants might have asked the waiter for a glass of "white wine," by the mid-1980s they were ordering a glass of "Chardonnay."

In the spring of 1984, Chalone Vineyard in Monterey County was planning a public stock offering, a brave step in the life of any company, particularly a winery when the grape glut was still causing headaches. While preparing a prospectus, Chalone asked Jon Fredrikson to do some market research that would make the case that sales of premium wines, such as the ones Chalone made, were growing rapidly and had a great future. Realizing that he had to back up such a thesis with solid statistics, Fredrikson asked key wineries to break down their sales by price category.

The resulting document described the American wine market with a clarity not previously available. For starters, Fredrikson divided sales into two major segments: low-cost popular and more expensive premium, which "generally sold at retail prices greater than $7 per 750 ml bottle. Premium-priced table wines are characterized by production in small quantities." That sector was growing 20 percent annually. Chalone's argument: "The Company's wines are sold in this market segment and typically sell at retail prices from $8 to $25 per 750 ml bottle." Chalone's shares easily sold out.

Through the late 1980s and early 1990s, baby boomers were reaching their peak income years and had plenty of disposable income. They were also paying more attention to what they were eating and having good wine with good food. As Fredrikson says, "People stopped eating and began dining."

On November 17, 1991, *60 Minutes* provided the stimulus that the American wine business needed to finally get out of the doldrums. The program broadcast one of its long segments on a phenomenon that Dr. Serge Renaud of the University of Bordeaux called the French paradox. It pointed out that although the French eat more rich food such as foie gras, cheese, and duck than Americans, they have much lower levels of heart disease. The explanation for this paradox was that the French also drank large amounts of red wine. If Americans wanted to enjoy the pleasures of French cooking, they had to drink red wine like the French. People in the California wine business still tell of how Americans went rushing out to buy bottles of red wine that Sunday night. The traditional toast "To your health" suddenly had a new meaning. Red wine sales soared, and a small winery named Blackstone that made an inexpensive Merlot went from selling a few thousand cases annually to 412,000 in 2000.

With business now booming, the glut of the 1980s turned into the shortage of the 1990s. Demand for wine was so strong and supplies so short that by the mid-1990s, Robert Mondavi was buying surplus bulk Merlot wine in France for his Woodbridge brand, which sold for less than $5 a bottle.

Jon Fredrikson often says that developments that might take a year in any other field of business require a decade in wine. A new winery could spend ten years buying raw land and planting a vineyard, then making the wine, launching a brand, and finally realizing success. The 1990s were the decade when the California wine business exploded. Americans were feeling flush. They had seen their stocks and homes dramatically increase in value. Some executives were making fortunes at start-up companies in Silicon Valley, not far from Napa Valley. Those people admired the sophistication that wine represented. Robert Mondavi became the poster boy for the wine lifestyle of good food, good art, and of course good wine. Rich people wanted to buy into that by owning a winery. As writer James Conaway wrote in *The Far Side of Eden: New Money, Old Land, and the Battle for Napa Valley*, a personal wine label for the status conscious had become "the twenty-first-century equivalent of a coat of arms."

New wineries seemed to be opening every day. The number of California wineries jumped from 807 in 1990 to 1,950 in 2000. One would expect that with all the new wineries prices would stabilize, but they soared. The average price of an acre of vineyard-ready land in Napa County jumped from $35,000 in 1990 to $180,000 in 2000.

Premium wines such as Chalone were no longer the most expensive. Fredrikson created a new ultrapremium category that sold for between $14 and $25 and a luxury one, $25 and above. Both were hot, and the wine press was thick with stories about California's next cult wine. Merlot was the favorite grape because it was soft and easy to appreciate, even for novices. California during the 1990s also enjoyed a string of outstanding vintages, while France was having a run of bad ones. Even aficionados on the East Coast, who had traditionally looked to Europe for quality wine, began paying as much attention to America's left coast as they did to Bordeaux's left bank. Helping feed the frenzy were regular reports on the health benefits of wine. It was the antithesis of neo-Prohibition: if you drank a glass of red wine a day, you would live as long as Methuselah.

Premium-wine prices went higher and higher, especially for low-production brands that got high scores from the most influential critic, Robert M. Parker Jr. Even in poor-quality years such as 1998 and 2000, the worst in a decade, California prices marched ever higher, far outpacing inflation.

"The biggest problem for wineries in the mid-1990s was allocating their limited supplies to customers and restaurants," says Fredrikson. "Winemakers didn't want to offend their loyal customers, but they didn't have enough product to satisfy everyone who wanted to buy their wine." Hot brands such as Silver Oak, which under its main label sold only two wines, both Cabernets—a Napa Valley and a Sonoma—allocated customers just six bottles of the Napa Cab the day it went on sale for the first time. Savvy consumers got around the restriction by bringing relatives to join them in line and buy a half dozen. The most popular wineries could charge just about whatever they wanted, and they would still sell out. By the middle of the 1990s, both new wineries and existing ones were planting more and more vineyards to keep up with seemingly endless demand.

No winery is an island. In this era of easy and relatively inexpensive international transportation as well as global tastes and interconnected markets, a winemaker's decision in Modesto or Mendoza can have an impact on the price of a wine at a store in Los Angeles or a restaurant in New York City. In the first years of the twenty-first century, the market was being hit by two important new developments: an international economic downturn and a global wine glut.

On the economic front, first came the end of the go-go 1990s and the dot-com bust on Wall Street. Billions of dollars invested in stocks simply melted away, and with them, people's perception that the world's new wealth class could drink $100 bottles of Napa Cab every night. The international economic crisis in 2008, the worst downturn since the Great Depression of the 1920s and 1930s, reinforced people's sense of economic uncertainty. A seismic shift in wine took place almost overnight. Conspicuous consumption was suddenly out of fashion. Wine lovers around the world, though, didn't stop drinking; they simply dialed down the price they were willing to pay for a bottle. After two heady decades of growth for premium products, those bottles were suddenly gathering dust on store shelves.

At the same time, a global wine glut was occurring in markets all around the world, thanks to record planting in the 1990s. According to the International Organization of Vine and Wine, world wine production in 2009 totaled 268.7 million hectoliters, while global wine consumption was 236.5 million hectoliters. That surplus translates into 359 million cases more wine than the United States consumed in 2009.

The region hit hardest was Europe. Domestic consumption was down one-third in a generation and yet production levels until recently had remained high. The strong euro also pushed export prices higher and hurt sales. Europe's share of the world wine market fell from some 80 percent in the 1980s to about 60 percent today.

The biggest decline in Europe has been in the old reliable *vin ordinaire,* because of changing tastes dating back to the 1960s. Higher-quality wines held their markets somewhat better, but they still had to scramble. The French slogan in recent years has been *boire moins; boire meilleur* (drink less; drink better). Other traditional wine-consuming countries in southern Europe adopted the same attitude. Wine is now more popular in northern European countries such as Sweden, Britain, and Ireland, but the growth there has not made up for sales losses in France, Spain, and Italy.

Europe is unlikely ever to return to its former glory. For years the European Union has been annually producing 150 million more cases of wine than it could sell at home or abroad. For many years, the Europeans turned that surplus into industrial alcohol, including ethanol to be used in automobiles. But in April 2008, the European Community switched the thrust of its wine policy by adopting a plan to pay growers to take 175,000 hectares (432,434 acres) of grapes out of production over a three-year period. Yet even after that, Europe will still be making far more wine than it can sell in the commercial market and will have to resort to unloading the excess in the bulk market at heavily discounted prices.

Australia also has a huge wine surplus. A generation ago, that country saw wine as a product to drive its economy. During the 1980s and 1990s, government policies to increase wine exports stimulated excessive vineyard planting. Soon the country was producing far more wine than it could sell. Australia also suffered from an overly strong currency, caused by the demand, largely from China, for its minerals and other raw materials. That has pushed up the price of all Australian exports, including wine.

At first Australia sold its surplus at home in unlabeled bottles, called clean skins, for about $3. In more recent times, though, the country has sold the excess in the international bulk market—often for less than fifty cents a liter. The head of the country's Wine Grape Growers Association says that Australia needs to reduce its vineyards by 20,000 hectares (49,421 acres) from the current 177,000 hectares (437,377 acres). Australian wine exports have already dropped 10 percent since the peak in 2006–07.

All the world's major wine-producing countries are now selling surplus wines at reduced prices, operating in the unregulated and little-known bulk market, where tanker ships of wine are daily bought and sold. Australian companies, for example, ship tankers of wine to Britain, where supermarket chains bottle it and sell it with a house label. Australian wine sold in the United States can go for about seventy cents a liter, even though the U.S. has its own surplus. China has become a major buyer in the bulk market, especially for wines from France and Chile.

The American market has been changing in several ways that help both wineries and consumers by letting them deal directly with each other and reducing the power of distributors. Some 70 percent of the cost of a bottle of wine has traditionally gone to distributors and retailers. The repeal of Prohibition in 1933 required all alcohol sales to go through the three-tier process of producer, distributor, and retailer. The number of distributors has been falling dramatically in recent years, from three thousand in 1999 to about five hundred. During that same period, though, the number of American wineries increased from eighteen hundred to sixty-two hundred. The remaining wholesalers were not interested in selling little-known products from small wineries. They wanted to work with big producers and large volumes.

The system, though, began to break down in May 2005, when the U.S. Supreme Court ruled in *Granholm v. Heald* that a state could not permit in-state wineries to ship directly to consumers while prohibiting out-of-state ones from doing so. The decision opened the door, at least partly, for consumers to buy directly from wineries, which generally charge lower prices, especially to their wine club members. Wholesalers have attempted to get new legislation passed that would roll back that decision, but so far the ruling stands. This offers an important business opportunity to both wineries and consumers.

The other major development has been the growth of wine sales on the Internet. Wineries with excess production are now selling them at attractively low prices through discount sites such as Lot18, WinesTilSoldOut, and Cinderella Wine. The cost is routinely about half the list price, and the wines include famous brands. Archaic U.S. laws unfortunately forbid the companies from shipping to all states. Internet wine sales are likely to continue growing rapidly.

Looking back on a half century of wine history and trying to foresee what is likely to happen in the future, a couple of lessons stand out. The first is that this business continues to be a graveyard for large corporations with little experience in wine. Giants such as Coca-Cola, Nestlé, and Pillsbury bought up wineries in the 1970s in expectation of easy and large profits, but a decade later, they were rushing to get out. At the end of 2010, a host of major companies that had entered the field in the boom years were heading for the exits. Australia's Foster's, France's Pernod Ricard and Rémy Cointreau, and America's Constellation Brands and Brown-Forman were selling off all or part of their wine holdings. The history of the Robert Mondavi Winery, when it blurred its public's perception by selling both very expensive and bargain wines under the same label, showed that even companies who know the business have trouble when they get too big.

The second lesson is that surplus wine production, which has spawned so many new companies going after the bargain segment of the market, is likely to continue. Production has become global, with companies far and wide looking to make new products and enter new markets. It is inconceivable that there will ever be an OPEC of wine, with just a few producers controlling output and dictating price. The free market may not work in many fields, but wine is a textbook case of how it operates to the benefit of consumers.

The first decade of the new century turned into a wonderful time for wine consumers, and that trend is likely to continue. Savvy companies are rushing to offer bargain wines. In April 2010, Wegmans, a supermarket chain with stores from New York to Virginia, started a program of $6 wines to help consumers expand their horizons at an attractive price. Stores carry dozens of different wines currently from six countries, including some discovery varieties such as Chenin Blanc from South Africa, Torrontés from Argentina, and Cava from Spain. Says Michael Riley, the director of wine operations: "Customers experiment with different wines and continue to grow in their knowledge as they become wine fans."

As Jon Fredrikson told me, "Intense competition from thousands of wineries both in America and from around the world has created a dream market for American wine consumers at all price levels. Most Americans consume wines priced under $10, and today that huge segment, making up about four-fifths of all wine sales, delivers better-quality wines than ever before. The widespread availability of good wines at reasonable prices bodes well for American consumers."

That's the greatest story never told.

PART TWO

The Iconoclasts

A small cadre of wine people are challenging old ways of thinking and doing things. They are not united by anything except radical ideas and defiance of conventional wisdom about how people taste, whether experts and judges are reliable, the kind of packaging to use, and who should be recommending wines. In the process, these iconoclasts are changing the way millions of people think and drink.

CHAPTER THREE

Unraveling the Mysteries of Taste

Tim Hanni was one of the first two Americans to be recognized as a Master of Wine, the most prestigious honor in the field. In order to put the letters MW after their names, they had to pass a rigorous written and oral examination plus write a thesis on a wine topic. Founded in 1955, the London-based organization has fewer than three hundred members worldwide. Originally an exclusively British organization, the Institute of Masters of Wine opened its membership to other countries in the late 1980s. Along with Joel Butler, the longtime director of wine education at Ste. Michelle Wine Estates in Washington, Hanni passed the entrance exam in 1990.

A little over two years later, Hanni admitted to himself that he couldn't control his drinking. Being one of the world's top wine experts but also an alcoholic results in a complex personality. Hanni today is challenging the wine business from within. An intense person who often recognizes patterns where other people see only chaos, Hanni for nearly two decades has been trying to understand the physiopsychology of how human beings actually perceive and experience wine, and in doing so he is debunking some of the field's most universally accepted maxims. With the unbridled enthusiasm and confidence of a true believer, he urges people not to be ashamed of liking sweet wines, which most gurus consider only a small step above poison, and not to castigate themselves for being unable to understand why everyone else is going into ecstasy over a highly rated Bordeaux First Growth or a California cult Cab.

Hanni has a background in both food and wine. He got into cooking early in life and bounced around restaurants for years. He first worked at Bern's Steak House in Tampa, which then claimed to have the largest wine list in the world, with some six thousand labels. There followed many other food-and-wine jobs as he increased his knowledge of different cuisines, including Chinese. In most restaurants, he was also responsible for the wine list.

In 1979, Hanni became the wine buyer at Happy Herman's in Atlanta, an early gourmet grocery that boasted fifty single-bean coffees and hosted regular wine dinners, where Hanni both selected the wines and prepared the food. In 1985, he started his own wine importing business in Atlanta, but closed it only three years later to join Nestlé's Wine World Estates. For the next eleven years, Hanni worked with Beringer Wine Estates, which owned Beringer Vineyards, Meridian Vineyards, Chateau Souverain Winery, and a wine-importing business. For years he ran the wine-education program, working with longtime winemaker Ed Sbragia and with master chefs from around the country. Hanni was later the Director of International Development, which involved managing the company's business in Canada and Asia. He says that his jobs in those years involved promotion, education, and evangelism.

Despite the achievement of passing the Master of Wine test, Hanni in the early 1990s was having a difficult time. He was drinking heavily, his first marriage was on the rocks, and he had to file for personal bankruptcy. Although he had the MW pedigree and had been a professional chef for more than a decade, he felt he really couldn't come to grips with the food-and-wine combinations that were the foundation of so much of his work. Moreover, he knew enough about both wine and food to realize that much of what was being passed along by others was quackery. "I knew something was really wrong, but I didn't know what it was," he recalls.

After struggling with these issues for a couple of years, Hanni in the summer of 1992 invited thirty leading sensory scientists from eleven countries to a luncheon at Beringer Vineyards' Culinary Arts Center in Napa Valley. None of them was a wine scientist or even knew how to make wine. He wanted to talk to people outside the wine trade, who were not contaminated by its conventional thinking. He set a splendid table and pulled out some of Beringer's best old wines, then forced the guests to sit through his long and rambling talk and preliminary thoughts about the way people taste wine and the shortcomings of food-and-wine pairings. Hanni ended his speech by describing some classical combinations and encouraged people to tell him whether they thought that, in his terms, they were "truth or fertilizer." One by one, the scientists said the pairings were "fertilizer." How about red wine and meat, the mostly universally approved combination? Fertilizer. Red wine actually makes New York strip steak more astringent. The real reason it works is that chefs usually put salt, a bitterness blocker, on steak and that causes the illusion of a smooth taste. Tuscan cooks serve steak with lemon and salt—plus a glass of red wine—but again it's the seasoning that makes the pairing work.

The group went on to find plenty of fertilizer in the belief that complex foods go best with complex wines, and that salt and acidity are wine enemies, when they are clearly its best friends. They tried combinations of fish with red wines and meat with white wines, and concluded that people should serve the wine they prefer. The largest piece of fertilizer adhered to the concept that there exists a perfect consistency between the taste experiences of two people. The lunch had turned out to be a disaster for conventional wisdom. "That day everything I had been taught was completely trashed," Hanni told me. "So I decided to start working with individual scientists to understand what was really going on."

By the end of the year, Hanni was feeling better about things. As a result of the luncheon conference and what he had learned since, he had concluded that his real job at Beringer was to become a disruptive innovator, throwing bombs and breaking all the rules. Life also looked better because he was playing guitar in a band called the Toasted Heads and dating the lead singer, Kate Costello.

For Christmas that year, Tim and Kate drove north from Napa Valley to Eureka to celebrate the holiday with her mother, Joanne Cottongim. Tim was meeting Kate's mother for the first time, and he was naturally a little nervous. Kate had told him that her mother had a PhD in economics, had taught at nearby Humboldt State University, and had played golf at St. Andrews in Scotland. She was a great fan of food, but Kate also mentioned that her mother's favorite wine was White Zinfandel, a popular sweet wine that aficionados hate. As a popular slogan among wine geeks goes, "Friends Don't Let Friends Drink White Zinfandel." It is profoundly *déclassé*. "Kate's mother was supposed to be unsophisticated trailer trash for drinking White Zin, but she was a lot smarter than anyone she met," Tim says. Finally, Kate confided that her mother had really liked her daughter's first husband. Tim was obviously facing a serious challenge.

Looking to capitalize on his training in food and wine, Tim volunteered to cook the holiday meal and bring the wine. The day before Christmas, Tim showed up at the house with a leg of lamb under one arm and a case of Beringer White Zinfandel in the other. "Joanne saw Kate and me at the door with gifts in hand, and said to me with great enthusiasm, 'Son, welcome, and let me show you the kitchen.'"

The holiday was a great success, and Joanne enjoyed Beringer White Zinfandel with the leg of lamb. The experience, though, shattered what Hanni had been learning in nearly thirty years in the wine business. "Joanne did not fit my vision of a White Zinfandel drinker. She wasn't one of 'those people.'" Here was a sophisticated, educated woman who likes a sweet wine that is the butt of jokes. "I clearly had to revise my view of things and became passionately curious about what was going on. That began my journey into understanding sensory sensitivity and how we all end up with our individual wine preferences." It would turn out to be a long and difficult journey.

In 1993, Tim and Kate married, but they got off to a rocky start because he was still drinking heavily. For a while he tried studiously to spit out wines he tasted, as judges do in competitions, but that didn't work. Finally Hanni realized that if he kept on, drinking was going to ruin his second marriage just as it had the first. Along with many another recovering alcoholic, Hanni clearly remembers his last drink—a glass of Meridian Chardonnay on December 16, 1993, after playing a round of golf in Phoenix, Arizona. The following day, he started six months of rehab.

Hanni returned to his job determined to do some serious research on why there were so many differences of opinion among wine and food professionals, quickly concluding there was an even greater disconnect between experts and the general public than he had realized. Most people just assume that everyone has the same experience, whether they are eating a piece of chocolate cake or drinking a glass of Champagne.

Hanni soon learned about an obscure event that challenged that notion. In 1931, DuPont chemist Arthur Fox accidently released a cloud of the chemical phenylthiocarbamide, a compound known by the initials PTC.

Colleagues working in the lab near Fox that day had different reactions to the chemical. Some said it had a repugnant bitter smell, but Fox, who was much closer to the cloud than the other workers, did not detect that. Fox then tested several friends and more coworkers and found that their reactions varied greatly. Additional studies showed that some 70 percent of people could generally taste PTC, but the numbers ranged from 58 percent for native residents of Australia and New Guinea to 98 percent of indigenous Americans. Nonsmokers and people who didn't drink coffee or tea were also more likely to recognize it. Fox and others concluded that there must be a genetic relationship between those who could taste PTC and those who could not. That link, indeed, is so strong that the ability to identify the chemical was used to detect paternity, before the advent of DNA testing. In the 1960s, Roland Fischer, another researcher, showed that people who tasted PTC also showed specific food preferences. It was becoming obvious to Hanni that people experienced taste differently. In fact, more recent studies have shown that people have a range of sensitivity to sight, smell, hearing, and taste. A concert pianist hears differently than an average person, and a master painter has more sensitive color perceptions.

Hanni became interested in the work of Linda Bartoshuk, a professor then at Yale and now at the University of Florida, who has studied the variations in people's sense of taste. She discovered a phenomenon known as burning mouth syndrome among postmenopausal women that results in a diminished sense of taste. Doctors had earlier thought the loss was psychosomatic, but Bartoshuk proved that some women actually had damaged taste buds. Her work showed that some people have an elevated sense of taste, while others have a much more subdued one. The heightened sensitivity to taste has nothing to do with experience or training, but is simply due to the fact that some people have more taste buds on their tongue. The number can vary between five hundred and ten thousand. Bartoshuk explains, "We may live in completely different sensory worlds."

Bartoshuk originally placed people into two categories: medium-tasters and super-tasters, but later work divided them into three categories: 25 percent non-tasters, 50 percent medium-tasters, and 25 percent super-tasters. There is nothing good or bad about being a super-taster or a non-taster—it's simply part of the human condition.

Hanni found a number of academics plowing through the same fields of study and recruited an informal brain trust. Among them were Charles J. Wysocki of the Monell Chemical Senses Center in Philadelphia, Virginia Utermohlen of Cornell University, Michael O'Mahony and Rie Ishii of the University of California–Davis, and Lionel Tiger of Rutgers University. His mentors broadly confirmed the conclusions Hanni was starting to reach and pointed him toward other academic work. They were also adding some intriguing pieces of information. Utermohlen, for example, in her work on the relationship between a person's sensitivity to taste and smell and choice in food, drink, and even profession had found that if a pregnant woman has severe morning sickness during pregnancy, the child is more likely later to be a super-taster. Not surprisingly, Hanni received strange looks from people when he asked what kinds of wines they liked and whether their mothers had suffered from morning sickness. They usually didn't know the answer and had to call their mothers to ask.

One of Hanni's early and controversial conclusions was that a person's palate does not mature over time or through education. "You can't rewire yourself," he says with passion. No amount of training to identify wine flavors is going to change a person's fundamental sense of taste. Some might be trained to better identify such tastes as cork taint or oakiness, but that will not change the type of wine the person prefers. When it comes to tasting, people are as stuck with what nature gives them, just as they are with the color of their eyes.

As Hanni reexamined his wine research with his team of advisors, he grew more and more irritated by what he considered the dogmatic condemnation of sweet wines and the people who drink them. "Mankind has been making wine for eight millennia, and until the last fifty years people mostly drank sweet wine," he says. The Bible has several hundred references to wine, and many of them refer specifically to sweet wine. The Romans praised "honeyed wines."

Tilar Mazzeo, author of *The Widow Clicquot: The Story of a Champagne Empire and the Woman Who Ruled It,* recounted how after the Napoleonic Wars the widow captured the Russian market by selling them Champagne that was incredibly sweet by modern standards. A bottle routinely contained 300 grams of residual sugar. The 2001 Château d'Yquem, the most prized Sauternes, has about half as much sugar, and California's popular Grgich Hills Violetta, a late-harvest blend of Chardonnay and Riesling grapes that is considered a dessert wine, has roughly 250 grams.

In the summer of 2010, divers in a Baltic Sea shipwreck between Sweden and Finland discovered a cache of Champagne bottles believed to date from the 1780s—some of the oldest authentic bottles ever found. The divers called in sommelier Ella Grüssner Cromwell-Morgan to sample one, who said, "It tasted fantastic. It was a very sweet Champagne, with a tobacco taste and oak."

Hanni has collected historic wine menus and merchant price lists showing that in the nineteenth century, quality sweet wines cost more than the great dry wines of Bordeaux and Burgundy. Queen Victoria was a fan of sweet German Rieslings from the Rhine village of Hochheim. The British still today call all German wines Hock.

When Americans started becoming interested in wine in the 1950s, the top-selling imports were mostly sweet wines: Blue Nun, Riunite, Lancers. Top-selling California Chardonnays today, such as Kendall-Jackson, Conundrum, and Rombauer, are a little sweet, although their winemakers rarely discuss that, because Americans like to *talk* dry, but *drink* slightly sweet. Jess Jackson, the owner of Kendall-Jackson, sued his former winemaker, Jed Steele, for passing along the K-J touch of sweetness when he became a consultant and also using that technique in his own Steele Chardonnay. The judge ruled in favor of Jackson, but the little bit of sweetness continues to be practiced in California.

Sweet White Zinfandel was first made by Sutter Home, which accidently discovered it in 1975, when winemakers had a problem with so-called "stuck fermentation" in a batch of Zinfandel grapes. Fermentation had stopped because the yeast died before consuming all the sugar. The resulting product had a sweet taste and pink color. Sutter Home gave it the name White Zinfandel, and it was soon the best-selling wine in America. Sutter Home, Gallo, Beringer, and Mondavi annually sell millions of cases.

The head of the wine department at H-E-B, one of the largest food retailers in Texas, told me in the summer of 2010 that his top-selling wine at the time was Fratelli Moscato d'Asti, a sweet Italian wine selling for $10.98.

Moscato is almost never mentioned in wine publications. Hanni says, "We've disenfranchised and intimidated sweet-wine drinkers. If the wine business wants to regain the confidence of consumers, it will have to make a massive change in the perception of sweet wines and the people who like them."

Because the experts have such disdain for sweet wines, consumers can get great deals on all of them with the exception of Château d'Yquem, which can cost $500 a bottle. White Zinfandel and Moscato sell for less than $10, and even some highly rated Sauternes go for about $25.

Hanni's continued praise of White Zinfandel led to some complaints that he was only pushing the wine because it was one of Beringer's biggest sellers. He insists that was not true—but his outspoken views on wine and food were making it difficult for him to stay at the winery. So, in 1999, he left to start WineQuest, a website that helps hotels and restaurants make wine lists and manage sales.

During his research into food and wine interactions, Hanni's mentors introduced him to umami. Traditionally, all tastes were broken down into four basic types: sweet, sour, bitter, and salty. But in 1908, Japanese chemistry professor Dr. Kikunae Ikeda put forth evidence of a fifth taste that he called umami, a Japanese term that means "good flavor." Hanni has evidence that the taste is similar to what the French gourmand Jean Anthelme Brillat-Savarin (1755–1826) called *osmazome*, which he considered the main taste component in meat. Umami is a highly sought after quality that humans love and is found in meat, poultry, seafood, fermented and aged foods, including wine, and also in tomatoes, fruits, and vegetables. Hanni believes that modern winemaking techniques such as increased ripeness, longer maceration of red wines, stirring the lees of white wines, and the use of specialized yeasts have increased the umami taste in wines. Online, Hanni is known as the Swami of Umami, and Robert Mondavi called him Mr. Umami.

Eventually Hanni came up with his own system for classifying wine drinkers, which is slightly different from the one Linda Bartoshuk developed. He didn't particularly like the terminology of super-tasters and non-tasters, which seemed to imply that one is superior to the other. Hanni and Virginia Utermohlen have since introduced a form of phenotyping that divides people into four groups. A phenotype is the combination of physiological and behavioral traits someone exhibits when it comes to taste. Hanni and Utermohlen postulate that a simple series of questions, such as whether a person puts sugar in his coffee or has a passion for salt, provides the basis for determining a person's overall taste sensitivity and insights into his or her wine preferences. The best indicator, for reasons that are still not clear, is whether the person's mother had morning sickness during pregnancy.

The differing sensitivities between phenotypes explain why highly qualified wine experts can have totally opposite impressions of the same wine. One may think it causes a burning sensation, while another says it is smooth and rich. Hanni found it amusing that in the same week in January 2010, wine critic Dan Berger wrote an article about all the bad Cabernets on the market, calling it the "collapse of California Cabernets." He said this was due to their high alcohol content and overripened grapes. At the same time, Steve Heimoff, another highly regarded wine expert, wrote a piece declaring that Napa Cabernet Sauvignon was "pretty much as good as it can get." Hanni concluded they have different phenotypes and seem to live in different sensory worlds.

The four Hanni phenotypes:

- Sweet. These people appear to have the most taste buds and simply like sweet things. In a restaurant, rather than being embarrassed by ordering a White Zinfandel, they will often order a sweet cocktail before or with dinner. Hanni says this is his mother-in-law and a lot of closet sweet-wine drinkers.

- Hypersensitive. They like delicacy and finesse and unoaked Chardonnay. They are very sensitive to bitterness. Sarah Abbott, a Master of Wine, could be the poster child for the hypersensitive phenotype. She is an internationally recognized wine authority, but her wine preferences so frequently ran counter to those of her colleagues that she once said, "Often I wonder whether something is wrong with me."

- Sensitive. They like coffee with a little bit of milk and perhaps sugar in the morning, but black in the afternoon. They like salt, but can't stand the taste of sugar substitutes. Hanni suspects that Britain's Jancis Robinson, who generally has a balanced view, is a good example of a sensitive taster.

- Tolerant. They like Scotch, strong black coffee, and oaky, intense, high-alcohol wines. They also prefer big and bold wines with lots of tannins and intensity. Hanni says Robert M. Parker Jr. is the quintessential example of this phenotype.

Hanni has witnessed many interesting battles of the phenotypes over the years. In 2004, a brouhaha broke out among wine critics regarding the 2003 Château Pavie, a prized St.-Émilion. Robert Parket gave it 98+ points out of 100, writing that it "hits the palate with a dramatic minerality" and "comes across like a hypothetical blend of limestone liqueur intermixed with black and red fruits." Jancis Robinson gave the exact same wine twelve points out of twenty, labeling it a "ridiculous wine reminiscent of a late-harvest Zinfandel rather than a red Bordeaux." Parker later wrote on his website, "Her comments are very much in keeping with her nasty swipes at all the wines made by Gérard Perse." To which Robinson shot back, "Am I not allowed to have my own opinion? Only so long as it agrees with Monsieur Parker's, it would seem."

Domenic Cicchetti, a research scientist at Yale University, studied the ratings Parker and Robinson gave to the 2004 Bordeaux wines and found that Parker gave two wines above-average scores that Robinson scored unacceptable. Parker also judged nineteen wines excellent that she called only average.

Hanni says that such battles only reflect the different tasting profiles between Parker and Robinson. One is not wrong, and the other is not right. They're simply different, in exactly the same way that some people like the music of Brahms and others prefer Copland.

Some wine experts have stepped forward over the years to support Hanni's conclusions. Robert Mondavi, for example, said, "What Tim is proposing represents a quantum leap forward for expanding the enjoyment of wine and food. His message is easy to grasp, empowering, and useful to anyone who is in the least bit curious about wine." The *Wall Street Journal,* in a flattering profile of Hanni in January 2008, called him the Wine Antisnob.

In June 2006, Hanni and his theories faced their toughest audience during a three-day Institute of Masters of Wine international symposium attended by two hundred fifty of the world's top wine experts at the Silverado Country Club in the Napa Valley. Hanni was, in effect, pleading his case in front of the Supreme Court of wine. For support, he invited four of his taste mentors to join him: Charles J. Wysocki, Michael O'Mahony, Linda Bartoshuk, and Lionel Tiger.

Wysocki at one point had attendees taste jelly beans and smell various compounds to show the discrepancies that can occur even in an audience of great tasters. He also pointed to studies showing that identical twins are more likely to have similar tastes than fraternal ones. In another part of the presentation, Hanni asked people to smell a compound on a diamond-shaped piece of paper and say whether it was bitter or pleasant. The audience was equally split. Some thought it smelled like Parmesan cheese, while others said it was a sweaty sock. The compound was androstenone, a steroid that smells like wet wood, flowers, or urine to different people.

The speakers kept driving home the point that people don't taste exactly the same, but are influenced by learning, experience, and expectations. A person's genetic mix is much more important than is generally realized. Wine is simply not something where one size fits all, a fact not sufficiently recognized by winemakers or critics. Jancis Robinson, the first woman Master of Wine, summed up the presentations later on her website: "The main point of the session was to suggest that there are all sorts of populations of people who will perceive wine differently, thanks to our own sensitivities and preference, and that the wine business is crazy to act as though one message, or even one sort of wine, suits all."

Robinson continued the discussion on her blog under the title "Super-Tasters and Non-Tasters, Sensitivities and Preferences." One commenter made the interesting point that the taste vocabulary of European and American critics is culturally biased. Robinson agreed, writing, "A sizeable proportion of flavours (particularly fruits) described in standard wine texts are simply unknown to the Chinese." Another blogger, from Chile, noted that critics describe wines as tasting like licorice, a product rarely found in his country.

Despite the scholarly background of his research, Hanni collects enemies, especially among wine critics. In early 2010, while Hanni was on a speaking tour in Britain, the *Guardian* ran an article proclaiming, "[Hanni's argument is] so radical that self-professed 'experts' wouldn't even bother responding to it were it not for the fact that Hanni is one of them." Nearly a week later, Tim Atkin, the wine critic for *The Times* of London and another Master of Wine, wrote a spirited defense of his craft. That was followed by another blog defense of wine critics from Steve Heimoff: "I don't agree with Tim's premise, though. He can call me a dinosaur, an industry gatekeeper pushing back furiously against the onslaught of change. But none of that changes the truth. A wine taster can learn to understand and talk about wine."

Many of Hanni's critics proclaim that his biggest fault is that he doesn't believe in food-wine pairings, as if that were the most outrageous and unthinkable position any human being could hold. Hanni maintains that traditional wine pairings are inaccurate and do not provide a relevant basis for what to eat and drink together. So throw away all those tomes on matching wine to food. Instead of trying to remember all the details of what's in them, just keep a few basic principles in mind: light wines go with light food; heavy wines go with heavy food. He says to put a little salt and lemon on beef and then drink red wine with it. Adjusting salt, acidity, and sweetness can pair any food with any wine without compromising the taste if the wine is within the person's realm of preference. In a testament to the growing acceptance of Hanni's work, the Wine & Spirit Education Trust, a British organization that trains alcohol-beverage staffs for companies, in September 2010 asked him to revise its curriculum to reflect his conclusions on wine and food.

Hanni consults with top hotels and restaurant chains, speaks to professional groups, and roams the world driving the wine establishment crazy. He also gives lectures to groups as part of his New Wine Fundamentals education program.

One of his favorite projects is developing new wine lists for hotels and restaurants that reflect the conclusions he has reached. For many years, he has been advocating what he calls the "progressive wine list," which groups wines not by geographical region or by grape variety but by wine style, going from light and sweet to big and bold. A *Wall Street Journal* survey concluded that about one-third of all American wine lists are now organized this way.

Hanni showed me a prototype of a next-generation wine list that he prepared for a major hotel chain. He calls it the Affinity Wine List. At the top it states, "The wines are selected and grouped into flavor categories by flavor likenesses for persons who share the same taste affinity: Sweet, Delicate, Smooth or Intense. Each flavor section includes wines marked as Discovery, Connoisseur, and Favorites, if you would like to explore new wines. It is designed to offer you a broad and balanced range of selections for every personal preference, wine and food match and occasion." The wines were priced by the glass (from $8 to $21) and by the bottle (from $36 to $225).

Hanni also works with some of Napa's biggest wineries developing wine products that will appeal to new audiences. In 2009, one of those projects involved repositioning and increasing the price of a modestly successful, inexpensive Moscato. He suggested making the wine sweeter, not drier, and nearly doubling the price. The wine now annually sells more than one million cases.

Another Hanni project is the Napa Seasoning Company, which he started in 2006. It has only two products, Vignon, a flavor-balancing seasoning, and Vignon Seasoned Almonds, which he developed with a food scientist. The Vignon list of ingredients starts with sea salt, natural lemon juice flavor, and yeast extract. The goal is to simplify the technique of flavor balancing by sprinkling Vignon on something with the umami taste to offset the unpleasant interaction of umami with wine. Asparagus and artichokes are two foods that any wine expert will insist do not go with any wine. Wine connoisseurs say that when these foods are served, people should drink water, but Hanni says just sprinkle a little Vignon on either vegetable and then enjoy the wine of your choice.

Tim Hanni extols the message that people should have confidence in their own tastes. "Don't be ashamed of buying either a sweet wine or an inexpensive one," Hanni says. "There's no categorical right or wrong. Don't let yourself be a victim of the tyranny of a minority."

The Tim Hanni Taste Sensitivity Assessment

Tim Hanni prepared this simple test for readers to determine their Taste SQ (Sensitivity Quotient). Choose your answers to the following questions. Remember that there are no right or wrong answers. The more expert or involved you are in wine appreciation, the more your tastes may have evolved beyond this simple test. Also bear in mind that the Sweet and the Hypersensitive Taste SQ are similar, and the difference between them is whether or not you like sweet wines. This test, though, will provide an indication of your general taste sensitivity. Give yourself the points to the left of your answer.

Gender
0   Male
3   Female

Salted snacks such as nuts, pretzels, potato chips
0   I find most snacks too salty.
1   Yeah, I like salty snacks.
3   Yum! I am addicted to salty snacks.

Salt preferences (answer by taste preference, not from a health standpoint)
0   I find many foods too salty.
1   Food usually tastes fine as is and/or I add a modest amount of salt when I cook, or I avoid salt for health reasons.
2   I usually add a little extra salt to my food, or would like to but don't for health reasons.
3   People give me a hard time for adding too much salt to my food.

Coffee or Tea
Describe the perfect cup of coffee or tea:

0   I like it very strong (espresso or English Breakfast tea).
1   I like it strong (Starbucks and Peet's coffee or Earl Grey tea).
2   I like it medium (the weak coffee served at work, green or herbal tea).
3   Coffee tastes so horrible I can't stand it.

Sugar in your coffee
0   None.
1   A touch.
2   One teaspoon or the equivalent.
3   Two or more teaspoons.

Cream/Milk
0   I drink coffee black.
1   Touch of cream/milk.
2   Moderate cream/milk.
3   Lots of cream/milk.

Do you enjoy coffee with steamed milk or flavoring such as almond, vanilla, Irish Cream?
0   No.
1   Cappuccino, Latte, but not flavorings.
2   Sometimes I have both.
3   Usually both.

How do artificial sweeteners in diet sodas taste (try to answer by your taste preference, not from a health standpoint)?
0   No taste problem.
1   Don't know. I never tried a diet soda in my life.
1   Taste funny, but not too bad.
2   I can tell a big difference but have adapted OR some taste much better than others.
3   Yuck! They taste horrible.

Bonus question: do you have an occasional drink of straight Scotch, Cognac and/or Armagnac?

-3   Yes!

0   Sometimes.

1   No way.

When you finish, add up all your points to get your Taste SQ score and see your group. The classifications: Sweet: 15–25 points (prefers sweet wines); Hypersensitive: 16–25 points; Sensitive: 5–15 points; Tolerant: 3–7 points.

Keep in mind that this is an oversimplified, yet valid and useful, way to determine where you are on the taste sensitivity continuum. Psychological dimension plays a very important role in shaping your personal preferences. There is some overlap between the groups and you may determine which group best suits your preferences if you fall on the cusp between two. Over time, you might change your entire sensitivity category because of changes in wine fashion, aesthetics, learning, and experiences. For example, I know a Master of Wine who is a Sweet phenotype but also very passionate for the bold flavors of Italian Barolos. At the end of the day, feel free to pick and choose whichever group seems to have the wines you love the most.

In the general population, about 30 percent of people fall in the Sweet category, 25 percent in Hypersensitive, 25 percent in Sensitive, and 20 percent in the Tolerant group. Professional wine people tend to lean much more toward dry and more intense wines. As a result, they are more likely to be Sensitive or Tolerant tasters.

Tim Hanni's recommendations below will help people in all four groups understand the types of wine they might like. Keep in mind that the more experienced and confident you are around wine, the more likely it is that you will have already developed strong preferences through those personal experiences.

Sweet

Note: This group is only for people with a preference for sweet wines. If you scored 20–25 points and like dry wines, go to the Hypersensitive group.

In most cases, you have the highest taste sensitivity, the most taste buds, and you love sweet wines. Don't let anyone intimidate, embarrass, or harass you! If a sommelier tries to sell you on a dry rosé, hold your ground.

WINE RECOMMENDATIONS

Favorites: You probably tend to go for Rieslings, Moscato, Chenin Blanc semi-sec, White Zinfandel, Liebfraumilch, Sangría, and fruit wines. If you want to try something less sweet, demand delicate and smooth flavors.

Discovery Wines: You may want to try Moscato from the United States, Australia, and Italy; Vouvray (demi-sec) or Coteaux du Layon from France; sweet Rieslings; Moscato d'Asti from Italy; and wines made with the Symphony grape, a cross between Muscat of Alexandria and Grenache Gris. California's Ironstone Vineyards makes a wine named Obsession Symphony that sells for about $8; Vendange also makes Symphony. Many sparkling wines and French Champagnes have the sweetness you crave, provided you like the bubbles.

Connoisseur Selections: Coulée de Serrant from the Loire Valley, true French Sauternes, most German Rieslings, Ice wines, and sweet Alsatian wines. Anything sold as a dessert wine may appeal to you anytime!

Hypersensitive

If you drink coffee, you probably add plenty of cream and sugar. You are also likely to be extremely opinionated and passionate about the roast level and origin of the coffee you drink. You are picky, picky, picky about food, music, art, and wine—even the tags in your clothing irritate you and have to be cut out! Delicacy and finesse, smoothness, and lower alcohol levels are paramount. Make sure to interview your wine merchant carefully and look for descriptions on bottles that fit your heightened sensitivities. The key thing to communicate is your desire for finesse and not the "high point scores" among intense white wines and monster reds. For you, refined and elegant, please.

WINE RECOMMENDATIONS

Favorites: Pinot Grigio, dry or slightly sweet Riesling, Soave, Viognier, Merlot, and Pinot Noir tend to be high on your list, along with many of the unoaked or even sweeter Chardonnays. You may also be a sparkling wine and Champagne lover.

Discovery Wines: White Albariño and Rioja reds from Spain, Grüner Veltliner from Austria, a wide range of Italian wines including such reds as Chianti, Barbera, and Dolcetto.

Connoisseur Selections: Alsatian whites (not too high in alcohol), Condrieu, silky red Burgundies, and high-quality, drier German wines; many of the finest Italian white wines, and Sauvignon Blanc from New Zealand.

Sensitive

You like variation, such as coffee with a little milk or cream in the morning, black in the afternoon and espresso at night, or vice versa. You may be pulled to intense Chardonnays and big Cabernet Sauvignons at first, but over time find they may become too much. You tend to be more adventurous with your choices. Jancis Robinson's recommendations should suit you perfectly.

WINE RECOMMENDATIONS

Favorites: Chardonnay and Cabernet Sauvignon are your bread and butter, along with Syrah/Shiraz, red Zinfandel, Merlot, and many red blends. Sauvignon Blanc may have great appeal along with Viognier, Pinot Blanc, and Pinot Gris.

Discovery Wines: Modern-styled reds from Portugal and Spain, Grenache blends, Syrah/Shiraz, Mourvèdre from Australia, and obscure Italian reds and whites. You can also find great satisfaction in almost any of the Tolerant and Hypersensitive recommendations as long as the wines have enough, but not too much, intensity and richness.

Connoisseur Selections: The world is your oyster, and it is almost impossible to tell you where to look because there are so many choices! Beware the high-scoring wines with off-the-chart alcohol content. You will like white and red Burgundies, Chardonnay, and Pinot Noir, as well as Australian Shiraz and red blends, and American Meritage.

Tolerant

In addition to your strong, black coffee, Scotch or Cognac, and even cigars, you almost exclusively like big red wines, Cabernet Sauvignon and Zinfandel, regardless of whatever food is being served. You might also like Chardonnays that stand up and shout at you.

WINE RECOMMENDATIONS

Favorites: Cabernet Sauvignon, old-vine(s) Zinfandel, Petite Sirah, Rhône reds and whites from France, Italian reds such as Super Tuscans, Barolo, and Brunello di Montalcino.

Discovery Wines: You will like monster reds such as Cahors from France, reserve reds from Chile or South Africa, and in-your-face Australian Shiraz and Argentine Malbec. Try a Cannubi Barolo from Michele Chiarlo, Peter Michael Chardonnay, and St. Francis Old Vines Zinfandel.

Connoisseur Selections: Let Robert M. Parker Jr. of *The Wine Advocate* and Jim Laube from *Wine Spectator* be your guides. They love the style of wines you prefer and are the perfect authorities for you.

To take a more extensive Taste Sensitivity assessment and get additional wine recommendations from Tim Hanni, go to www.yumyuk.com.

CHAPTER FOUR

Are Gold Medals Worth Anything?

Robert T. Hodgson, retired professor of oceanography and statistics at
California's Humboldt State University, is hardly the type of person
one would expect to throw stink bombs into the dignified world of wine
competitions. He's a soft-spoken, deliberate person, who weighs his words
as if they were grams of gold placed on the finely calibrated precision balance
scale that he keeps in the lab at his Fieldbrook Winery in Eureka, California.
With a full white beard and pleasant smile, Hodgson looks a bit like a
comforting Santa Claus. Yet this mild-mannered man in recent years has
shaken the very foundation of wine competitions.

Stroll through any wine store and you are likely to see bottles on shelves
with notices about the medals they have won in this or that wine competition. You may never have heard of the event, but the awards give an allure
of importance, and it might be enough for you to pick up the wine with
the prize rather than the one right next to it without an award. Medals on
bottles must work, since so many wineries promote them. Barefoot Chardonnay, a wine that sells for $5, has a sticker on its bottle announcing a gold
medal often without naming the competition in which it was won. HRM
Rex-Goliath, which sells at about the same price, has a stamp on the neck of
its bottles, that reads, "30 Gold Medals," but again doesn't reveal the events.
Oak Leaf Cabernet Sauvignon, which costs $3 at Walmart, mentions on its
label that it has won "over 40 medals since 2008."

One of my favorite wines is d'Arenberg The Dead Arm Shiraz, which
comes from the McLaren Vale region of South Australia. Just above the label
for the 2000 vintage is a panoply of insignias for seven gold medals plus
one trophy and Top 100 designations from Australian wine competitions.
Every time I open a bottle of The Dead Arm, I'm reminded of Bastille Day
celebrations I used to see while living in France. Old soldiers would wear all

the medals attesting to their valor in combat and then march proudly in parades. The veterans had so many awards hanging on their chests that they seemed to stoop slightly forward.

Wines that have received awards often hike their prices, but Hodgson's research challenges the very validity of the prizes.

A look inside the world of wine competitions raises lots of questions. To begin with, they can be very profitable ventures for the organizers, who are often publications, whether wine-related magazines or general-interest daily newspapers. A few sponsors, such as the Orange County Fair in California, have no entry fee; but most charge about $100 per wine to participate. In addition, the winery has to provide four or so free bottles of the wine being entered. Judges are generally not compensated for their time. Organizers will usually pick up out-of-pocket expenses for travel and hotel, but don't give any honorarium. Big-name wine gurus such as Robert M. Parker Jr. undoubtedly get paid, but they are the exception and rarely participate in public tastings. Do the math on two or three thousand wines being entered for $100 each and relatively low overhead, and you'll see it's a profitable business.

The wines judged at big competitions generally come from lesser-known wineries hoping to strike gold. They like competitions because there is little risk. If they don't win or they score poorly with the judges, no one ever knows, and they might get some useful feedback that could lead to their changing their winemaking styles to appeal more to judges and consumers.

Famous wineries with well-established labels or high scores from wine critics such as Parker or *Wine Spectator* are not interested in wine competitions. Have you ever seen France's Château Latour or California's Screaming Eagle touting its awards? They have little to gain from them and rarely enter. Stag's Leap Wine Cellars, which won the famous 1976 Paris Tasting over top Bordeaux reds, for example, almost never enters wine competitions. If it doesn't win, in the eyes of some people it has actually lost. So the safe strategy for famous wineries is to avoid competitions.

I have been a judge at several wine tastings around the United States, and it has been interesting to witness them from inside the tent. The judges usually come from one of two broad groups. They are either winemakers or wine journalists. There might also be a few academic wine experts, sommeliers, wine salespeople, and sometimes, but not often, enthusiastic and seasoned wine consumers. I've found winemakers to be the best judges. They have extensive experience tasting their own wines at various stages of development, and perhaps into their decline. They have probably also examined wines made by their competitors and are good at picking out what they like and don't like and any technical faults. Wine journalists are good at articulating what they taste, but their expertise is usually not as evident as that of winemakers. Of course, the name of the wine competition goes on the award, not the name of the judges. So when a consumer sees that gold medal, he doesn't know whether the judges were qualified or not.

The organizer often announces before the competition starts how many gold medals are expected to be allotted, which is usually about 10 percent of entries. The *San Francisco Chronicle* wine competition, which gets nearly five thousand entries and six thousand paid visitors who can taste along with the judges, has a reputation in the wine trade as being an easy place to win a gold medal, which helps it get more entries. San Francisco is also a demanding event, with judges often tasting well over two hundred wines.

The wine competitions in which I've participated all followed a similar script. Staff workers in a back room pour a small amount, two or three ounces, in a standard wineglass that has a number written in ink on the stem. Wines are presented in flights of somewhere between six and fifteen wines, usually but not always the same type of grape. Judges are told only the grape variety. There are normally somewhere between four and six judges in each panel, and at a large wine competition judges will taste at least one hundred wines a day and sometimes more. One often tastes several flights of the same type of wine, thus for example scoring thirty Cabernet Sauvignons in a morning. If a judge thinks he or she has spotted a corked bottle, another bottle of the same wine is generally opened and new samples are provided. During their tastings, judges usually nibble on pieces of bread, cheese, or olives to cleanse their palates between wines. The brand of choice for olives is Graber from California, which are usually consumed with gusto. Bottled water is always available.

In all my experience the judges were serious about their task. They rarely talk as they work their way through the wines. They always spit out the wine after they have tasted it, so that they do not consume any alcohol. Old-timers at the Indy International Wine Competition, which is part of the Indiana State Fair and annually attracts some three thousand entries, still tell of the winemaker who was sent home before lunch on the first day because he was not spitting and had already become tipsy.

After all the judges on a panel have finished a flight, they discuss their individual scores and whether to award a medal. There is usually some consensus about the wine's quality. It's rare for one person to want to award a gold, while another doesn't think it deserves any medal. Most judges are not dogmatic about their opinion unless it is a question of an obvious fault, such as oxidation. It's not unusual for a judge to change his or her score during the discussion, although rarely does he or she go from giving no medal to awarding a gold.

Just as in the deliberations of a jury trial, some panel members can influence others. I have participated in many discussions when one judge changed the votes of others. Chip Cassidy, the wine director of the Crown Wine & Spirits chain in Florida and a veteran of many wine competitions around the world, told me that he thought the most honest judging he has ever attended was at the annual Vinitaly show, where the judges tasted alone and could not discuss their scores with anyone. That is a complicated way to organize an event, which is why the method is rarely used, but it eliminates outside influences.

Robert Hodgson grew up in Seattle, and became interested in winemaking while working on his PhD at Oregon State. His first venture into the field was making blackberry wine, which he remembers tasting while it was still fermenting. As his hobby continued, Hodgson began looking for sources of good grapes and in 1969 drove an old Volkswagen Squareback station wagon to the Napa Valley to buy five hundred pounds of grapes.

In the early 1970s, Hodgson landed a teaching job at Humboldt State University, which is located amid the redwood trees in California's far northwest. There he taught physical oceanography and elementary statistics. In 1976, Hodgson's Fieldbrook Winery made its first vintage, and he was soon producing about one thousand cases annually. He bought quality grapes from Mendocino County, located just south of Humboldt County, which was a leading California wine region in the mid-nineteenth century.

Hodgson's wines were soon selling well, with about one-third of them going into the San Francisco market. While that was encouraging, he always wondered whether they were any good, so, in the early 1980s, he began looking for ways of getting some third-party opinions. Wine competitions seemed like a good way to achieve that, and he first entered one at the Los Angeles County Fair. He won a bronze medal, and for a few days felt ten feet tall. He then entered more county competitions as well as the one at the California State Fair, the state's biggest. The inconsistency of the results at the various competitions, though, bothered the scientist in him. Sometimes one of his wines would win a gold medal, but then the next time that same wine wouldn't even get a bronze. Bewildered, he set out on a quest to see if he could find an explanation.

The professor first decided to become personally involved with the California State Fair Wine Competition. Working on panels, Hodgson grew to appreciate fellow judges for the seriousness with which they approached their task. He noted how most of them took copious notes about each wine and recognized that the good judges had an uncanny ability to describe taste sensations on paper. He concluded that he wasn't a good judge because he had trouble expressing his opinions in writing.

Hodgson also began noticing the inconsistency of the results, and took his concern to chief judge G. M. "Pooch" Pucilowski. Hodgson told him that he didn't think he should continue being a judge. Pucilowski, though, urged him to stay with the competition because as a small winemaker he brought a different point of view to the panels, which were mostly staffed with big-winery people. Richard Peterson, a top winemaker in Napa, even recommended that Hodgson join the State Fair Commercial Wine Advisory Task Force.

From his new position, the professor began a systematic study of results at the California State Fair Wine Competition. Because of his professional work with statistics, Hodgson became highly uncomfortable with the inconsistency of the scores he was seeing. Results were all over the board. One judge might give a wine a gold medal, while another gave it no medal. That might just reflect the opinions of two different people, but shouldn't there be some objective standard of quality? The judge, Hodgson thought, might as well be rolling dice to determine who gets an award. In no other field would such random results be considered acceptable. The state fair, Hodgson concluded, needed to figure out why there was such a high level of statistical disparity and whether anything could be done to reduce it and improve results.

Hodgson's first hypothesis was that the fault lay with the judges. So, at the 2005 California State Fair Wine Competition, he studied their results closely and noted that they had widely varying tasting styles. Some would only smell a wine before passing judgment, while others pondered and agonized over a score. Hodgson finally proposed to Pucilowski that the judges be monitored without telling them that their results were being watched. In those days a panel of four judges would quickly assess wines one day, voting to accept or reject them for further consideration on a second day. If at least two judges voted to accept the wine, it went to the second round on the next day. Hodgson introduced one of his own wines, a Pacini Vineyard Zinfandel, into the mix, placing three samples from the same bottle in front of the judges for evaluation. In two instances three or more judges voted to eliminate his wine from further consideration. However, the third sample received two positive votes. The following day, in the final round, the same judges gave that wine a double gold medal, meaning that all four judges gave it a gold! "Something is clearly wrong," Hodgson told Pucilowski.

Pucilowski agreed that it seemed unusual, but was not surprised. At the same time, he realized there had to be another way to judge wines that provided more consistent results, and he thought Hodgson could help him find it. So the state fair competition began changing procedures. Rather than using the retain-eliminate method on one day followed by a second day of reevaluating the retained wines, the fair divided the entries equally between both days and proceeded at a slower pace.

At state fairs 2005 through 2007, Hodgson carefully judged the judges. The objective was not to see whether they agreed with each other, but whether individual judges were consistent in their own scoring of the same wine in different tastings. Judges were unaware that they were being tested. Each panel of four received a flight of twenty to thirty wines that included three poured from the same bottle. Judges were asked to vote on a scale of 1 to 8, going from no medal to gold. Competitions involving Chardonnay and Cabernet Sauvignon wines were the easiest to study because those varieties have the most entrants.

The results were tabulated, and Hodgson analyzed the findings. "Some of the judges did pretty well, and some were pretty awful," he recalls. In some cases, a judge gave no medal, no medal, and then a gold to the same wine from the same bottle. Such results clearly called into question the ability of the judges to rate wines accurately. As Hodgson explained to me, if a radiologist were to read the same X-ray three times and not come up with the same diagnosis, he wouldn't be in that profession for long.

In the second year of testing, the results were similar, but with a surprising twist. The judges who had excelled in consistency the first year did not repeat their performance the next year. One who did well in 2005 might do poorly in 2006, and vice versa. No judge was best in both years. The results to Hodgson seemed almost to be a question of chance: "If ten people are rolling dice, someone might throw an unusual series of doubles. Is that because he is skilled at throwing doubles or just lucky?" he asked. "Unless the dice are loaded, it can be explained by chance." The results Hodgson was getting were discouraging, because they meant that a good judge could not be used to train other ones to be more consistent.

For three years in a row, Hodgson wrote up his results just as he would if he were preparing the material to be submitted to a professional publication, and he presented them to state fair officials. Pucilowski and others were very interested in the results and asked the professor for suggestions on how to improve the quality of the program.

In January 2007, Hodgson and Karl Storchmann, an associate professor of economics at Whitman College and also the managing editor of the *Journal of Wine Economics,* started an e-mail exchange about the work being done at the state fair. Hodgson explained it in some detail, but also pointed out that he had promised the people running the tastings not to release any results. Storchmann responded enthusiastically in an e-mail, "Bob, wow, this is intriguing!!!! . . . You need to write something for us!!"

He also forwarded to Hodgson papers others had done on the quality of wine judges and another on the prices of wines that won tastings. The two then began considering whether to publish a paper based on Hodgson's research. The state fair people were anxious for the results not to be released to the general public out of fear that they would reflect badly on their competition and that people would not understand that the research was an attempt to find a way for judges to be more consistent. Hodgson, on the other hand, believed the public had a right to know.

Hodgson in 2007 wrote a paper and sent it to Storchmann, who circulated it to the journal's other editors for a peer review. They were all leaders in their fields: Kym Anderson was a professor at the University of Adelaide and consultant to the World Bank; Victor Ginsburgh taught at the Free University in Brussels; Orley Ashenfelter of Princeton University was about to become president of the American Economic Association; and Robert Stavins was from the John F. Kennedy School of Government and director of the Harvard Environmental Economics Program. They all urged Storchmann to publish Hodgson's paper.

The state fair's Commercial Wine Advisory Task Force met to come up with a position to be passed along to its board of directors on whether to publish. In hopes of overcoming opposition, Hodgson said he would leave out the important fact that the paper was done on the basis of results from the California State Fair Wine Competition. Task force member Mike Dunne, the wine editor of the *Sacramento Bee,* told the others that leaving out the fair's name would be meaningless and any competent journalist would be able to figure out in fifteen minutes where the study had been conducted, so it might as well be made public. Darrell Corti, a longtime judge who had been active in California wine for decades, warned that releasing the paper could mean the end of the state fair competition. By a close vote, the task force agreed to recommend that the paper be published and that it be stated that the research was based on data collected at the Sacramento wine competition. When the issue went to the board of directors, state fair general manager and CEO Norbert Bartosik urged members to authorize publication, which they did.

Hodgson's work was the lead article in the winter 2008 issue of the *Journal of Wine Economics,* under the headline "An Examination of Judge Reliability at a Major U.S. Wine Competition." The nine-page document is scholarly in tone and heavy with charts and graphs. The abstract stated the results starkly: "About 10 percent of the judges were able to replicate their score within a single medal group. Another 10 percent, on occasion, scored the same wine Bronze to Gold. . . . An analysis of variance covering every panel over the study period indicates only about half of the panels presented awards based solely on wine quality."

While working on his paper, Hodgson had come across an article in *The California Grapevine* that had published results on four thousand wines entered in thirteen American wine competitions. That gave him the raw material for a new paper that would examine whether there was consistency of results over several competitions. During a winter vacation in 2009, Hodgson crunched the numbers and analyzed the results, examining what had happened to wines that had been entered in five competitions and won at least one gold medal.

The *Journal of Wine Economics* published his conclusions in its spring 2009 issue with the title "An Analysis of the Concordance Among 13 U.S. Wine Competitions." His results were even more stunning than those in his first article. Out of the 2,440 wines entered in more than three contests, 47 percent received gold medals, but 84 percent of those same wines did not receive any award in another contest. So there was no consistency from competition to competition. Hodgson wrote in his abstract: "Many wines that are viewed as extraordinarily good in some competitions are viewed as below average at others." His final conclusion: "(1) there is almost no consensus among the thirteen wine competitions regarding wine quality, (2) for wines receiving a Gold medal in one or more competitions, it is very likely that the same wine received no award in another, (3) the likelihood of a Gold medal can be statistically explained by chance alone." One winemaker told him that "if you want to win gold medals, all you have to do is enter a lot of competitions and sooner or later you'll win one." Hodgson's second *Journal of Wine Economics* paper proved that theory.

Hodgson, though, wasn't finished with his research on wine judges. The 2009 fall issue of the *Journal of Wine Economics* published a third paper. This one was entitled "How Expert are 'Expert' Wine Judges?". It drew on research done by experts at Yale and New York University as well as the results of Australian studies on competitions. Hodgson's conclusions: both the California and Australia results "suggest that less than 30 percent of *expert* wine judges studied are in fact 'expert.'"

Hodgson's work originally had a limited audience outside the world of wine economists and statisticians, but it caught the attention of Leonard Mlodinow, a professor at Caltech who, with Stephen Hawking, wrote *A Briefer History of Time* and was also author of the best seller *The Drunkard's*

Walk: How Randomness Rules Our Lives. Mlodinow used Hodgson's work as the basis for an article that appeared in the *Wall Street Journal* on November 20, 2009. Mlodinow cited earlier studies that reached similar conclusions, writing that in view of the research, the average wine consumer should be "refusing to pay for medals and rating points."

Hodgson's research has led other statisticians to venture into the world of wine competitions. Jing Cao and Lynne Stokes of Southern Methodist University examined some of the results for judges at the 2009 California State Fair, looking at bias, discrimination ability, and variability. They concluded that their results could be helpful in the future selection of judges. The *Journal of Wine Economics* published their paper in 2010.

Hodgson still labors in the statistical vineyards of wine competitions, using the one he runs at the Humboldt County Fair as a forum for trying out new ideas. One of his latest concepts is to have judges score wines on three criteria: anticipation, balance, and satisfaction. The works of Hodgson and others are likely eventually to improve the results of wine competitions and the validity of gold medals.

Despite his own trailblazing research, Robert T. Hodgson continues to enter his wines in competitions, and there is a gold sticker proclaiming "California State Gold Medal" on the bottle of his Fieldbrook *il montaggio* Sangiovese. The Fieldbrook website also lists Hodgson's sixty-two medals dating back to 1992. If the public continues to pay attention to medals despite his research, he told me, he might as well get credit for the awards he's won.

In 2008, David Akin, a winemaker in the Lodi wine region, was looking to start a wine tasting that would highlight the area's products. Lodi was once known primarily for its bulk wines and as the home of Woodbridge by Robert Mondavi, but in recent years it has been making better wines and now has higher aspirations. Akin took his idea to the local Rotary Club and also to "Pooch" Pucilowski of the California State Fair Wine Competition, who is a resident of Lodi. Pucilowski then went to Tim Hanni, who thought this might be a way to do more research on his theories about how people taste. Pucilowski also saw the Lodi event as an opportunity to do experiments in judging that would be difficult to undertake at the historic state fair event.

The first Lodi International Wine Awards in 2008 operated along the lines of a normal wine competition, except organizers did not permit judges to talk among themselves, lest they influence each other. In 2009, it introduced some average wine consumers as judges, but kept their scores separate from those of experienced tasters. The results showed that the two groups liked totally different wines.

The third year, the organizers revamped the tasting and changed the name to the Consumer Wine Awards. On the basis of work with sensory specialists, they gave the judges a longer time to evaluate a wine. Instead of presenting them with a flight of perhaps a dozen wines of the same grape variety, they sampled one wine at a time and had up to three minutes to evaluate it. Also rather than tasting perhaps one hundred wines a day, judges rated only forty in 2010 and thirty or fewer in 2011.

The competition is now in its groove and provides an interesting contrast to other programs around the country because the judges are average consumers. The 2011 contest pulled in seven hundred entries, with the vast majority coming from California, although some were from Virginia. The 120 volunteer judges were a good cross section of the wine-drinking public and not professional tasters.

The range in prices for entries went from $4.75 to $90, with plenty of bottles at around $30. The most expensive wines as a group came from Napa Valley, but only two of the fifteen best of class hailed from there. The most expensive product in the competition was a Cabernet Sauvignon from Oakville Ranch in Napa. It won a gold. The most expensive wine to win a best-of-class award was Dancing Fox Merlot from Lodi at $29.50.

Five best-of-class winners sell for $10 or less: Gallo Family Vineyards unoaked sweet Chardonnay ($5.99), HRM Rex-Goliath Red Blend ($7.99), Motos Liberty Pinot Grigio ($8.99), Cellar No. 8 Cabernet Sauvignon ($10), and Simply Naked unoaked Chardonnay ($10).

Among superpremium wines, Gallo performed best. Its Family Vineyards won three golds and a platinum among six entrees. The Barefoot Cellars brand had fourteen products in the competition and won three golds and a platinum. The company's Turning Leaf, though, did less well, getting only one gold among six entries.

Concluded Hanni after the 2011 competition: "The Consumer Wine Awards at Lodi is helping develop a better understanding of personal preferences and empowering wine consumers."

When I asked him whether average consumers should pay any attention to medals, Robert Hodgson responded, "I tell people that they should find out what kind of wines they like. They should believe in themselves. That's much more important than believing in wine judges."

CHAPTER FIVE

Thinking Outside the Bottle

Anyone looking to spend less money on wine should be considering alternative packaging to the standard glass wine bottle that holds 750 milliliters. Depending on whether or not the pourer has a heavy hand, the bottle holds roughly five servings. As a container it's a convenient size for two people to consume at a meal, and the shape—which first became popular in the 1600s—has been perfected. But larger containers, especially nonglass ones, can dramatically bring down the cost of wine.

In addition, environmentalists are now challenging the practice of shipping wine in heavy glass bottles thousands of miles around the world. Wine was one of the first products in history to be widely transported, going from winemakers in rural areas to nearby cities. During most of that time, though, the mode of transporting wine was totally different from what it is today. It traveled for hundreds of years in clay amphoras aboard ships, then starting in about the fifth century in wooden barrels. Once the wine arrived at its destination, it was poured into pitchers for serving at table, but in the early seventeenth century, after the advent of the rugged English bottle, it was locally transferred to those containers. The size of the bottle was determined by how much air the glassblower had in his lungs to make the container. Over time the size was standardized, though the shape was much rounder than the ones in use today.

The most heavily traveled international wine route was from Bordeaux to London, with wine shipped in barrels and then bottled at the destination. It was only in 1927 that Baron Philippe de Rothschild inaugurated bottling at the château in an attempt to eliminate the common problem of wine fraud, when inexpensive wine was shipped to London and put in famous bottles. As a sign of authenticity, Baron Philippe printed on the label *Mise en bouteille au château* (literally: Put in bottle at the château). The British called this château bottling. As late as the 1960s, some top Bordeaux wineries were still bottling part of their production in London, but eventually the vast majority of wine was shipped around the world in 750ml bottles.

Some wine producers offer so-called large-format bottles, which are particularly popular for special events such as weddings or anniversaries. These start with the magnum, which contains 1.5 liters, the equivalent of two regular bottles, and go up through ever-larger ones named after biblical kings such as Jeroboam (4.5 liters) and Nebuchadnezzar (15 liters). Standard-size bottles and magnums are common, but bigger ones are rare. The biggest bottle made to date is a Five Virtues Shiraz from Australia that stands six feet, five inches tall and weighs 1,300 pounds. It holds the equivalent of 387 regular bottles. There's no special name for that one.

Many wine professionals consider the magnum to be the ideal bottle size because it allows the wine to mature at just the right pace. It's also convenient to use at parties since fewer corks have to be pulled, and the sight of a magnum gives a festive air to any occasion.

Many producers of wines selling for less than $10 for a standard bottle sell magnums for only slightly more. Affordable wines in magnums became popular in the 1970s as part of the success of California's fighting varietals. Brands such as Glen Ellen and Fetzer sold well and continue to be popular in that size, as do imported wines such as Cavit Pinot Grigio and Lindeman's Chardonnay. Prices vary greatly depending on the state, but a 750ml bottle of Glen Ellen Chardonnay or Cabernet Sauvignon will cost about $4, a magnum $7. That brings the average price of the two bottles down to $3.50. A standard bottle of [yellow tail] for those same two varieties is $6.99, the magnum $10.99, reducing the cost of 750ml of wine to $5.50.

The first new wine container since the development of the English bottle in the seventeenth century came out of Australia. In 1955, William R. Scholle was looking for a way to safely transport battery acid. His solution was to put the liquid into a tough plastic bladder that ensured the acid would not leak, and the bag was housed inside a corrugated fiberboard box. A decade later, Thomas Angove, another Australian, applied this invention to wine. He was the managing director of Angove, a family winery in Renmark,

South Australia, and saw it as a good way to sell bulk wine to consumers. His son John was not impressed when his father showed him the container. "I remember when I was about fifteen, he brought home a prototype, and I said to him, 'This is ridiculous. Nobody is gong to buy wine out of a cardboard box and plastic bag.' But he persevered, and didn't listen to me. He was determined."

Thomas Angove called his product a wine cask, and Australians commonly referred to it as a "bag-in-box." His company patented the invention on April 20, 1965. Angove's boxes originally held one gallon of wine and were not very consumer-friendly. People had to cut off the corner of the bag of wine, pour out a glass, and then reseal the bag with a peg that came with the box. As the wine was poured, the bag collapsed, so the wine never came in contact with air, which would have spoiled it. Two years later, Penfolds, another big Australian wine company, patented a more convenient bag-in-box that had a tap for dispensing wine, and later even better spouts were introduced.

That packaging quickly became the industry standard. Wine boxes were a hit in Australia, and now some half of all the wine consumed there is sold in those packages. They are also popular in Europe, particularly the Scandinavian countries, for daily wines. The French came up with a *franglais* name for the container, calling it *le bag in box*. By the 1970s, big French wine companies such as Nicolas were selling Beaujolais and Côtes-du-Rhône, two daily wines, in boxes. The French generally liked three-liter boxes better than the five-liter ones popular in Australia.

Bag-in-box offered consumers several advantages: The wine was less expensive in the larger containers, initially selling for only a few dollars a gallon. Also, people could enjoy just one glass with dinner and didn't have to worry about finishing a whole bottle. Boxes eliminated the danger of corked wine, which occurs when the wine picks up bad smells and tastes from corks tainted with the chemical compound 2,4,6-trichloroanisole, or TCA. Finally, wine could be stored for long periods, thanks to the airtight container. Wineries promised that the wine could be drunk for a month or more after being opened.

Boxes, though, can have problems with air getting to the wine. Over time, it seeps into the bag, both through the walls of the plastic container and around the tap. The wine then oxidizes and loses much of its fruit flavor. Box manufacturing has gotten somewhat better, but air remains a problem. Somewhere on the package consumers can find the date by which the wine should be consumed. François Lurton, a major producer of inexpensive wines around the world, once told me that he never ships wine in boxes if they have to make the long and often hot trip from the Southern Hemisphere to the Northern.

Americans were slow to pick up on box wines, although soon all the mass wine producers had box brands. The Wine Group was a trailblazer in the field and is now the top U.S. company in boxes. It was originally a subsidiary of Coca-Cola, but in 1981 the soft-drink company wanted to get out of the wine business, so the group's managers bought the wine operations. The Wine Group annually sells 60 million cases of largely inexpensive products, making it the second biggest company in wine after Gallo. One of its early successes was the five-liter Franzia box, which is now the world's most popular wine, annually selling the equivalent of thirty-three million cases of 750ml bottles. Currently it comes in both five- and three-liter boxes. Gallo offers Peter Vella, Carlo Rossi, and Livingston Cellars in boxes. Box wines now have their space in retail stores and a following with the public, but the wine press dismisses them as the successor of jug wines, of interest only to winos and college students looking for a cheap high. Many of the box wines still carry names such as Chablis that have nothing to do with the grapes used in their production, and they are often sweet. The Wine Group and Gallo are both highly secretive companies that don't release their sales figures, but there is no doubt that box wines have found a large market.

Ryan Sproule in 2003 changed the way many Americans thought about box wines. A software engineer by training who had worked in Silicon Valley, he lost his job when his firm was caught in the dot-com bust of 2001. Being unemployed wasn't a disaster for Sproule. He was forty-one and had been living a hectic, intense existence for nearly two decades at high-technology start-ups, and he welcomed the chance to take some time off and travel. Along with many people his age, he had enough experience to know how businesses work but was still young enough to think big. So he packed his dreams in a suitcase and went on the road. After six months of travel, Sproule decided to go back to work, but not in the tech world. While visiting Europe, he had seen box wines and thought they were a great idea. He was surprised that no one in the United States was putting quality wine in a box, as they were in Europe and Australia. The box wines then on the market, such as Franzia, Almaden, and Peter Vella, all had negative reputations, considered simply junk wines. Sproule concluded that he could solve that problem. All he had to do was sell better wine in a box and then market it heavily.

In the spring of 2002, using the skills he had learned working for Silicon Valley start-up firms, Sproule launched a company to make a better box wine. Sproule ran his idea past four wine business experts. Three of them told him he was crazy because no one would buy quality wine in a box. The fourth, though, agreed with him that it was just a matter of educating consumers on the benefits of upscale box wine. Just as many successful innovators do, Sproule ignored the three nays and went along with the one yea.

He had seen tech firms get into trouble by spending too much capital early, so he was averse to putting cash on the line. Nevertheless, he sold his house to finance his venture and eventually invested about $500,000 to get going. Sproule began as a virtual company that at first had no other employees, relying mainly on consultants who were paid for specific work and didn't get a salary or benefits. His office was in his rented home in Walnut Creek, a modest town of sixty-five thousand people located sixteen miles east of Oakland.

Sproule's first decision was to use a three-liter box, rather than the five-liter ones then on the American market. He also wanted to keep the price under $20 to reduce the danger of sticker shock. "Anything over that would seem like a bigger purchase psychologically," he says. He wanted consumers to be able to put a $20 bill on the counter and get back some change. Sproule then did a focus group with friends, who all liked the idea.

The early years of the new millennium were one of those periods when surplus wine was sloshing around the bulk market. With a consultant winemaker helping him do the tasting, Sproule sampled wines for sale by the tanker load. He set a price limit of $6 a gallon, which he thought was the highest he could go and still keep the retail price at less than $20.

When it came to designing the box, Sproule wanted it to look serious, but not pretentious. "It had to exude quality," he says. At first he put an actual wine label on the box, the same kind and size consumers would see on a bottle, but that was later dropped. He wanted the box to be black because he thought it was the color of luxury. In addition, black made his product stand out from the five-liter wines, which mostly had white containers. The consultant graphic artists wanted him to go with flashy packaging, but he stuck to his original concept: simple, classic, luxury. He named the new product Black Box.

Sproule decided his first wine would be a Chardonnay, the most popular wine on the American market, but he didn't want what he calls the "big, buttery, oaky" style that was then popular. He thought average people drank only a few glasses of that kind of wine before becoming sated. He wanted an easy-to-drink, crisper flavor designed to go with meals. He and the winemaker consultant blended wines from several producers to get the exact taste they wanted. Sproule bought most of the Chardonnay for $6 a gallon from one of Napa Valley's oldest and most prestigious wineries. Its Chardonnay retails for nearly $40 a bottle. Sproule says he could have put out an even better-quality wine from another wine region, but he wanted the prestige of the Napa appellation to be on his first box. The second wine in a Black Box was a Sonoma Merlot.

The heart of Sproule's sales pitch was that he was selling a premium $10–12 bottle for half price to people who drank wine every day. Those people, he believed, won't spend more than $15 for a daily wine. "I was one of those people, and so I was targeting myself," he says. When he started taking his product into liquor stores, Sproule ran into difficulties with owners because of the box. He soon developed the ploy of taking a bottle of his wine into the store for tasting and saying he was going to sell it for $5. When he got the expected good reaction to a quality Chardonnay at that price, he would pull out the box and explain the packaging.

Sproule was initially both the company's salesman and its delivery person, trying to convince store managers to stock his unusual product and taking along a few cases in his pickup truck. He didn't try at first to sell through grocery outlets, and only went to wine stores that had knowledgeable staffers who could explain the Black Box concept. The first boxes of the vintage 2001 Chardonnay with the proud Napa Valley appellation on the label went on sale in January 2003. PlumpJack Wines, a high-end San Francisco liquor outlet that also owns a pricey Napa Valley winery, was the first store to carry Black Box. Sproule's modest goal was to sell eight thousand cases in the first year.

Within a month following the launch, he realized he had a huge hit on his hands. He started getting reorders from stores much earlier than anticipated. Sales also got a boost in February, when Black Box Chardonnay won a silver medal at the *San Francisco Chronicle* Wine Competition, and he promoted that heavily in stores. The *Chronicle* followed up with a story by respected critic Dan Berger with the subtitle, "Premium wine is no longer strictly a bottled affair." Accompanying it was a picture of a waiter in a tuxedo and white gloves holding a box of Black Box Chardonnay. Instead of the 8,000 cases Sproule hoped to sell in the first year, he actually sold 140,000.

Only ten weeks after the launch, Sproule was at a Monterey wine festival promoting his new venture. Winery booths were arranged in alphabetical order, so Black Box was located right next to Blackstone Winery, which is owned by Constellation. The Blackstone people showed interest in his product and started asking him questions. Finally, an unassuming guy whom Sproule didn't know came up and asked him if had ever considered selling the company. Sproule thought he was just another Blackstone sales rep, but when the man left his business card behind, he learned it was José F. Fernandez, Constellation's chief executive officer.

At around the same time, Sproule got a call from Michael Mondavi, who was then running the family wine business. He invited Sproule to a private multicourse lunch at the winery, complete with Robert Mondavi's best wines. Mondavi also wanted to make a deal. Eventually Sproule got written offers from Constellation, Mondavi, and Trinchero Family Estates. Fetzer made an overture but never a firm offer.

Sproule was reluctant to sell, because all the signs were that he was going to have a big hit. Wine distributors were beating down his door to carry his boxes. Sproule eventually concluded that he was interested in something less than an outright sale, such as a licensing agreement. He finally went with a royalty agreement with Constellation, which he thought best understood his plans for Black Box and wanted him to be involved with the company for several years. The deal closed on September 1, 2003, only nine months after the product was launched.

Black Box now sells two million cases annually, the equivalent of twenty-four million bottles. If it were still an independent wine company, it would be about the tenth largest in the United States. It currently produces eight varieties: Chardonnay, Riesling, Merlot, Cabernet Sauvignon, and Shiraz from California and Washington State plus Malbec from Argentina, Sauvignon Blanc from New Zealand, and Pinot Grigio from Italy. Black Box still buys its wines in the bulk market and owns no vineyards, although Constellation has some.

While the bargain price for a quality wine was usually the impetus for people to buy Black Box, the company has found that the convenience of a box over a bottle soon became the driving force. Consumer studies said that equally as important as the price were factors such as the ability to drink only one glass at a time and to have several different wines open simultaneously, the compactness of two magnums in a small container, easy portability, and environmental friendliness.

Black Box has done well at some of the most prestigious wine competitions. It has won fifteen gold medals, including two at the California State Fair and one at the 2010 Finger Lakes International Wine Competition. The wines have also received scores in the 80-point range from *Wine Spectator,* some even in the high 80s.

Go into any American wine retail store today, and you'll see a section devoted to box wines. Some fifty companies are now making box wines. Bota Box, made by Delicato, is marketing itself as the eco-friendly wine. Hardys, an Australian company that Constellation also owns, has a line of three-liter boxes that have received good reviews. Franzia now sources much of its wines abroad, with the Chardonnay sometimes coming from South Africa and the Cabernet Sauvignon from Chile. Consumers, though, have to look closely at the box to see the country of origin in small letters.

Wine in Tetra Pak containers, which are airtight and made of coated paperboard, has been in Europe for many years, but only recently became popular in the United States. Wine snobs disparagingly call them "fruit-juice-box wines" or "picnic wines."

The Rebel Wine Company, a joint venture of partners Charles Bieler, Joel Gott, and Roger Scommegna, working in cooperation with Trinchero Family Estates, have long been innovators in wine packaging. Despite the negative reputation of wine jugs, the Rebels had an early success that appealed to a young crowd. In 2002, Rebel Wine launched Three Thieves Bandit, the first Tetra Pak wine in the United States, which came in a one-liter container. The company claims that the grapes come from premium California vineyards. Says Joel Gott: "You're going to see more and more Tetra. It's very convenient."

Tetra Paks got a big push when Target launched its Wine Cube, which is produced by Trinchero Family Estates and sells in two sizes, a 1.5 liter package that contains four small Tetra Paks, and a three-liter bag-in-box. The Target store clout means the company moves a lot of wine, and it is now Black Box's major competitor. Unfortunately for consumers, the Wine Cube is available only in states where alcohol can be sold in the same location as food.

American wineries continue to seek out innovative ways to package wines. Red Truck, a Sonoma winery, introduced a metal, three-liter mini-barrel that sold for about $30, but it didn't catch on and was dropped. A California company called United Natural Process Alliance is selling reusable stainless steel bottles to wineries that recycle them. The Gotham Project in New York City has plans to launch a metal twenty-liter container similar to a beer keg, for use at parties or in restaurants. It also can also be reused.

France's Jean-Charles Boisset, who owns DeLoach Vineyards in Sonoma, has introduced a mini wooden barrel that contains ten liters of Pinot Noir. The company calls it Barrel to Barrel, but it is actually a plastic bag-in-box inside an oak barrel. Boisset promotes this as a less expensive and more eco-friendly way to deliver wine. DeLoach says the wine will stay fresh for about eight weeks. Ten liters yield about seventy glasses of wine, so the barrel originally appealed in restaurants and bars. In November 2010, the company came out with a consumer size that holds three liters. The small barrel is $220, and the bigger original one is $250. The price of three-liter bags range from $52 to $96, depending on wine quality, and the ten-liter bags from $156 to $288. At that price point, DeLoach barrels are hardly bargain wines.

Consumers looking for the least expensive wine should consider box wines. They can get both value and good wine, which is why premium boxes are now the fastest-growing segment of the wine business, increasing about 25 percent annually. The next time you're drinking a quality wine from a box, raise a glass and thank Ryan Sproule.

CHAPTER SIX

Gatekeepers Old and New

There are critics, consultants, and specialists to advise people looking for a book to read at the beach, a dress to buy for a wedding, or a painting to hang in the living room. When it comes to wine, a plethora of people are waiting to help you select a bottle for that special event. Whether consumers are buying wine in a retail store or ordering it in a restaurant, they can get information through books, newspapers, websites, apps, or adult-education classes. The world of wine, though, resembles that of high fashion. The haute couture stars' creations that critics and magazines love this season are a long way from what women are wearing to work or dinner.

Many famous wine tasters and consultants have sipped their way through history because they seem to have a unique ability to identify and appreciate wine and brandies. In the early part of the twentieth century, there was Arnold Raleigh Morrow in California. He was a top executive with the California Wine Association, a wine cartel in pre-Prohibition years that limited production in more than sixty wineries in order to keep up prices. Morrow went from winery to winery around the state rating the quality of the association's members. He was so serious about his job that he never swallowed even a drop of wine out of fear that it would affect his ability to taste. That landed him in *Ripley's Believe It or Not* on March 23, 1935. The item read: "A. R. Morrow Dean of American Vintners was a professional wine taster for 47 years before he drank any." He also did not smoke, eat spicy food or sweets, and had only a light breakfast on tasting days.

People within the wine trade claimed that he was such a talented taster, he could tell whether a winemaker had a large mortgage on his property simply by sampling his wine. If it had a weak flavor it meant the winemaker was overcropping the vines so he could have a bigger harvest even though that reduced the quality. A California vintner once put Morrow to the test.

The winemaker showed up in Morrow's office with a bottle of wine and asked the taster to tell him the size of his mortgage. Morrow tasted the wine, paused a while, and then told him confidently that it was $10,000. The winemaker could have died; Morrow was right. The supposed savant later revealed that only a few days before the challenge he had been talking with the winemaker's banker, who told him that the man had just taken out a loan.

Morrow's strict rule about not drinking the alcohol he was sampling ended on January 16, 1919. That day he was rating several California brandies behind closed doors, when his secretary interrupted him to tell him that the day before, five more states had ratified Prohibition, pushing the total past the thirty-two necessary for it to be the law of the land. Figuring that his tasting job was over and showing his contempt for Prohibition, Morrow picked up a glass full of brandy that he had just sampled and downed it in a single gulp. After the end of Prohibition, he returned to being a wine taster and regularly had a glass with dinner.

Most Americans need help from gatekeepers such as Morrow, because few people have grown up in a culture like that in Europe, where wine is simply part of daily life and not a mysterious elixir. Americans have an international reputation for being pushy, loud, know-it-alls. That is not true, though, when it comes to wine. When the subject comes up, many are unsure what they should like or buy. Members of the Millennial Generation may be more confident about their likes and dislikes than their parents, but for most Americans, wine remains, as Churchill said of Russia, "a riddle wrapped in a mystery inside an enigma."

But it's not just Americans who need help. In 2010, the veteran British wine critic Michael Broadbent, on the occasion of his four hundredth column in the London wine magazine *Decanter,* wrote, "My feeling is that consumers have never had so much choice, but they have never been so confused. The whole world is making a good standard of wine today, and they need some guidance."

Most wine gatekeepers are self-taught. Only a few of the people deciding what others should drink have passed the demanding professional qualification programs to become a Master of Wine or Master Sommelier. The rest have learned what they know from personal experience. This is not to say that they are unqualified—there is no better way to learn about wine than to drink it. But there are few objective standards by which an aver-age consumer can judge or check someone's wine expertise, the same way that they might check out a person's law degree or medical diploma, for example. An old saw in the business is that anyone with a pen, notebook, and a few bottles of wine can become a wine critic.

Experts do not always taste wines blind, although many claim they do. As was so clearly seen in the Paris Tasting, blind tasting is the only way to be truly objective about the wine in the glass. Robert M. Parker Jr. admits that he sometimes knows the name of what he's trying. He also samples wine in barrels, and there are persistent rumors that savvy winemakers pro-duce specific ones tailored to his well-known preference in order to get high scores.

I was long curious about the reviews of supposedly blind tastings because the scores were almost never unexpected. Statisticians have developed the concept of outliers, which are examples outside the range of the great major-ity of the sample being studied. But in all the tastings of the top five First Growths of Bordeaux that I have ever read, there is never an outlier. None ever receives, for example, fewer than 80 points. Someone who had worked for a major wine publication finally explained why. Although the judges taste the First Growths without seeing the labels, they know that it is a sam-pling of just those top wines, which is why they never rate one low.

Whether they are writers, sommeliers, or store owners, gatekeepers are usually out to find the next big thing in wine, a special vintage, a little-known winery, or a new hot grape variety. As a way to show that they're in the know, sommeliers often recommend a wine that the customer may have never heard of. A few years ago, every publication and sommelier was abuzz about Grüner Veltliner, a white wine coming mainly out of Austria. The hot topic recently has been dry Riesling.

Consumers should remember that every gatekeeper has his or her per-sonal taste profile. If you prefer light white wines, find a writer or a critic who shares your interests and stay away from the ones who are always proposing wines you end up not liking. Don't drink big, bold Cabernets because that's the wine of choice for the arbiters of taste. Take some time to find your soul mate among critics. Gatekeepers can be helpful, but never forget that they have their own agenda, which may or may not coincide with yours.

The language of gatekeepers can show their prejudice. Coco Krumme of the Massachusetts Institute of Technology did an interesting study of the impact on the appreciation and price of wines from the words critics use. She looked at the descriptions of more than thirty-five hundred wines ranging from $4.99 to $137.99 retail. Her goal was to find the descriptors that best predict the price of a bottle. Her conclusion:

> Expensive wines are described in terms indicating authenticity or exclusivity (versus accessibility), fullness of flavor (rather than lightness), and with specificity (versus generality). For example, *old, elegant,* and *cuvée* best predict expensive wines, while *pleasing, refreshing,* and *enjoy* are associated with the cheap wines. "Dark" words such as *intense, supple, velvety,* and *smoky* are highly correlated with expensive wine; *bright, light, fresh, tropical,* and *pink* predict cheap ones. Expensive bottles see more specific descriptors, including a higher percentage of single fruits and flavors such as *tobacco* or *chocolate,* while inexpensive wines are described in more generic terms: *fruity, good, clean, tasty, juicy.*

The words can prejudice a consumer's view. Would you prefer an "elegant" wine or a "juicy" one?

The most important gatekeeper in the world of wine, without a doubt, is **Robert M. Parker Jr.** I once spent a day in St.-Émilion with a French wine exporter, who happened to have a copy of Parker's ranking of the region's wines a day before the official publication. Winery owners and winemakers treated the guy as if he possessed the secret for eternal life. They were going crazy to find out what Parker had written about them. Were their wines going to sell out upon release, or were they going to be stuck with unsold inventory? You could read the reaction on their faces when they learned their scores. Total elation at one winery; painful dejection at the next. Parker made their day, or ruined it. The title of Elin McCoy's 2005 biography perfectly describes Parker: *The Emperor of Wine.*

Many people have their epiphany with wine. Parker's took place in December 1967, when he followed his girlfriend to France, where she was spending her junior year abroad. Parker has an unusually acute sense of smell and taste, and the trip focused his senses on wine. He later become a lawyer, out of admiration for the muckraking of Ralph Nader, and set out in the late 1970s to bring that same approach to wine, a field rife with conflicts of interests for critics, producers, journalists, and retailers. In 1978, he began publishing a ratings newsletter called *The Baltimore-Washington Wine Advocate,* and a year later, he shortened the name to *The Wine Advocate.*

Parker burst onto the international wine scene when he went against the herd of critics and called the 1982 Bordeaux an outstanding vintage. That controversial judgment stood the test of time and established him as the world's leading expert on Bordeaux. Fame and fortune quickly followed, and he was soon writing best-selling wine books from his home base in rural Maryland, in addition to the newsletter, whose circulation has grown to more than fifty thousand.

Aside from having an outstanding sense of taste, Parker also had the luck, or the genius, to develop a scoring system that was easy for Americans to understand. At the time, both American and European wine critics used a 20-point system. Parker, though, introduced a 100-point one, like the standard in U.S. classrooms. Americans instinctively understood what the numbers meant. They knew that a 95 was a great grade, while 80 was just average. Parker had taken one giant step toward demystifying wine.

The Wine Advocate also introduced a new style of describing wines. European critics traditionally wrote rather prosaically on the subject. They seemed to agree with the French novelist Stendhal (1783–1842), who wrote, "Pleasure is often spoiled by describing it." André Simon, a giant among critics, wrote of red Bordeaux in his 1919 book *Wine and Spirits*: "The excellence of claret, and the reason why it may rightly claim precedence over all other wines, is that it is the most harmonious and natural of all wines." He also once compared a wine to "a girl of fifteen, with laughing blue eyes." His protégé Hugh Johnson, who started writing in the 1960s, followed that style: "The overriding hallmark of claret is to be slightly mouth-drying and at the same time to taste of fresh soft fruit. It is not what is known as fruity."

Parker, on the other hand, wrote with flair, drama, and similes. He gave the 2008 Ausone wine from St.-Émilion 96 to 100 points and this description: "The wine possesses dense fruit, full-bodied power, remarkably sweet tannins, and more elevated acidity. . . . The acidity seems low because of the wealth and density of the fruit. Everything is incredibly pure, and the cascade of blue and black fruits interwoven with notions of crushed rocks, flowers, and forest floor is as provocative as it is grand."

Not everyone likes Parker's purple prose. Richard Quandt, a Princeton economics professor and member of the Liquid Assets Wine Group there, counted words in Parker's wine vocabulary from his 2007 reviews and found more than 120 descriptive terms, ranging from the *a* for angular, animal, anise, apple, apricot, and austere to *v* for vegetable and violets. Quandt wrote that he could accept a word like *cocoa* to describe a wine, but he "really drew the line at scorched earth and spicy earth," because he had never eaten earth.

Critics claim Parker likes a particular style of wine: big, bold ones, powerful California Cabernet Sauvignons, red Bordeaux, and Rhône Valley Syrahs. He rarely writes, for example, about Tempranillo, a subtle red grown mainly in Spain. He also likes wines high in alcohol. If your taste matches his taste, then Parker's recommendations will be perfect for you.

Several studies have shown that a strong recommendation from Parker drives up the price of the wines. As a result, he has profoundly influenced the style of wines being made today all around the world. Many in the business complain that winemakers believe if they want a high Parker score, they have to make a Parker-style wine. Stores happily post Parker. Enology consultants such as France's Michel Rolland sell their services by implying, if not outright promising, that they can raise a winery's Parker scores if it will only follow their recommendations.

Parker met his match in Burgundy. He has been criticized for failing to appreciate the elegance and finesse of French Pinot Noir. He landed in a French court for statements made in one of his books alledgedly implying that one producer shipped lower-quality wines abroad and kept the best for France. Parker denied the claims and the suit ultimately was settled. He eventually turned Burgundy and California over to other tasters and sticks mainly with his first loves: Bordeaux and the Rhône Valley.

Robert Parker so towers over the gatekeepers that others tend to get lost. A few, though, have developed strong followings. Probably the second most influential critic is **James Laube**, who reports on California wines for *Wine Spectator*. He generally likes wines in the same style as Robert Parker.

Because of the power of the publication and the breadth of its readership, the *New York Times*'s main wine writer, **Eric Asimov**, also has clout. He writes feature articles and does tastings called Wines of the Times with *Times* colleague Florence Fabricant and visiting wine professionals. His personal tastes are broader than those of either Parker or Laube.

The sway of British critics, who long dominated the American market, is in decline. **Jancis Robinson** remains influential, more through her website than her weekly column in *The Financial Times*.

Consumers are likely to have their most personal experiences with gatekeepers at the **wine stores** where they shop. Dean Gargaro owns the liquor store at the California Club in downtown Los Angeles, an exclusive establishment catering to the area's business, civil, and social leaders. Given that clientele, Gargaro's shop offers lots of hands-on, personal service to wealthy people looking for the world's best wines.

Gargaro got into the wine business in the late 1960s, almost by accident. He grew up in the Los Angeles area, where his father owned the Beverly Hills Club. Dean hung around his father's club, learning the ins and outs of running a food and liquor operation. After his army tour in Europe ended in 1966, Gargaro returned to Southern California and went into the liquor business, working on the wholesale and retail sides as well as with importers. One of his first jobs was to teach wine to salesmen who had previously been selling only hard liquor and beer. In 1986, he bought the California Club shop and has run it since then.

Gargaro believes a wine retailer's job is to provide value for the customer. He says many people come into a store looking to buy a big name, no matter what the cost. Selling that bottle can be good business, but the consumer doesn't leave the store any wiser about wine. "A retailer should be objective and impartial, not attuned just to how famous a wine is, but also to the quality in relation to the price and to how well the wine was made."

The first thing a good retailer should determine, according to Gargaro, is the person's price range. He says that too often people come in saying that they want to buy a Zinfandel, when they should be telling the clerk that they want a full-bodied red Zinfandel at a certain price.

Gargaro says wine writers have to make recommendations to a broad public, rather than to the tastes of an individual consumer, and critics also have to recommend when a wine should be consumed. "That's impossible to do accurately," he says flatly. "A wine retailer can point out the level of enjoyment the consumer will have now and perhaps the potential for improvement with bottle aging." A retailer is also in a position to know a customer's palate and listen to what the person is seeking. "No wine writer can possibly provide that kind of service," he says.

Sommelier is the French name for consultants who recommend wines to restaurant customers. This is another important group of gatekeepers, especially when it comes to expensive wines. Jean Arnold, president of Sonoma's Hanzell Vineyards, once told me that sommeliers have the greatest influence on the sale of her outstanding, but expensive, Chardonnay and Pinot Noir.

Unfortunately, too many sommeliers try to push consumers into buying more expensive bottles that may or may not be any better than what they initially ordered, a practice called upselling. A customer selects a wine at a price he's comfortable with, but the sommelier—often in front of the orderer's guests—suggests another one that might cost $50 or $100 more. Bad show, but it happens all the time.

Most sommeliers are self-trained wine experts who have picked up their knowledge in a restaurant. Doug Frost, however, has earned the two most prestigious honors in wine. He is both a Master of Wine, one of about 275 worldwide, and a Master Sommelier, of which there are only slightly more than one hundred in North America. Frost is one of only three people in the world to hold both titles.

After graduating in 1977 from Kansas State University, Frost worked at Plaza III, a fine-dining steak house in Kansas City. Within a week, he was helping the sommelier there do private tastings. Soon he was into wine wholesaling and eventually all parts of the business, including working for several years as a sommelier. He now mainly does wine consulting.

Frost sees the job of the sommelier as being the restaurant's wine director, working equally with the owner, the chef, and the diners. His mantra is that wine should be a complement to the food and make it taste better. He admits that the caricature of sommeliers as self-important wine snobs is "still out there." He adds, though, that in recent years restaurants and sommeliers have learned that success means getting return business, and that comes from a happy customer who liked his food and wine.

Many traditional wine gatekeepers have blatant conflicts of interest. The most important is that they have a prejudice for expensive wines. Everyone writes or talks about France's Domaine de la Romanée-Conti, but almost no one mentions California's Barefoot, Gallo's top-selling brand. Wine shops, of course, make more money when a customer buys a $100 bottle than if he buys a $10 one. That's the reason inexpensive bottles are usually on the bottom shelves of stores, while the more costly ones are at eye level. The same is true for sommeliers, and you seldom see a $20 bottle of wine on a restaurant list. Magazines know that big-name wineries with expensive products are the ones that take out full-page glossy ads. You rarely see ads for bargains such as Charles Shaw or Cupcake, two of the hottest wines on the market, and magazines write about them infrequently.

In addition, many of the old gatekeepers may be quietly on the take. Few put out their own or their company's money to buy wine in stores. Wineries are anxious to get their products out to the public, and a bottle is an inexpensive way to get some publicity. One reporter working in Napa Valley told me that his publication is so deluged with unsolicited bottles that it is difficult to get rid of them. Often the samples come from small, unknown wineries. Winemakers know that if they want to be included in the annual tasting of a particular variety in a magazine's upcoming issue they had better send a bottle to the publication. The most famous critics say they don't request bottles, but they rarely send them back. Wine distributors are also always armed with free samples for sommeliers and retailers.

The *Wall Street Journal*'s longtime wine critics, Dorothy J. Gaiter and John Brecher, were an exception to this practice. They bought all the wines they sampled, often purchasing fifty or more bottles for a column on a topic such as California Cabernet Sauvignons selling for more than $50, or inexpensive Chardonnays. They even bought their own expensive Bordeaux First Growths for an annual column. Their reports were respected for the writers' honesty and reliability. It was undoubtedly an expensive way to organize a tasting, however, and many people in the wine business speculated that that is why the *Journal*'s new owners dropped them in December 2009, after twelve years and 579 columns. Their successors, Lettie Teague and Jay McInerney, focus on profiles of wines and regions rather than the extensive comparative tastings conducted by Brecher and Gaiter, but still recommend wines.

Some established gatekeepers also enjoy junkets to wine regions around the world. These are particularly important for writers working for smaller publications that cannot afford to send them to Bordeaux or Mendoza. National wine organizations are all too happy to put together trips to their countries and pick up the bills along the way because they know they will get favorable press. The more famous critics don't make such voyages, but they are often wined and dined while on the road.

In the spring of 2009, the blog *Dr. Vino* and online magazine *Slate*, plus the *Wall Street Journal*, revealed tales of Robert Parker's reviewers taking trips paid for by foreign wine promotion groups. Wine Australia confirmed it paid for the air travel, meals, and accommodations for Parker's Jay Miller, who covers that country's wines. Wines of Chile and Wines of Argentina said he also took their free trips. In addition, Mark Squires, another Parker contributor, has had travels paid for by national wine groups. That news darkened Parker's Ralph Nader image, and he replied on his website that he had "serious guidelines regarding conflicts of interest" that applied to his staff as well. Both Miller and Squires are still Parker reviewers.

The Internet is producing a new army of gatekeepers who are guiding consumers to the wines they may love or at least buy. This group is able to avoid the conflicts of interest that haunt its predecessors, and many in this group advocate inexpensive wines. Wine blogs are popping up so fast that it is difficult to keep track of them. There are thousands, and they will play an increasingly important role in wine education. Wine bloggers now meet regularly to make contacts and improve their craft. The first conference was in Rioja, Spain, in July 2008. Then the North American Wine Bloggers Conference followed in October of that year in Santa Rosa, California. The 2011 American session was in Charlottesville, Virginia, while the European one was in Franciacorta, Italy. Another group of writers covering regional American wines has started a website called drinklocalwine.com, which promotes wines from "the forty-seven states that are not California, Washington, and Oregon." It also has an annual meeting. The innovators and iconoclasts in wine communications are new gatekeepers.

The most important member of the wine blogosphere is **Gary Vaynerchuk**. In just a few years he has gone from an unknown to America's most influential critic after Robert Parker Jr. and even has the potential to eclipse the muse of Monkton, Maryland. Vaynerchuk's first platform was his Internet series *Wine Library TV,* which had more than one thousand episodes before being replaced by the similar *Daily Grape,* which is also available on smart phones. He makes sure people pronounce his name correctly by saying it slowly at the beginning of each program: vay-ner-chuk. For those who still can't get it right, he is simply Gary V, and fans call themselves vayniacs. Vaynerchuk calls his followers the vaynernation, creatively combining one of the world's oldest products with the latest information technology and making both of them lots of fun. He speaks to a new generation with the directness and candor that young people like, but at the same time the older generation generally seems comfortable with him.

Born in Belarus in 1975, when the country was still a Soviet republic, Vaynerchuk three years later moved to the United States with his parents. Their story is an immigrant's dream come true. Gary's father, Sasha, bought the modest Shopper's Discount Liquor store in blue-collar Springfield, New Jersey. Naturally the son worked in the family business while growing up. He also began reading wine publications and started tasting things that critics mentioned in their reviews, such as grass, tobacco, and even rocks, to see if he could identify them in wines. He soon realized he had a good sense of taste. After graduating from Mount Ida College in Massachusetts, Gary took over managing the store and renamed it The Wine Library. One of the first things he did was to sample every wine on the shelves.

The store did well, thanks in large part to the uncomplicated advice about wines that Gary handed out freely to anyone who came into the store. Vaynerchuk's business really took off, though, on February 21, 2006, when he launched *Wine Library TV,* his video blog about wine. The show was simple and inexpensive to produce. Gary sat in a corner of his office talking about wine. A clerk from the store ran a simple video camera and didn't stop taping no matter what happened. *Daily Grape* is shorter and reviews fewer wines. He often tapes it himself.

Near the end of the first show, Vaynerchuk revealed the secret of his success, saying, "I'm a serious guy about our business, but really not all that serious." In a field filled with inflated egos, Gary has an over-the-top personality and enthusiasm for his subject that show through. His other passion in life that he mentions endlessly is the New York Jets football team. He repeatedly says that his dream is one day to own them. The show is now delivered not only on the web but also on Twitter and Facebook, making Vaynerchuk the first wine superstar in the social media. His gonzo style makes him a popular guest on television shows, and in April 2009, Vaynerchuk signed a ten-book deal for $1 million. The first one, *Crush It!,* was not even about wine, but on how to use the new media to promote your career or business. His second was entitled *The Thank You Economy.* Both immediately hit the best-seller lists. Vaynerchuk is a workaholic who labors nonstop over his various media platforms, selling both himself and his products. The audience for some of his videos now exceeds a hundred thousand.

Although the focus of his attention is generally on the high-priced, premium wines that give him the best profit margins in his store, his shop carries a good range of less expensive bottles. In fact, the day I visited, the first thing I saw was a display of $10 wines. He also stocks four varieties of Avia wines from Slovenia that sell for less than $5. Though bargains are not his specialty, he has many.

When it comes to tasting styles, Vaynerchuk seems to like elegant wines more than powerhouse ones, putting him more in line with Jancis Robinson than with Robert Parker. He dumps ridicule on wine scores, but still uses the 100-point system. He is not too pompous to do a whole show on what wines go with what breakfast cereals. He concluded that Cap'n Crunch pairs perfectly with Germany's sweet Reichsgraf von Kesselstatt Scharzhofberger Riesling Spätlese. After tasting the two, he waxed, "The most hedonistic eating event I can think of." (Rap star Eminem, on the other hand, in the song "Bagpipes from Baghdad," recounts having Cap'n Crunch with red wine, but doesn't get more specific.)

Vaynerchuk is turning into a one-person wine conglomerate. In addition to the store and *Daily Grape,* he has a weekly radio show on Sirius, and is accumulating other wine websites and Internet discount locations. He also has a subscription newsletter and does wine cruises and tasting extravaganzas. Vaynerchuk is as ubiquitous as his impact.

Jeff Siegel is known in the blogosphere for *The Wine Curmudgeon,* which is ranked regularly among the most popular wine blogs. Some people in cyberspace can be flaky, and their sites are more promotional vehicles for their egos than a place to learn about wine. Although he came to wine by accident, Siegel has solid experience in journalism, which serves him well. He says, "I'm a wine writer, and the Internet happens to be my platform of the moment."

After growing up in suburban Chicago and earning a journalism degree at Northwestern, Siegel's dream was to cover the Cubs for the *Chicago Tribune.* He started as a sports reporter, and became a journeyman journalist working for four papers, three of which, he notes, are no longer around. His last full-time job was with the *Dallas Morning News,* which ceased publication on December 9, 1991. Sensing the end was near, Siegel had already gotten into freelance journalism, writing out of Texas about any topic he could sell. Eventually he drifted toward wine, writing especially about local and inexpensive ones that no one was covering.

The top feature listed on Siegel's website is his $10 Wine Hall of Fame, which he originally created in the early 1990s for Southwest's in-flight magazine. The idea behind it was simple: "The average price of a bottle of wine sold in the U.S. is $6. So that tells you about what people are drinking, but no one at the big magazines was writing about them." He adds that people are "really desperate" for recommendations of $10 wines. A recent Top Ten list included Bogle and Toad Hollow from California; Yellow+Blue Malbec from Argentina; Notorius, a white wine from Sicily; and Casamatta Toscana, which he called "perhaps the best cheap Sangiovese I've ever had."

Siegel's reviews run about two hundred fifty words, and each notes the price and whether he bought the wine or received it as a sample. Originally he purchased all his own wines, but now wineries give him about half. He thinks that buying their own wines keeps him and other bloggers honest. Siegel was inspired one day to do a column on 2009 Bolla Valpolicella when he was walking through a grocery store and spotted it. That used to be his father's favorite wine, so he paid $6 for it and reviewed it. He wrote it was "young and disjointed," but also noted, "It's an incredible value at this price, a wine for winter stews and red meat and tomato sauce."

The Wine Curmudgeon is one of the few media outlets to pay attention to Gallo's Barefoot, one of the top-selling wines in the United States. Siegel says, "Gallo understands its customers better than anyone else. Barefoot wines are professionally made, and you get your money's worth. Are they interesting? No. I think there are more interesting ones at the same price."

Siegel predicts that the message from the bloggers is unlikely to change, but the medium will be different. "How will the Millennials communicate about wine?" he asks. He believes they will use handheld devices and says his reviews of two hundred fifty words will then seem like books. Twitter allows messages only up to one hundred forty characters.

Robin Goldstein, another innovative gatekeeper, has become a leading advocate of inexpensive wines and plans to use all the new media to get his message out. Goldstein has a gold-plated résumé: a graduate of Harvard University, where he studied neuroscience and philosophy; a law degree from Yale; an academic year in 2010–11 as a visiting scholar of economics at the University of California–Berkeley. Goldstein has never practiced law, and had a brief career researching and writing for Fodor's travel guides in Europe, South America, and Asia. After returning to the United States, he started a series of restaurant, wine, and beer books under the corporate title Fearless Critic Media.

Goldstein got into wine during his senior year at Harvard. He and three housemates opened a bar named the Mask and Spear Pub in the building where they lived. They were all twenty-one, so drinking was legal, although they couldn't sell liquor. They accepted bottle donations from fellow students and, mimicking endowed academic chairs, they named the gift after the donor (for example, the David F. Elmer Bottle of Sweet Vermouth). Whenever anyone got a drink from the bottle, he had to toast the donor. At the pub they began blind tastings to see whether customers could tell the difference between high-priced vodkas and cheap brands. Students often preferred inexpensive ones. Goldstein even discussed wine tastings in his 1998 senior thesis, and the experiences at the pub inspired his later books on wine and beer. He was also motivated to do the wine book because he felt the media were covering only the expensive top of the market, while virtually ignoring the mainstream sector.

Mild in manner and soft of speech, Goldstein appears more comfortable in academia than in bare-fisted wine pits. At the same time, he has an inner toughness. He researches his subjects carefully and writes like a lawyer. For example, he tests the quality of judges by putting two samples of the same wine from six being tasted and then weights the scores of better judges higher. *The Wine Trials,* his most successful product, is based on blind tastings done by people who work in various parts of the wine and food business. The book's stated objective is to "help you better navigate the inexpensive wine shelf." In the 2011 edition, the judges started with five hundred widely available wines selling for less than $15.

Goldstein has an impish side that seems to delight in deflating the proud and the powerful. He did that famously in 2008, when he paid a $250 fee to enter a fictitious Italian restaurant in the *Wine Spectator's* Awards of Excellence program for eateries with outstanding wine lists. His theory was that the supposed contest was a scam designed to raise money for the magazine. He speculated that all he had to do was enter, and he'd get an award. He named his fictitious Milan restaurant Osteria l'Intrepido, which translates loosely as Fearless Restaurant. The wine list he submitted with his application included a reserve list consisting largely of wines the publication had previously panned, giving them scores as low as an insulting 58 points. Goldstein says that once the magazine collected his $250, he did not receive any communication from *Wine Spectator,* until someone from New York City called and left a message on an answering machine asking if he wanted to take out an advertisement in a forthcoming issue that would report on Osteria l'Intrepido's winning an Award of Excellence. After Goldstein went public, the red-faced magazine had little to say in its own defense, claiming only that it had made phone calls and internal inquiries to verify the restaurant's existence.

In April 2008, Goldstein, Johan Almenberg, Alexis Herschkowitsch, and three other colleagues published a research paper in the *Journal of Wine Economics* based on the blind tastings they had conducted in producing *The Wine Trials*. The title: "Do More Expensive Wines Taste Better?" Their conclusion was clear and direct: "Individuals who are unaware of the price do not derive more enjoyment from more expensive wine. In a sample of more than six thousand blind tastings, we find that the correlation between price and overall rating is small and negative, suggesting that individuals on average enjoy more expensive wines slightly *less*. For individuals with wine training, however, we find indications of a positive relationship between price and enjoyment." In short, if you are a novice at wine, you'll probably like inexpensive wines better than costly ones. But if you're a wine consumer with plenty of experience, you may appreciate costly wines more. Of course, there are hundreds of thousands of novice tasters for every sophisticated one.

The 2011 book sent forth a clarion call to consumers to declare their independence from wine gatekeepers, writing, "By questioning wine prices, you will become less of a slave to expectations and more of a student of your own palate." The authors urged consumers to do their own blind tastings, saying it would help them train their palates, better understand their own taste preferences, and appreciate all wines more.

The most shocking result in the three years of Goldstein's blind tastings was in the first year, when the $9.99 Domaine Ste. Michelle Brut sparkling wine from Washington State scored far better than a $150 bottle of France's esteemed Dom Pérignon Champagne. Goldstein has repeated the face-off several times, and two-thirds of judges have always preferred the Domaine Ste. Michelle.

The night I tracked Goldstein down in Italy, he was most excited not about a great Barolo he had just had at dinner, but about the app that he was about to release that would allow consumers to download the material from the *Wine Trials* books onto a computer, smart phone, or some other mode of communication yet to be discovered. Goldstein's enthusiasm about a new age is palpable. The marriage of wine information and new technology is just beginning, he believes, and the potential is endless.

The roles and influence of the traditional and new gatekeepers will be played out over the next few years. Wine is inherently confusing, and people will always be looking for someone like Robert Parker but increasingly also to Gary Vaynerchuk, Jeff Spiegel, and Robin Goldstein to help them find their way through the grapevines. Two conclusions, though, are already clear. First, the old guard has a built-in prejudice for expensive wines, while many new arbiters of taste lean toward less costly bottles. Second, don't leave your brain at the bar. Although these experts can tell you which wines they like, those may not be the right wines for you. In the first century, the Roman philosopher Seneca warned of "the danger of allowing others—not just friends and colleagues, but the masses—to exert too much influence on one's thinking." That wisdom remains valid today. The final decision about a wine is yours, and yours alone. A person's taste is as unique as his fingerprint.

The rarely reported reality is that average consumers, unlike gatekeepers, don't spend hours bloviating over whether the wine in their glass expresses hints of a cigar box or has gobs of red-fruit flavors. They taste it and quickly decide whether they like it or not. If they do, they will probably buy another bottle. If they don't, they won't. They might also wonder if the wine is worth what they paid for it. That's a pretty rational approach to wine appreciation.

PART THREE

Wine Revolutionaries

The two most successful wineries of the last decade are located 7,761 miles apart: one in California's Central Valley, the other in Australia's little-noted wine region of Riverina. Both became successful by offering quality wine at a great price. Others have tried to emulate their model for success, but they remain the towering giants of the business. Just behind them, though, are Chinese companies, still mastering the magic of making wine but growing at a rapid rate.

CHAPTER SEVEN

The Rebel from San Joaquin Valley

Every Friday afternoon at the offices of the California magazine *Wines & Vines* in San Rafael, staffers would gather informally to drink some wine and recover from the rigors of another week of working on the monthly publication. They often opened interesting bottles that they might have recently discovered. In late September 2002, they were having one of those regular encounters, when Tina Vierra, the publication's advertising coordinator, went out to her car and brought in a bottle of Chardonnay. The label, printed with a classic font in black and gold, read "Charles Shaw." Vierra explained she had bought it recently for $1.99 at Trader Joe's, a slightly quirky grocery chain then doing business largely in California. Without any promotion or advertising, Trader Joe's had introduced the Charles Shaw brand in February of that year. The front label identified the wine as simply coming from California, and the back one said it had been cellared and bottled in Napa and Sonoma, but that didn't mean the grapes had been grown or the wine made there.

Another bottle opened that Friday afternoon was a Chardonnay from the Dry Creek Valley of Sonoma County, an area renowned for the popular white wine. That Chardonnay had a list price of $67, although *Wines & Vines* has never revealed its brand name. After the staff tasted both wines, they decided that they actually liked the $1.99 wine better than the $67 one. The expensive Chardonnay tasted a little funky in a way that no one could exactly identify, but the Charles Shaw wine was clean and faultless, with rich fruit tastes of apricots and white peaches and just a hint of sweetness.

Tina Caputo, who wrote a column of short news items for *Wines & Vines* called "Wise and Otherwise," did one about the office tasting, reporting that the $1.99 Charles Shaw Chardonnay was considered better than the unnamed $67 one. It was the first time the wine had been mentioned in print, and the tasting at the magazine was the beginning of a wine legend.

Two months later, Michalene Busico, the food editor of the *Los Angeles Times,* asked reporter Corie Brown to do a story about the many surprisingly inexpensive wines the editor was seeing in grocery stores. What was going on? As Brown started digging into the story, the Charles Shaw brand captured her interest. It was available only at Trader Joe's and sold at the unbelievable price of $1.99. She talked to the Trader Joe's wine buyer and eventually learned that Bronco Wine Company, located in Ceres, just outside Modesto in the San Joaquin Valley, produced it. Brown's fifteen-hundred-word story, the first major article about Charles Shaw, appeared on Saturday, December 7, 2002, nearly a year after the wine was originally launched. Brown wrote colorfully: "Since it was introduced in February, Charles Shaw wine has gained a cult-like following in Southern California, with wine drinkers backing their cars up to the loading dock of the Los Angeles-based discounter to lay in a supply of the Trader Joe's exclusive."

Brown's story also provided the background on the eponymous Charles Shaw. He was a Stanford Business School graduate who dreamed of having his own wine brand after working as a banker in France, where he fell in love with Beaujolais, a wine made with Gamay grapes. So that's what he was going to plant in Napa Valley. In 1974, Shaw and his wife, Lucy, bought land and converted an old barn on the property into a winery. The Charles Shaw label had a drawing of a gazebo that was also on-site. The Gamay sold for $8, which at the time was more than most French Beaujolais and was probably the reason the Shaw wine flopped. As often happens when a husband-and-wife business goes bad, the marriage was soon on the rocks and a divorce followed. In 1994, the Charles Shaw winery was auctioned off for $1.6 million, but the brand was not included in the sale. Since it was known in wine circles that California's Bronco Wine Company was buying unused labels, a bankruptcy trustee offered the brand to them, figuring it was worthless and that Shaw might get some quick money for the asset. Without any idea what they were going to do with the brand, Bronco bought it for $18,000.

Until the *Los Angeles Times* story, news of Charles Shaw wine had spread entirely by word of mouth. Happy consumers picked up a bottle, liked it, then told their friends and went back for more. Initially only four varieties were available: Chardonnay, Cabernet Sauvignon, Merlot, and Sauvignon Blanc, although White Zinfandel and Shiraz were soon added. For many first-time buyers it was undoubtedly an impulse buy. If it turned out to be bad, they could always pour the bottle down the drain without any great regrets. In fact, the price was so low that many people for the first time began buying cases of wine to have on hand for daily drinking. Charles Shaw was quietly changing the way people thought about wine. It was no longer something just for special occasions. America finally had its *vin de table*.

Wine brands usually bear the name of the owners such as Robert Mondavi or Charles Krug and labels showing castles or mountains, but Charles Shaw soon picked up a fun moniker. At one point in the early days, a Trader Joe's employee wrote in an Internet posting, "The stuff is moving so fast we call it Two Buck Chuck." The press and public loved the nickname, which was soon part of the national vocabulary. Two Buck Chuck was cheap chic.

Songs were soon written in its honor, and videos celebrating it started showing up on YouTube. Drew Weaver wrote a tune entitled simply "Two Buck Chuck," with the opening stanza:

> *When I'm lonely, what makes me feel so fine*
> *Why it's Two Buck Chuck—a mellow affordable wine*

A YouTube video by Craig Nuttycombe and Piper Heisig rhapsodized about the wine with a catchy rock beat and urged people to run down to Trader Joe's and raise a toast to Charlie Shaw. In another YouTube video by a group called The Fresh, Chuck was rhymed with the most famous four-letter word in the English language. Kealoha Cruiser Rue, a sometime songwriter, taped a YouTube video extolling the inspiration he got from drinking "three bottles of Two Buck Chuck." Ellen DeGeneres did a skit about it on her television show.

After someone cast a write-in vote for Charles Shaw in a California election, Bronco's public relations consultant Harvey Posert printed up bumper stickers promoting "Charles Shaw for Governor" and "Charles Shaw for President," which became hot collector's items. Even Jon Fredrikson, the California wine-market expert, had one on the back of his car.

More than 600 million bottles of Charles Shaw wine have now been sold. In California the price remains $1.99, while in other states it is usually $2.99. Trader Joe's explains that the higher price is due to transportation costs. With some 6 million cases now being sold each year, Charles Shaw should reach the billion-bottle milestone sometime in 2017. No brand of wine has ever come even close to that achievement.

Charles Shaw wine hails from the most underappreciated area in American viticulture. California produces 90 percent of all American wine, from the north among the redwood trees close to the Oregon border, to the desert near the Mexican border. The state's most glamorous wine country is the Napa and Sonoma valleys, but most production comes from the region Californians call the Central Valley, made up of the Sacramento Valley in the north and the San Joaquin Valley in the south and meeting in the delta formed by the Sacramento and San Joaquin rivers. The Central Valley is about the size of Tennessee and calls itself "the greatest garden in the world." Its boundaries are fixed on the north by the Cascades, Trinity Alps, and Klamath Mountains; on the east by the Sierra Nevadas; on the west by the Coast Ranges and San Francisco Bay; in the south by the Tehachapi Mountains. The northern section gets plentiful rain, while the south is semi-desert. Many mornings in the winter the valley is socked in with thick fog that makes driving dangerous. The average temperature in July in Modesto, the heart of the valley, is close to 95 degrees.

British wine writer Jancis Robinson most clearly recognized the potential of the Central Valley, which many Americans long overlooked, writing in 2000, "There seems to me no reason why the vast Central Valley of California could not be producing seriously well-made, reliable, extremely inexpensive wine."

In the Central Valley, everything grows profusely, from almonds and tomatoes to cotton and grapes. The small town of Escalon (population six thousand) northwest of Modesto calls itself the Land of Peaches and Cream. John Steinbeck wrote of the area in the *Grapes of Wrath:* "The spring is beautiful in the California Valleys in which the fruit blossoms are fragrant pink and white waters in a shallow sea. Then the first tendrils of the grapes, swelling from the old gnarled vines, cascade down to cover the trunks." The Central Valley demands much of the people who work the fields. It is not a place for the weak of heart or back. Steinbeck also wrote, "In the souls of the people the grapes of wrath are filling and growing heavy, growing heavy for the vintage."

In 1870, the Central Pacific Railroad established Modesto, the Central Valley's unofficial capital, as a stopping point for east-west trains. The town was originally going to be named after W. C. Ralston, a San Francisco banker, but he modestly refused, so people decided to name it after the Spanish word for modest: Modesto. It's now an unpretentious town with a population of more than two hundred thousand, and chopped up by four-lane freeways. Modesto has never lost its modesty or its blue-collar roots.

Sol P. Elias, a Central Valley historian, wrote about the early days: "Like every frontier village that grew up with a rush, Modesto, in its infancy, suffered its period of open lawlessness, its era of unbridled gambling, its reign of brutal thuggery, its sway of the malign saloon influence, and its season of brazen, flaunting vice." In the late 1800s, hardy and determined Italian immigrants began arriving there. The main attraction was inexpensive land, a lot cheaper than in the neighboring Napa Valley. An added bonus was readily available water for farming.

Rafaelo Petri, a bon vivant who wore a large, diamond stickpin and carried a gold-headed cane, was an early member of the migration of Italian winemakers to the Central Valley. He came to California, probably in about 1880, from Tuscany, where he had made wine, and started to work in San Francisco hotels. Soon he was buying wine in bulk for his rooming houses. In 1886, he bought a small winery in the San Joaquin Valley and named it the Petri Wine Company. The night before Prohibition started on January 16, 1920, people lined up for blocks outside Petri to buy wine, at first for about twenty-five cents a gallon, but as supplies ran low, for several dollars a gallon.

Another of the early Italian winemakers was Giuseppe Franzia, a native of a village near Genoa, who also first went to San Francisco, then moved to Stockton in the Central Valley, where he grew and sold vegetables. Giuseppe soon had saved $100 and sent it to a girl back home. He told her that if she would join him in California, he'd marry her. She was insulted rather than flattered, and let it be known around the village that she wouldn't accept the offer. The proposal sounded good, though, to Teresa Carrera, who wrote Giuseppe and told him she'd take him up on it. He replied, telling her to use the $100 to pay for transportation to California. She arrived on July 4, 1900. The couple soon married and began a family of five boys and two girls. In 1906, Giuseppe bought a ranch in Ripon, northwest of Modesto, planted a vineyard, and in 1915 started a winery. He was soon one of the most successful grape growers in the valley.

Giuseppe Gallo, who grew up in the village of Fossano in Italy's Piedmont area, arrived in San Francisco in about 1905. He worked at first as a ditch digger, but then began buying wine from small winemakers and selling it to Italian boardinghouses. Gallo later ran a boardinghouse for miners in the Sierra Nevada Mountains and a saloon in Oakland. Prohibition shut down the bar in 1918, and he went into farming, buying a small vineyard a few miles north of Modesto. Gallo knew little about agriculture and turned to Franzia, who told Gallo that he had a poor piece of land for a vineyard and should sell it and get something better. Gallo followed the advice and in 1926 bought forty acres in Modesto.

Cesare Mondavi, from Sassoferrato, a village northeast of Rome, migrated to Minnesota in 1906 to work on the Iron Range. During Prohibition the local Italian community sent him to California to buy grapes for their homemade wine, which was permitted even in the dry years. In 1923, Mondavi moved to California and opened a produce company in Lodi in the northern San Joaquin Valley. After Prohibition he started making and selling bulk wine and bought Lodi's Acampo Winery.

As social outsiders in the Central Valley, the Italians stuck close to each other and often intermarried. In 1931, one of the Franzia girls, Amelia, married Ernest Gallo, one of Giuseppe's sons. Four years later, Rafaelo Petri's grandson Louis Petri married Flori Cella, whose family owned the Roma Winery, then the largest in California.

By mid-1933, it was clear that Prohibition was going to be repealed, so the families started making plans for the new era. Many wanted to move out of supplying grapes to winemakers and start making their own wine because the profits were better. The Petri family, which had sold its wine business at the beginning of Prohibition and was making cigars in Tennessee, got back into their original trade quickly by leasing three wineries.

In 1933, while her husband was on a trip to Italy, Teresa Franzia mortgaged the family ranch for $10,000 to start the Franzia Brothers Winery. Joseph, the youngest son, who was known as Joe Jr. since Giuseppe was Joe Sr., became president, John was secretary and treasurer, and Frank, Louis, and Salvador were vice presidents and ran different parts of the business.

Also in 1933, Ernest and Julio Gallo started the E. & J. Gallo Winery with $5,900 of capital and some rudimentary knowledge of viticulture and enology that they gleaned from books they read at the Modesto public library. Ernest was twenty years old, and Julio was twenty-three. Ernest borrowed $5,000 from his mother-in-law, Teresa Franzia, for the bulk of his start-up capital.

The Italian families expanded and prospered despite the slow growth in American wine consumption. They made what people in those days wanted: mainly sweet and high-alcohol products. The Franzias sold sweet port and sherry as well as Sauternes and Rhine-style wines. The Gallos had Carlo Rossi jug wine, André sparkling wines, and high-alcohol fortified wines such as Ripple and Thunderbird.

Some of the Italian families began looking beyond the Central Valley. In 1943, the Mondavis bought the Charles Krug winery in Napa Valley, which became the focus of interest for Cesare's elder son, Robert. After the Petris bought Italian Swiss Colony in 1953, they began to center much of their activity at its winery in Asti, a town in northern Sonoma County.

The five Franzia brothers, however, stuck to their roots in the Central Valley, and the next generation of Franzias grew up expecting to take over the family business when their turn came. The main players in this group were cousins John Franzia, who was born in 1939, Joe Franzia, born in 1942, and Fred Franzia, born in 1943. Joe and Fred were the children of Joe Jr.; John was their cousin, named after his father. In their youth, the three were fast friends and worked harvests at the Franzia winery, set amid expansive agricultural fields between the towns of Manteca and Escalon. Although Fred was the youngest of the three, he was always recognized as the leader of his generation. Even at an early age, the other two deferred to him.

The two elder brothers received Jesuit educations, attending boarding school at Bellermine College Prep in San Jose and then nearby Santa Clara University. Fred studied Latin and Greek in high school. His favorite course was English, and he was also a member of the altar boy society. Joe and Fred Franzia were both on the Bellarmine football team. Joe was a multiple threat in the backfield, while the smaller Fred was a kicker. Fred's senior high school yearbook praised him for a point after touchdown against rival St. Mary's, and in another game he kicked a forty-two-yard field goal.

Joe was a football star at Santa Clara University. Fred's playing days were over, but he became vice president of the Finance Club. He already knew where he was going.

After receiving a degree in finance in 1965 from Santa Clara, Fred immediately went to work for the family business, starting in Stockton in sales. He still says today, "You soon learn in business that nothing happens until someone sells something." Then he moved to Southern California to direct Classic Wines of California, the company's wholesale operation.

By the time the young Franzias got into the family business, the Gallos were the dominant winemaker in the Central Valley. The two families, though, remained close. Even when he was a child, Fred Franzia impressed Ernest Gallo, who recognized the young man's maturity and treated him with respect. Fred says Ernest Gallo and Robert Mondavi were his mentors, but he adds that you still have to do things your way. "You listen to a lot of people, but in the end you have to decide things yourself," he says. The two men met frequently until Ernest died, in March 2007. Fred remembers having dinner with Ernest one night and asking him where the finish line was for a company. Gallo replied that he would know it when it arrived.

In addition to leadership and an almost compulsive drive to succeed, Fred early on showed a rebellious streak. While working in the Los Angeles area, he took a wine appreciation course at UCLA from Robert Balzer, the famous wine critic of the Los Angeles Times. One day Franzia was in the back of the class tossing off a steady stream of wisecracks until finally the frustrated Balzer pulled the errant student aside and told him, "Young man, when I am talking, you do not. Do you understand?" The two later became good friends. This pattern has been repeated throughout Fred Franzia's life: he pushes, and pushes, and pushes—until someone pushes back.

Initially, the two Franzia brothers and their cousin were only getting started in the family business, when three Franzia siblings from the previous generation sold their shares of the company to an investment banker, who then convinced the two remaining owners to sell their shares also. The Coca-Cola Bottling Company of New York then bought Franzia for nearly $50 million, calling its new division The Wine Group.

The elder generation's sale of the family business shocked Fred, Joe, and John Franzia. Fred, who was so mad at his father for agreeing to sell his share that he didn't talk to him for seven years, told one interviewer that his father, unlike himself, wasn't a "fighter." Fred and his father eventually reconciled, but the incident left a deep scar on the son, from which he never totally recovered. He still refuses to talk about it today, yet has not forgotten what it was like to lose the family name. Fred rarely shows any signs of weakness or compassion in a negotiation. Everything is business. Many years later, he was negotiating to buy the Grand Cru winery in Sonoma, a family firm started by Walt Dreyer that had a brand called Dreyer Sonoma. At one point in the talks, Walt Dreyer asked if he could keep the Dreyer name after the sale. Fred said he would take the brand name until he had sold off the inventory he was also buying, but then would give it back to the Dreyer family.

After only a few months of contemplating what to do now that they would be working for Coca-Cola rather than their family, Fred, Joe, and John incorporated a new company on December 27, 1973. They called it JFJ Bronco. Soon their initials fell off the name, and it became simply Bronco Wine Company. Fred Franzia likes to keep everything he does under a fog of secrecy, and says that he can't remember the origin of the name, but the connection is Santa Clara University, whose mascot is the Bronco. Many years later, when Bronco bought property in Napa, the company gave it the address 33 Harlan Court—that was Joe Franzia's number during his football glory days at Santa Clara.

In January 1974, Bronco began building its business. Fred became CEO, while Joe and John were copresidents. Over time, a clear and easy division of labor developed among the three. Fred remains the boss and takes the final, tough decisions. Joe runs sales, and John handles production. The three share profits in an equal split. The only outsider in the tight family circle of top management is Bronco's vice president Dan Leonard, a former executive with Almaden. In February 2010, when Bronco had troubles with financial mismanagement at Red Truck, a Sonoma winery it controls, Franzia sent Leonard to clean up the mess.

Fred proudly points out that the company started at zero. The first employee was Barbara Raetz, who had been Fred's assistant at Franzia Brothers. She received the first company paycheck, before the three owners were paid, and still works for Fred.

Bronco soon bought pastureland in the small town of Ceres outside Modesto and built its headquarters. Initially Bronco was simply a wholesaler selling wine in Southern California. There was no master plan about how the company was going to develop, but soon it was making wine for established wineries. Through their Italian connections, the three partners knew the key players, who were all potential clients. Bronco made some wine on its own that it sold mostly in gallon jugs under the label CC Vineyard and also a JFJ sparkling wine.

In the early days, contract winemaking was the heart of the company. Making wine for client companies is a profitable business for those who know how to do it. When a wine variety or product suddenly becomes hot, a big-name winery may not have the capacity or staff to ramp up production to meet demand. So it turns to an outside company, which buys grapes or juice in the bulk market from companies that have more than they need. Since the buyer is a wine business, it makes tough demands. A top official from the client winery usually tastes tanks that the contract winemaker has for sale and picks the one he wants to buy.

When White Zinfandel became a hit in the early 1980s, the two largest producers, Sutter Home and Beringer, couldn't keep up with demand, so they turned to Bronco, which was soon making most of the White Zinfandel on the market. When wine coolers became popular about the same time, Bronco also produced those, for Seagram.

Success in running a contract winery is based on two things: first, the product has to be good, since the buyer is going to put its own label on it; second, the public should never know that the wine was not made by the winery whose name is on the bottle.

Fred Franzia already knew the business because of his family, but he soon became the grandmaster of it. A born deal maker, he loves the give-and-take of bargaining. "People don't understand that we're both buyers and sellers," Fred told me. "We buy grapes, and we buy wine. But we also sell grapes, and sell wines. We try to sell for more than we pay. We buy at $4 and sell at $6. And we do the same thing every day."

In its first year in business, Bronco built a large production and transportation facility at its new property in Ceres. Trucks brought in empty bottles, Bronco filled them, and then other trucks hauled them to the client winery. Soon John Franzia added crushing equipment, so they could purchase either grapes, juice, or wine. Whatever Fred found at a good price, Bronco bought.

Doing wine production for other wineries gave Bronco an insider's view into what was happening in the market. From one day to the next, Fred knew what some of the biggest companies were selling . . . or not selling. He continues to make market intelligence part of the planning strategy for his company.

Bronco for years operated below the radar screen of the press and public. People who drank its wine had no idea who made it because Bronco's name wasn't on the bottle. In fact, the Bronco name is still not on any label. Although the company fought to keep the names of its clients private, over the years it became known that it had made wine for some of the biggest names from the Napa Valley, including Robert Mondavi, Sutter Home, and Beringer.

Fred Franzia is not a business manager who spends a lot of time on abstract concepts. Instead, he is a master of management by opportunity. In 1976, only three years after he got started, the bulk-wine market was starting to tighten, so he went in search of a more reliable source of grapes. He soon signed a lease with Getty Oil, then the largest landowner in the state of California, to grow grapes on its vineyards west of Fresno. Getty was primarily interested in the oil in the ground, but also wanted to get a good return on the crops grown in its fields. Getty had previously done business with Gallo, but struck a new deal with Bronco, which had begun operating its first vineyards.

In the mid-1970s, still in his thirties and unknown to people outside the wine business, Fred Franzia moved into a powerful position in the California wine business, becoming part of the leadership group of the Wine Institute. In 1976, John De Luca, the Institute's new president, was meeting the organization's leaders and listening to their issues. One of the people De Luca was anxious to talk with was young Franzia. They held a first meeting at San Francisco International Airport, and later De Luca visited the Bronco facility and was struck by its austerity. The three Franzias worked in makeshift offices: two trailers parked near an industrial building made of corrugated steel.

Franzia, though, impressed De Luca as he explained his part of the wine business. After swearing the Institute president to secrecy, Fred told him about his deals with Getty as well as the names of some of his customers, such as Robert Mondavi and Beringer, and his contract to make the sparkling wine that Western Airlines served on its Champagne Flights up and down the West Coast. Later De Luca visited a new Franzia vineyard in Lodi. Bulldozers were preparing the ground for planting, and Fred told him that he had great hopes for the Chardonnay and other varieties he was going to plant there. He had studied weather patterns and found that the area was blessed with the same cooling breezes off San Francisco Bay that made wines from the southern Napa Valley so good. Fred also talked at length about the importance of drip irrigation, telling De Luca it was vital for the development of California wine and would open new possibilities for Franzia's San Joaquin Valley.

Franzia served as an officer of the Wine Institute from 1976 to 1981 and was chairman in 1981–82. Around the table were the founders of California wine, Ernest Gallo, August Sebastiani, Joe Heitz, Robert Mondavi, and others. They were all twice Fred's age, but that didn't intimidate him. Franzia, who has a way with swear words that would make a sailor blush, spoke his mind and defended his ideas. At one point he told his elders that it wasn't good enough for them just to be on the Wine Institute board and pay their dues. They also had to go on Institute trips to Sacramento and Washington to promote wine's political agenda. Franzia chastised some of the old guard for importing foreign bulk wine that competed with local producers.

Though Fred Franzia never cleaned up his language or his provocative comments, he paid homage to the pioneers of California wine formally in 1982, when he dedicated a new cellar room at Bronco's Ceres plant. He invited De Luca to be the master of ceremonies, and barrels were named in honor of Ernest and Julio Gallo, Robert Mondavi, and August Sebastiani. The event was a celebration of their shared Italian and wine heritage. In a rare moment of sartorial splendor for a guy who normally looks as if he sleeps in his clothes, Franzia showed up in a Brioni suit from Italy bought especially for the occasion.

After his year as the Wine Institute chairman, Franzia turned his full attention back to Bronco and began sending Dan Leonard to attend its meetings. The nearly six years that Fred had worked closely with the organization showed him how state and national politics are played. Franzia, though, still needed to maintain a low public profile.

By the early 1980s, Bronco was growing rapidly. In 1986, the ten-year-old vineyard deal with Getty ended after Texaco bought the oil company. Franzia decided to become master of his domain by buying vineyard land. Many myths have grown up about Fred and his empire. One is that he has been able to sell inexpensive wines only because the glut of California wine allows him to buy bulk product at bargain prices. As a result, some people have concluded that eventually his source of grapes will disappear and that will kill off his bargain wines. The reality is that Bronco, now the largest vineyard owner in California, grows most of its own fruit.

Franzia in 1986 bought his first property, which he still remembers was exactly 1,437 acres. His timing was either terrible or brilliant. The wine business was in a slump because of declining consumption. Wells Fargo bank had published a report about bad times ahead for both grape growers and winemakers. If someone believed in the long-term prospects for the business, however, it was an ideal time to buy vineyards. One wine insider told me, "Fred started picking up land at ten cents on the dollar from the top of the Central Valley to Bakersfield, and even some in premium areas such as Sonoma County." Franzia talked at company meetings about planting five miles of new vines annually, and it was only later that his staff realized he meant five square miles, which is 640 acres! That's more land than most wineries have under cultivation. Experts in the business say Bronco now owns 45,000 acres of vines, but with his customary obfuscation Fred allows, "You can safely say that we have more than fifty square miles of vineyards planted."

Although Franzia remains an important player in the bulk wine market, and a shrewd buyer and seller, he is no longer dependent on it. Prior to 1986, Bronco-owned vineyards supplied none of the company's grapes. Franzia told me that now "maybe 55 to 60 percent" comes from his property. He then quickly added, "We have no intention of ever providing 100 percent of our own grapes." Nonetheless, Bronco's holdings are many times greater than Gallo's. Today, Bronco's self-sufficiency is actually closer to 80 percent.

Franzia's role in the bulk market combined with his own vineyard holdings provide him with better knowledge of the wine business than anyone. If consumers want more Pinot Noir and less Merlot, as they did after the movie *Sideways,* he adjusts his planting accordingly. If wine drinkers are looking for a white-wine alternative to Chardonnay, he plants Pinot Grigio and Viognier. If Argentine Malbec is hot, he makes California Malbec.

Bronco has benefited from the quiet revolution taking place in Central Valley winemaking—for example, professors and researchers at Fresno State University had been changing winemaking technology to adjust to the area's warm climate. Fresno State has long been the poor cousin of California wine education. The University of California–Davis is older, more prestigious, and works mainly with Napa and Sonoma wineries. Fresno State is younger, less famous, and cooperates more with Central Valley companies. Davis stresses enology, or the making of wine; Fresno spends more time on viticulture—the growing and handling of grapes. Fresno State offers more hands-on experience and has long had a bonded winery on campus; Davis is more theoretical and only recently built a winery with money donated by Robert Mondavi. Davis is white collar and white lab coat; Fresno is blue collar and blue jeans. Davis is from Venus; Fresno is from Mars.

The biggest issue facing wineries in the Central Valley is heat. Grapes grow abundantly, and harvests can be huge. The flip side, though, is that too much heat reduces quality. The changes in recent years in Central

Valley winemaking, however, are both manifold and important. New and better vine rootstock and clones, the building blocks of viticulture, have been introduced and continue to be developed. Oak is more widely used—not necessarily expensive French oak barrels, but less costly substitutes in the form of oak planks or chips from inexpensive producers in the United States or other countries. These have nearly the same effect on the wine, at a fraction of the cost. New canopy management systems involve trellising and pruning techniques to better protect grapes on the vine from the sun's harsh rays. Drip irrigation, which Fred Franzia told John De Luca about in Lodi three decades ago, is now widely and efficiently used to give grapes just the right amount of water. Airplanes flying over fields have instruments that can monitor moisture levels in the soil. Perhaps most important, grapes are often picked early in the morning or late in the day to protect the fruit from midday heat and then shipped in refrigerated trucks and kept in cooling tanks at the winery to preserve the fruit's freshness.

As a result of this spread of knowledge, the wines being made in the Central Valley are today better than ever before. Wineries there are also producing grape varieties that were unimaginable only a few years ago. Who would have thought of making cool-climate Pinot Noir in the hot Central Valley? In recent years, though, Bronco has experimented with dozens of Pinot Noir clones in search for the best one to use in the valley. Fred Franzia is particularly proud of a new Pinot Grigio variety that Bronco patented in November 2008. A workman in the field discovered a plant in a vineyard near Arvin southeast of Bakersfield that had different colored shoots and pointed it out to his boss. The two workers were soon propagating that Pinot Grigio vine, which produces more fruit and has a superior taste. The result was the Tehachapi Clone (U.S. Patent No. 19,435), which was introduced in Bronco's Forest Glen Pinot Grigio. Franzia maintains it's the best produced in California at any price, and sells for about $6 a bottle.

Although he is neither a viticulturist nor enologist by training, Fred Franzia has been a quiet adaptor of all the new technology and keeps his company close to academic research. Bronco in 2005 pledged $1 million to Fresno State to endow a chair in the department of viticulture and enology. When another donor fell through on payments for a similar chair, Bronco quietly picked up the cost. When I asked him about the donated chair, he replied that he wanted to make sure that the latest technology is not lost in the hectic pace of harvest. "Knowledge wins every game," he says.

The longtime chief winemaker at Bronco is semiretired Ed Moody. He received a bachelor's degree at the University of California–Davis, and then in nine months, the shortest in school history, earned a master's degree in enology. After that he worked for United Vintners, where he did research on the use of oak and the development of new wine styles. Moody learned the tastes of American wine drinkers while working at the Italian Swiss Colony winery in Asti. Each day researchers made four sample cases of wine that had varying levels of oak, sugar, and other flavors. The cases then went directly into the tasting room, where people were asked to share their preferences. They clearly liked the ones with a touch of oak. Moody later directed winemaking at the Escalon Cellars and at Monterey Bay Wine Company, a contract producer that made wine for Beringer, Robert Mondavi, and Delicato. Moody has been at Bronco since the summer of 1989. From 1992 to 1994, he did extensive studies with an American barrel-making company and UC Davis on the effects of oak on wine. At one point Bronco owned eighty thousand oak barrels, undoubtedly the most of any California winery.

After spending his entire career at large-production wineries, Moody insists that the much-touted superiority of artisan winemaking is overstated. Bronco makes ninety million gallons of wine a year, crushing two million gallons of juice a day during harvest. "Little wineries need to get high prices in order to be able to make wine in small quantities," says Moody. "You make better wine in a seven-hundred-thousand-gallon tank than you can in a seven-hundred-gallon one because there is less exposure to air, and oxygen is the enemy in winemaking," he adds. Moody says Bronco's winemaking is built on rigorous controls that guarantee consistent quality.

In the early 1980s, Bronco's distribution business suffered setbacks when it lost the Robert Mondavi and Glen Ellen accounts to Southern Wine & Spirits, the biggest in the field. Fred Franzia told an interviewer it was a painful experience, since Bronco had to lay off 175 employees. After investing heavily to help build up those brands only to see them go off to another distributor, the Franzias decided that in the future they were going to control their own fate and start building their own brands with labels they owned.

Fred Franzia's strategy was always to be ready when a business opportunity came along, and the way to do that now was to buy up wine labels from owners who wanted to unload them for one reason or another. He bought existing labels because it was cheaper to buy those than to go about the time-consuming job of designing and producing a new one. It might cost $10,000 just to get a label designed, and he could buy one for less. In a matter of three years, Bronco purchased some forty brand labels and put them aside for future use. Among them were little-known brands such as Forest Glen, Montpellier, Black Mountain, and Crane Lake.

Bronco's breakthrough into retail wine sales took place in December 1992, when it purchased Sonoma County's Hacienda Cellars. The company was already selling wine to the rapidly growing Trader Joe's grocery chain, which then had about one hundred stores in California. The chain has a South Seas motif and offers exotic products such as soy veggie meatballs and spicy Thai peanuts. It also likes to have exclusive rights to products. Trader Joe's is a new-age firm, with a young staff and laid-back style. Instead of using a loudspeaker, employees communicate with each other by ringing fire-engine bells. Theo Albrecht, a major German food retailer, bought the company in 1979 and began a rapid expansion. The chain now has some three hundred fifty outlets in the United States.

Hacienda handed over to Bronco its dealings with Trader Joe's, and soon Fred Franzia was pulling labels out of his folder and putting them on wines to be sold exclusively at its stores. Central Valley wines were given the broadest possible designation of simply California and sold for about $3.99, but Bronco's Sonoma or Napa wines cost slightly more, at $4.99 or $5.99. It was the beginning of a mutually beneficial arrangement. Trader Joe's became the largest seller of wine in California, the state with the largest wine consumption, and Bronco became a leading purveyor of inexpensive wines. The Bronco–Trader Joe's deal was a perfect marriage, and Two Buck Chuck its historic offspring.

Fred Franzia has spent a lot of time in court. The agreements Bronco had to distribute Robert Mondavi and Glen Ellen wines both ended up in lawsuits, and he would later have a legal battle with Napa wineries that went all the way to the Supreme Court. Franzia's most serious legal problem, though, arose on December 9, 1993, when he was indicted in federal court for passing off inexpensive grapes as much more expensive ones, in violation of the laws of the federal Bureau of Alcohol, Tobacco and Firearms (ATF).

Investigators had spent nearly a decade uncovering the biggest wine scandal to hit California since Prohibition. Some players in the wine trade were trying to take advantage of a rapid run-up in Zinfandel prices, largely because of the success of White Zinfandel. From 1985 to 1988, the per ton price of Zinfandel grapes soared from $100 to $900. During that same time, though, the cost of similar-looking grapes such as Mission, Grenache, Barbera, and Valdepena remained steady at some $150 to $200 per ton. It was tempting for growers or brokers simply to switch the field tags that identify the grapes or make false claims about the variety on official documents. The scam was simple: sell a $150 ton of Valdepena as a ton of Zinfandel for $900, and pocket the profit.

In 1987, Michael Licciardi, a partner in a family-owned Central Valley brokerage firm, was sentenced to five years in jail for mislabeling grapes that ended up in Charles Krug and Robert Mondavi wines. Delicato, another winery, unknowingly bought from Licciardi 4,900 tons of grapes valued at $3.1 million, but then hurriedly altered company records to cover up their wrongdoing after federal officials started asking questions. Delicato president Anthony Indelicato eventually pleaded guilty to falsifying federal documents, and prosecutors forced him to sell his company stock and barred him from working there for five years. The federal government also fined the company $1 million.

Federal officials began hearing from people inside the wine business that

Bronco might also be mislabeling grapes. Suspicions were raised because the company was processing too much Zinfandel juice for the amount of plantings then in the ground. At the end of 1989, R. Steven Lapham, assistant U.S. attorney in the federal Eastern District of California, was handed the case.

The feds began their investigation by following trucks carrying grapes from the fields to the Bronco Winery and then verified the company's statements to the ATF that the government subpoenaed. After four years of investigation, a federal grand jury on December 9, 1993, handed down a fifteen-page indictment against "Bronco Wine Company and Fred Franzia" on charges of conspiracy to defraud. The indictment maintained that Franzia started the illegal action no later than August 1987 and continued it through April 1992. The alleged criminal activity was clearly not just a mistake. Said the indictment: "During the course of the conspiracy, the defendants misrepresented approximately one million gallons of wine valued on the wholesale market at approximately $5 million." The document contained colorful details on how Franzia would "instruct various individuals to sprinkle Zinfandel leaves on non-Zinfandel grape loads to give the false appearance that the loads contained Zinfandel grapes." The indictment said Franzia referred to this as the "blessing of the loads."

Only a month later, on January 19, 1994, Fred Franzia pleaded guilty in U.S. District Court and paid a $500,000 fine. Under the settlement, he was banned from being Bronco's CEO for five years, could not participate in the company's viticulture or winemaking during that time, and had to serve five hundred hours of community service, which he did at a child-abuse center in Modesto. Bronco Wine Company had to pay a $2.5 million fine.

The combined $3 million fine against Bronco and Franzia was the highest levied up to that point in the Eastern District of California. The other parts of the plea bargain, though, were a good deal for Franzia. During the plea bargaining, he argued that he had the key management role in the company. If he were forced to go to jail, he claimed, the company would likely fail and many Modesto residents would lose their jobs, causing harm to the whole community. Some bankers reportedly supported his arguments in talks with federal officials. In the end, Lapham bought the argument, and Franzia was let off easy, and ran the company for the next five years just as he always had.

When I interviewed Franzia, he refused to discuss the case, saying, "It was twenty-five years ago, and I don't want to talk about it." In 2008, Bronco's lawyer tried to get Franzia a presidential pardon from George W. Bush before he left office, but it was not granted. Franzia today remains a convicted felon.

One of the most complex parts of Fred Franzia's personality is his obvious resentment toward Napa and Sonoma winemakers. He seems to believe that they look down on the hardworking people of the Central Valley. It angered Franzia that Robert Mondavi hid his Lodi and Italian heritage and assumed the airs of Napa Valley. Franzia pointedly corrects people for using the commonly used term Central Valley, saying that they should be calling the area the San Joaquin Valley.

Such attitudes were perhaps behind his other long and costly legal fight with the Napa Valley. In the 1990s, Franzia slowly and quietly started looking for ways to associate his wines with Napa. He bought Napa Ridge, then a Beringer property, in 2000 for a hefty $40 million. He also picked up Rutherford Vintners and Napa Creek. Federal law required wines to have at least 75 percent of the grapes from an area claiming a geographic brand name such as Napa Ridge or Rutherford Vintners, but a grandfather clause exempted brands born before July 7, 1986, as long as they gave the origin of the grapes somewhere on the label. Beringer had been making Napa Ridge that way with little opposition. Franzia did the same thing by blending some of his Central Valley grapes with Napa ones, and soon he was selling Napa Creek wines at Trader Joe's for $3.99.

In 2000, Bronco opened a large bottling plant in the southern Napa Valley that was as flashy as the headquarters in Ceres are spartan. The structure looks like it might have been air-lifted from Tuscany and can bottle eighteen million cases a year, twice the Napa Valley's annual production. And best of all, Bronco could now legitimately print on its labels that the wine was "bottled in Napa Valley." Soon tanker trucks filled with wine from Ceres were rolling into the bottling plant. Critics called them "freeway-aged wines" for the drive from San Joaquin Valley to Napa Valley.

The Napa Valley establishment answered Bronco's ploys with shock, horror, and outrage. That no-good, despicable, cheap-wine guy from the Central Valley was going to destroy their successful business strategy of charging high prices for wines by stressing their low production and the uniqueness of Napa Valley *terroir.* The valley's wine establishment felt Fred Franzia was a blasphemy to everything Napa and needed to be stopped before he attacked again.

Napa Valley leaders pulled together to press for tougher state restrictions governing what could be called a Napa wine and eliminating the grandfather clause exception, which Governor Gray Davis signed into law in September 2000. It was due to take effect on January 1, 2001, but just before that, Bronco went into court to block the legislation. The case then worked its way through the judicial system, with Bronco winning the initial round in December 2002, but losing eventually on appeal in the California Supreme Court in August 2004. Bronco moved to the U.S. Supreme Court, appealing on several grounds. It lost on all of them, and in January 2006, the high court refused to hear the case, thus clearing the way for the laws to go into effect.

Fred Franzia also refuses to discuss his fight with Napa, saying it too is ancient history. "We bought the team with a goalpost at each end, but then they moved the goalposts," he told me ruefully.

Though Bronco wasn't doing well in its legal battles, Fred Franzia saw another new opportunity. During 2000 and 2001, there was once again too much wine sloshing around the bulk-wine market, and big buyers such as Gallo were pushing prices to dramatic lows. At one point, it was paying suppliers only fifty cents a gallon. Since Fred was buying and selling wine, he knew what was happening, and in fact he had to sell off some of his own product at extremely low prices in order to make room for the next harvest. Rather than continue selling wine at giveaway prices, he came up with the idea of bringing out a wine that would cost even less than the $2.99 Trader Joe's was then charging for his least expensive bottles. Fred Franzia insists that Trader

Joe's came up with the idea of the $1.99 price because the retailer, not he, sets prices, but others say that he was the driving force behind the project.

So, once again Franzia pulled out the list of labels he had bought and for no particular reason selected Charles Shaw to be the brand name. It took some time to get all the pieces together for the new bargain product. Franzia went to his suppliers and told them what he was going to do and pushed them to lower their prices. He told them that if the strategy worked, they would all be profiting from huge sales and everyone would benefit. Tough negotiations followed, and he won some concessions. The price of bottles, cartons, and labels all came down. A penny here, and a penny there, and pretty soon Bronco had a wine that Trader Joe's could sell for $1.99. In addition to reducing costs, Franzia told suppliers that they had to be ready to ramp up production. If the wine flopped, they could pull back and quietly walk away. They had to be prepared, though, for it to go really big.

Franzia paid close attention to the product's presentation. The clearest example was in the closure he chose for the bottle. Bronco puts only natural cork products on most of its wines, unlike Gallo, The Wine Group, and Robert Mondavi, and other bargain brands that use less expensive plastic corks for inexpensive bottles. Franzia says he could cut his cost of production by $3 million a year, if he simply moved to plastic corks. "We buy one billion corks a year, so saving a half penny on each of them would be big money," he told me. But Franzia knew people were going to be suspicious of the new product simply because it was selling for such a low price. As a result, Charles Shaw had to enjoy the quality image conveyed by natural cork.

Charles Shaw hit the stores in early 2002 with no one watching, but soon sales took off. Bronco realized it had a tremendous hit on its hands when sales went to one million cases in less than a year. No wine had ever had such a vertical takeoff. Each spring the Unified Grape & Wine Symposium takes place at the Sacramento Convention Center, when more than ten thousand people listen to Jon Fredrikson make his annual state-of-wine report. At the same time, he announces his winery of the year. In 2003, Fredrikson gave the award to the Bronco Wine Company. The attendees reacted at first in shock, and there was some grumbling, but soon it sank in that Charles Shaw had indeed changed the wine business as no product before. For Charles Shaw, Fredrikson even created a new category in his hierarchy of wine classifications: Extreme Value.

Sales were humming along in July 2007, when Charles Shaw shocked the world by winning the award as the best Chardonnay at the California State Fair for its 2005 vintage. The fair's annual Commercial Wine Competition has been held since 1854, making it the oldest and, it claims, "the most prestigious in North America." The competition brags on its website, "Award winners truly are the best of the best!"

Entries are limited to California wines, and each year some sixty judges taste about three thousand wines from approximately six hundred properties. All the judges are required to pass a qualification examination, which consists of a one-day advanced seminar taught by instructors from the University of California–Davis. Entries are put in a category by grape type, but not by price. The tasting is blind, so judges know neither the name nor the price of the wines. Only about 2 percent of the entrants at the California competition receive the highest honor, a double gold, when all the judges in a panel give the wine a gold medal.

Three hundred fifty-one Chardonnays were entered. The average price was $28.50. David Bruce and ZD Wines, which each cost $55, were the highest priced. Charles Shaw, selling for $1.99, was the least expensive. When the competition was completed, two wines, Charles Shaw and Wente Vineyards, had both earned double golds. Eight judges were then asked to decide between the two for best of show. After a taste-off, and by a split vote of five to three, they named Charles Shaw California's best Chardonnay! News of its victory even ran on national television shows.

The judges made no attempt to apologize for their decision. In fact, they reaffirmed it. Richard Peterson, who had been rating wines at the state fair for twenty years and was an enologist at top wineries, said, "Charles Shaw won because it is a fresh, fruity, well-balanced Chardonnay that people and judges, though maybe not wine critics, will like."

Charles Shaw continues to win major awards. In 2011, its 2009 Pinot Grigio was Best of Class at the Pacific Rim International Wine Competition, and its Shiraz won the same accolade at the New World International Wine Competition. That same year, the Cabernet Sauvignon, Merlot, White Zinfandel, and Sauvignon Blanc also won medals.

Despite the runaway success of Charles Shaw, Fred Franzia hasn't stopped looking for new opportunities. The Australian wine market was awash in wine by the middle of the first decade of the new century, thanks in part to government programs that encouraged grape growers to plant or expand vineyards. Following his own edict to fellow California winemakers when he headed the Wine Institute, Franzia had never imported any foreign wine. By 2009, however, the wine surplus in Australia offered an opportunity too good to pass up. He also worried that if he didn't take advantage of the situation, someone else would. As he told me, "The last thing I wanted to do was to displace California wine sales with Australian wine sales. But the second last thing I wanted to do was to have someone else do it. It was the lesser of two evils for me."

In June 2009, Bronco brought out a Chardonnay with a friendly looking koala bear on the label. The name: [Down Under]. The wine's original label noted in small letters that it was "by Crane Lake," another Bronco label. Putting it under an already established product got the product into stores faster, but that was dropped after [Down Under] received all the necessary regulatory approvals. The wine sold for $2.99, not only at Trader Joe's but also at other retail outlets. Fred Franzia was quoted in the press as saying that his target was Australia's hot [yellow tail] product that was then selling for about $7.

The screams and lawsuits emanating from [yellow tail] were almost instantaneous. Casella Wines filed a suit claiming that Bronco had infringed on its trademark by copying both the animal theme on the label and the brackets around its name. Once again, Fred Franzia had pushed and pushed until the other side pushed back.

By now, he had learned that legal fights are expensive, and Bronco dropped the brackets in favor of quotation marks, but kept selling the wine. "Down Under" now enjoys brisk sales of three varieties of Australian wine: Chardonnay, Cabernet Sauvignon, and Shiraz. For a July 2009 column, Dorothy J. Gaiter and John Brecher in the *Wall Street Journal* rated fifty Australian Chardonnays and named "Down Under" "best value." They wrote: "It's not rocket science. Just good fruit made in a clean, zippy wine with fresh-fruit tastes." After that and in a rare step by the penny-pinching company, Bronco took out ads to brag about the accolade. Some tried calling it the "three dollah koala," but the name never caught on.

Bronco Wine Company now has some two thousand employees, and Franzia is almost obsessive about continuing to improve his products and reduce the costs. He strives to keep selling Charles Shaw, at least in California, for $1.99. One minor change made in 2010 was to switch the paper for its cartons from white to light brown to lower the cost of the boxes by a few pennies. "We work hard to keep the price down," he told me. "If the automobile industry worked as hard on the costs of cars as we do, there wouldn't be any foreign cars sold in this country."

Although he didn't set out to play the role, Fred Franzia has become a spokesman for the wine consumer, fighting a lonely war against the big companies overcharging for wines that he feels are no better than his. His statement that no wine should cost more than $10 has become a mantra.

Bronco has a quality and price ladder for its many brands, even within the $2 to $10 range. One key determinant of price is the source of the grapes. Wines using Napa grapes are the most costly to produce because they are grown on high-priced real estate. Grapes from the California Central Coast, the Central Valley, or even Sonoma are less expensive, so the price of the wine is lower. Oak improves the taste of wine, but also the price tag. Bronco continues aging wines in oak, but uses less expensive forms of it, for example chips rather than barrels. American oak is also less expensive than French.

Bronco has eight winemakers, and each is responsible for about six brands. The company's top seller is Charles Shaw, followed by Crane Lake, which offers several more varieties than Charles Shaw and sells about two million cases annually. A few Bronco wines are priced at more than $10, but most go for less. Until recently, Bronco production was split in thirds among Chardonnay, Cabernet Sauvignon, and Merlot. But with the growing popularity of other varieties such as Pinot Noir, Shiraz, Riesling, Malbec, and Sangiovese, the Bronco palate has grown.

The company doesn't have the extreme value segment of the American wine market all to itself, but its success has forced the competition to lower prices. Gallo's Barefoot, which sells for about $6, has grown to be one of the most popular California brands. The Wine Group now makes the Oak Leaf line of wines exclusively for Walmart so it can compete with Trader Joe's. It sells for $1.97 in California and $2.97 in most other markets.

Despite their popularity with much of the wine-consuming public, Bronco wines rarely get good reviews either from magazines or from critics. *Wine Spectator* reviewed a few of its wines in 2006 to accompany a profile of Fred Franzia and gave three of them less than 80 points, almost unheard-of low scores. The 2004 Charles Shaw Merlot got just 77. The top-rated ones, 2003 Rutherford Vintners Cabernet Sauvignon and Charles Shaw 2005 Chardonnay, got just 83. Since only Trader Joe's carries Charles Shaw, other wine stores have no interest in saying anything good about it. Gary Vaynerchuk did a hilarious tasting of six Charles Shaw wines in episode number 212 of his *Wine Library TV* program, which he called "Two Buck Vaynerchuk." He gave the Sauvignon Blanc 83+ and the Shiraz 85, but condemned the rest as mostly undrinkable "sugar water."

Though dismissed by critics, Bronco does well at competitions. The bookcases in winemaker Ed Moody's cramped office in Ceres are filled with medal-bedecked bottles of wine that he has made. In addition to the famous double gold that Charles Shaw won at the 2007 California State Fair, Bronco has captured many medals at the annual *San Francisco Chronicle* wine competition: Forest Glen 2008 Chardonnay, Motos Liberty 2007 Merlot, Montpellier 2007 Merlot, and Montpellier 2008 Cabernet Sauvignon all captured awards. In a July 2009 blind tasting by Sonoma's *Press Democrat*, Franzia's Napa Creek 2007 Cabernet Sauvignon, which retails for about $10, tied for first place with Caymus ($70), Ramey ($50), and Buehler ($30).

Fred Franzia keeps his private life private. Despite a spectacular business career, he still seems ill at ease away from his closest friends and family. His glasses constantly slip down on his nose, making it appear that he's never looking directly at you. Franzia resembles the character Signor Ugarte, played by Peter Lorre in the movie *Casablanca*, who at one point says to the Humphrey Bogart character, "You know, Rick, I have many a friend in Casablanca, but somehow, just because you despise me, you are the only one I trust." That's something Fred Franzia might have said.

Although he is at an age when most executives slow down, it's unlikely Fred ever will. He simply enjoys the work too much. One thing he is certainly not going to do is repeat the mistake of his father and uncles and sell the business outside the family. There are thirteen Franzia children from the three founders, and all are associated with the company in some capacity, although some also have independent careers. The selection of the member of the next generation to lead a family company is always complex. Joey, Fred's son, who once worked in sales and was regional manager in New York, appears to have the inside track. In 2009, thirteen members of the fourth Franzia generation created the Panther Rock Wine Company. The managing partners are Joey, Damon, and Brian. They are sons of each of the three Bronco founders. Two of their new brands are Masked Rider and Motos Liberty, each selling for less than $10 and targeting young wine drinkers.

Bronco has assets of more than $1 billion and annual sales of some 20 million cases worth $500 million. That makes it the fourth largest wine company in the United States. Fred Franzia stands as the international king of bargain wine, and the most innovative California winemaker of his generation. He also claims to be supremely happy. As he told me, "No one is ever going to have as much fun as I had putting the pieces together."

CHAPTER EIGHT

John Casella Grabs the World
by the [yellow tail]

In the fall of 2000 at the White Plains, New York, offices of W. J. Deutsch & Sons wine importers, which had about 170 employees and distributed the popular Georges Duboeuf Beaujolais, owner William Deutsch and his son Peter were discussing how many cases of a new Australian wine they were planning to import to the United States. The father was not terribly impressed with it and said he thought it might sell twenty-five thousand cases. Peter was a little more optimistic, saying it might sell fifty to seventy-five thousand. The wine had a friendly looking wallaby on the label and the name printed in the style of computer code: [yellow tail]. More than five years later on April 26, 2006, Frank J. Prial, longtime wine columnist for the *New York Times* and the grandfather of American wine journalism, did a story about [yellow tail], writing, "Nothing like this has ever happened before in the American wine business." Indeed it hadn't. After first hitting the U.S. market in July 2001, [yellow tail] shipped one million cases in its first thirteen months, making it the most successful launch in American wine history.

The story of [yellow tail] begins centuries ago in Sicily near the Mt. Etna volcano. This was long one of Italy's poorest regions. Small houses were built of rocks and had makeshift roofs. Grapes were about the only thing that grew in the lava-rich soil, and peasants dug terraced slopes into the hillside and planted vines. Everyone made wine, which they both drank and sold to northern Italian merchants who paid a pittance for it. They blended the powerful Sicilian *vino* with their thinner ones to provide some heft.

No one was rich in the village around Etna, but the Casella family was a little better off than most because it owned one acre of vineyards, unlike their neighbors, who had to work other people's property. Giuseppe and

Rosa Casella had three children, including Filippo, who was born in the village of Vena. While his peasant parents couldn't read or write, Filippo's generation was the first to go to school. At the age of nineteen, in 1939, he volunteered for Mussolini's army, in part because he liked to hunt. In the army he was trained as a radio operator in the elite Bersaglieri Corps and fought in North Africa. British forces captured Filippo in January 1940 and sent him to a prison camp in Bangalore, India, where he stayed for six years and learned some English, plus history, math, and French.

When the war ended, the ex-POW slowly worked his way back to Sicily, finally arriving home in November 1946. It quickly became clear that his future there was dim. The family landholdings would have to be split between him and a brother, and the vineyard could barely support one family, much less two. Nonetheless, Filippo began courting Maria Patanè from the nearby village of Sciara, marrying her less than a year after his return. In a land of people with dark complexions and brown eyes, the two stood out. Filippo had blue eyes, and Maria had fair hair and was known locally as "the blonde from Sciara." (Her mother used to rub walnut skins into Maria's hair in an attempt to darken it so she would look like other Italian children.) The couple soon had two children, and Filippo put meat on the family table by shooting foxes, cats, and anything else that got within range of his rifle.

Filippo, though, soon began looking to make a living outside Sicily. In the years after World War II, Australia had a program called White Australia that encouraged Europeans to move there and help build the economy. For five years in the 1950s, Filippo traveled back and forth between Sicily and Australia, with each passage taking four weeks at sea. When he arrived in the land down under, he worked eight- to ten-hour days in the Queensland sugarcane fields in the country's northeast corner, where pay was good but he had to live in housing called "cane barracks." He also worked a jackhammer, helping to build the Warragamba Dam near Sydney, one of the engineering feats of the twentieth century. Filippo was frugal and regularly sent money home to Maria and the children. Finally the couple decided to move the family to Australia, arriving there in November 1957.

The family was finally together, but Filippo still faced the hard life of an itinerant farmworker. All year long he labored in the fields, harvesting one crop after another. He also tried his hand at growing flowers and tobacco, but didn't have much luck with either.

In Australia, Filippo and Maria had two more boys, bringing the family to four children. John was born in 1959 and Marcello the following year.

One of the areas Filippo worked was Riverina in the state of New South Wales, some three hundred fifty miles southwest of Sydney and three hundred miles northwest of Melbourne. In 1816, explorer John Oxley was struck by what he called its "barren desolation," writing, "I am the first white man to see it, and I think I will be undoubtedly the last." The arid area originally could support little more than cattle grazing, but the establishment of the Murrumbidgee Irrigation Area in the first decade of the twentieth century opened Riverina to agriculture. The first grapes were planted there in 1914, and the first harvest was two years later.

Filippo often worked as a fruit hand around Yenda, a village with a dirt main street seventeen kilometers (eleven miles) from Griffith, the largest town in Riverina. As the crops ripened, he first picked apricots, then peaches, prunes, grapes, and finally oranges. Maria sometimes helped in the fields.

In 1966, Filippo bought a fifty-acre plot of land in Yenda for £17,000 ($19,000). The property was designated Farm 1471, and was deemed suitable for farming. There was a small, three-bedroom wooden house with a corrugated-iron roof on the property. The most important thing about the farm was its dam, which provided water for the animals and crops. The family's drinking water came from a tank that collected rainwater. The farm was already planted with Shiraz, Grenache, Palomino, Pedro, Trebbiano, and Sémillon grapes, which the family sold to local winemakers. The Casellas also grew peaches and other fruit.

Filippo had been making wine since his childhood in Sicily, so it was only natural that three years later, in 1969, he made his first wine in a new building he constructed next to the family home. He called his winery Casella. Filippo also built an open concrete fermenter to hold crushed grapes, which is still there with the date etched into the concrete: 31.1.1969. In addition, he constructed iron tanks that could hold 1,575 gallons of wine, enough for 800 cases.

Soon Filippo was traveling to Queensland to sell wine to the Italian community there and to the few Australians who were slowly switching from drinking beer to wine. Filippo stored wine for the trips first in old beer barrels, but eventually switched to plastic drums. The sales trips to Queensland were an ordeal for a man then in his fifties. He had to lug heavy containers in and out of trucks and was away from his family for weeks on end. Sometimes Marcello or one of the other children would travel with him, and the two lived out of the truck. Filippo followed that routine for more than twenty years. But during a 1990 trip, and only a short time before his seventieth birthday, he suffered a heart attack and underwent triple-bypass surgery. That would be his last wine-selling trip.

The Casella family suddenly had to face the question of what would happen to their little winery in Yenda, which now included several buildings around the three-bedroom homestead. At the time, Casella Wines was basically a one-person winery, producing only about fifteen thousand cases annually and selling directly to customers. It provided Filippo and Maria with an adequate income, but the operation didn't have much of a future.

One option was simply to close it down, but that prospect was quickly rejected because of the family's emotional investment in Filippo and Maria's work. But who could take it on? Over many evening discussions around the kitchen table, the solution emerged. The obvious choice was the second son, John. While all the children had worked around the winery, John already had university wine training and plenty of hands-on experience in the business.

John had started a liberal arts degree program at the University of Wollongong, but dropped out in the first year because he couldn't see where his studies would take him. After a few months of reflection, John decided to return to school and take the wine course at Charles Sturt University in Wagga Wagga. Although he had been around wine all his life, watching his father make it and helping his mother clean tanks, this was his first formal training.

After graduating from the program in 1982, John went to work for Riverina Wines, which was located in nearby Tharbogang and had been started by another Italian immigrant. At the time, it was a bulk producer making annually about 250,000 gallons of wine, but with plans to expand. John started as assistant winemaker and stayed at Riverina for twelve years.

His responsibilities increased until he was general manager of a winery five times bigger than when he first started there. At Riverina, he handled everything, from buying grapes and making wine to sales and financial controls. Looking back on those years, John says, "I left university with a lot of theoretical knowledge, but no practical experience. But at Riverina Wines I learned everything about how to run a big winery."

The world of wine is filled with superegos and domineering executives. John Casella is the exact opposite. He's self-effacing and understated. He speaks slowly and deliberately. This is not to say that he's a pushover, but he doesn't rule by intimidation, as is so often the norm in this business. His office is located in an old building in the center of the company's now huge winery complex that grew up next to the old family home, which stands unoccupied. On a Friday during a school break when I was there, he left work early to spend time with his four children.

Building on his experience at Riverina, John slowly but systematically developed a plan for expanding Casella Wines. "You start with what you know, and we understood the bulk market," he told me. "It's easier to sell a tanker load of wine to another winery than it is to sell that tanker load of bottles of wine to one hundred different stores." Bulk sales, though, were only a temporary expedient. "We knew that going forward our future would be in our own branded wines."

John Casella's top priority was to earn enough to set up a fully vested retirement plan for his parents, so that no matter what happened to the company they would be financially secure. Since his father was now in his mid-seventies and had undergone the bypass operation, he couldn't get retirement coverage, but John made sure that the plan for his mother, who is seven years younger than her husband, provided enough financial support for both of them. Another sign of John's conservative approach to his new business was that in 1994 and 1995, he worked at both Riverina Wines and Casella before going full-time at the family winery.

At the time, John was still in his thirties and had the ambitions and confidence of youth. He didn't know exactly where he was going to take the company, and he didn't know what challenges he would face or how he would solve them, but he was sure he could handle whatever came his way. Since he had never had much money, he wasn't worried about failing financially. He had already worked for more than a decade for a leading winery and had developed a solid reputation, so, if worse came to worst, he was confident he could get a job at another winery.

The 1994 vintage was John's first at Casella, and he crushed only 2,000 tons of grapes that produced 120,000 gallons of juice; the following year he did nearly 3,500 tons for 210,000 gallons. In 1995, Joe Casella, Filippo's oldest son, quit his job in the insurance industry to join John at the winery. Soon other family members were also signing on at the expanding venture.

One of John's driving strategies was always to expand to where he wanted to be. In 1995, for example, he put in a bottling line, even though he was then selling bulk wine to bigger wineries that bottled it. When he went to his banker to get a loan of $500,000 to buy the equipment, the banker turned him down because it looked like a risky investment that Casella didn't need to make. John tried to explain that he was going to grow and needed to learn about bottling. He said he wanted the equipment so he could train his staff to operate it. That way everything would be in place. "I didn't want to wait until I actually needed something," John explains. There was no budging people at the State Bank of New South Wales, so he took all his business to the rival National Australia Bank in Griffith, which provided the loan. Casella is still with the bank, which would soon be financing the company's spectacular growth.

Shortly after the bottling line was installed, Arrowfield Estate, a winery in the Hunter Valley north of Sydney, had a fire that destroyed its bottling line. In desperation it turned to Casella, who bottled Arrowfield's wine for fourteen months while it rebuilt its facility. That short-term contract work paid for Casella's bottling line, so essentially at no cost, John got his own bottling equipment and trained his people. It's important for a business to plan, but good luck is priceless.

By 1997, Casella had decided it was time to get into the international market. First he had to increase staff, since the company had only fifteen employees. Despite plenty of self-confidence, John Casella knew he couldn't do everything and slowly started building for future growth, following his strategy of preparing for where he wanted to be. He hired John Soutter, who had worked for many years at Cranswick Estate Winery in New South Wales, and gave him the title of general manager for sales and marketing. Soutter was later quoted as saying that the company's toughest job then was to keep its infrastructure in sync with its ambitions. Six weeks later, John hired Graham Harpley, who just left a job in corporate banking at the State Bank of New South Wales, to be the company's top financial executive. Soutter and Harpley shared an office and answered their own phones. Revenues that year were AUD7 ($5.5) million, but would double the following year.

After six months on the job, Soutter went on the road looking for an international distributor. At the time, John Casella thought Britain, Australia's biggest wine export market, might be the best prospect, but Soutter began looking into other areas and learning what wine people there wanted. It was an expensive investment to hire Soutter and send him around the world on market research trips, but Casella felt he had to do it. Soutter soon concluded that the United States had greater sales potential than Britain. Australian wines were starting to make a big splash there, and Robert Parker and *Wine Spectator* were writing effusively about big, bold Aussie Shiraz. Americans also considered Australian wines good values.

In April 1997, Casella made his first trip abroad, going to the biannual Vinitaly conference in Verona, Italy. It was a massive event, with 2,337 exhibitors and 83,000 visitors from 68 countries. Walking around and looking at all the flashy displays from the world's most famous wineries, Casella was at first overwhelmed and slightly depressed. The global companies, he mused, were so big and had so much money to spend on marketing. "I thought to myself what bloody chance did my little Aussie company from the middle of New South Wales have," he told me. "No one knew the Riverina region, much less my company."

Later he thought that since so many companies were already in the market, there had to be enough room for one more player. Before heading back home, he traveled to Sicily to visit relatives and to see where his parents, sister, and brother had been born.

The European trip crystallized John's thinking. He'd have to get a foreign partner since he didn't have the money to start the kind of independent export operation that Rosemount and other big Australian wineries already had firmly in place. Rosemount Diamond Label Shiraz was then the best-selling Australian red in the United States, while Lindeman's Bin 65 Chardonnay was the top white. Each sold for about $8. And while Australia exported high-end wines like Penfolds Grange and Henschke Hill of Grace, 80 percent of Australian products sold in the United States for less than $10, and 40 percent for below $7. Pricing would be crucial.

The following year, in the spring of 1998, and with the help of the Australian Trade Commission, Casella went to the annual meeting of the Wine & Spirits Wholesalers of America, held that year in San Francisco. He, John Soutter, and Philip Casella met two potential American partners, W. J. Deutsch & Sons and Brown-Forman. The companies were studies in contrasts. Deutsch was based in New York, privately held, and liked working with family-owned companies. Its Georges Duboeuf Beaujolais was the top imported brand in the United States. All its sales, though, amounted to only about one million cases annually. Casella's timing was fortuitous. While relaxing by a swimming pool in Florida during the 1997 Christmas holidays, Bill Deutsch had told his son Peter, the company's CEO, that he thought the company should get into Australian wines.

Brown-Forman, on the other hand, was a big public company from Louisville, Kentucky, whose roots were in Old Forester bourbon and Jack Daniel's whiskey, although it also distributed wines. It would have lots of resources to throw into the U.S. market launch of unknown Casella wines.

The Casella delegation met with William Deutsch and his sons Peter and Steven in the cavernous breakfast area of the Marriott Hotel. John Casella, the man from the village of Yenda, remembers being overwhelmed by the size of the place. Bill Deutsch impressed him when he started the meeting with a brief talk about his fundamental six P's of business: people, product, package, price, promotion, and potential. The concept made sense to John. Deutsch also stressed the importance of family firms working together. The meeting was cordial, and John left with a good feeling about Deutsch. "I had a sixth sense that he was the kind of person with whom we could work," John recalls.

That same night, Casella met with representatives of Brown-Forman, and they tried some Casella wines, including a Chardonnay-Merlot rosé that the winery had just developed. The Brown-Forman people promised to invest heavily in a product launch.

Brown-Forman, though, was also talking with McPherson Cellars, a Southern Australian winery, and eventually decided to go with it over Casella, which fell into Deutsch's arms. In July 1999, Casella Wines and W. J. Deutsch & Sons signed a contract. The two sides have never revealed the terms, but it has been widely reported that Deutsch owns 50 percent of the [yellow tail] label in the United States, although Casella retains the brand rights worldwide. The two agreed that Casella would take its profits in Australia on the basis of what they produced, and Deutsch would take its in the United States from what it sold. That was an unusually generous arrangement benefiting Deutsch, but John Casella felt he didn't have many options, realizing he couldn't tackle the U.S. market alone. After the signing, John asked Bill Deutsch what he thought about giving the wines the brand name Casella. Deutsch politely, but firmly, said he thought it would be confusing to have an Italian name on a line of Australian wines.

Ever prepared for an opportunity, John Casella had a product ready for the U.S. market. The brand name was Carramar Estate, and it was already for sale in the British market. The product looked modern in a curved bottle that had a drop of wax on top. It was a trendy touch Robert Mondavi had made popular a few years earlier, and Australia's Rosemount was also using it. The wine was going to be offered in three varieties: Shiraz, Chardonnay, and Merlot. The retail price was about $10. Early reviews reported that it was good, but nothing special.

Then, a few months after the release, and just as Carramar was trending toward disappointing initial annual sales of twenty-five thousand cases, disaster struck. The Shiraz wines turned out to be badly corked, and many bottles gave off an offensive smell. It wasn't just a question of an occasional bad bottle here or there; a whole batch of closures was flawed. To protect the company's integrity, there was no alternative but a massive recall, and even then irreparable damage might already have been done. To John, the experience was shattering, and he wondered if his company could recover from the setback.

At the annual Wine & Spirits Wholesalers of America meeting in May 2000 in Boston, John Casella and Bill Deutsch met to talk turkey. Casella offered his regrets, and Bill Deutsch explained that he understood it had been a problem that no one could have foreseen. When Casella asked Deutsch if he wanted to end their relationship, the American replied, "I still believe in you; nothing has changed." He then told John to go home and come back with a new product.

Every company makes mistakes from time to time, but the smart ones learn from their mistakes. Looking back on the Carramar experience, John Casella admits that it was the wrong product, at the wrong price, and with the wrong label. He says, "We were basically another wine at $8 or $9 with fairly ordinary packaging." An imported wine that might sell only twenty-five thousand cases a year in the U.S. market was not going to make it financially. He needed much bigger volume to be successful. Casella also admits that the Carramar's flavor profile was wrong. It was a me-too wine similar in taste to some other Australian wines that were already estab-lished on U.S. shelves and selling at the same price point. Consumers had expectations that Carramar wasn't meeting. The label was also dull, with an image that looked like an Italian coat of arms. The new wine had to be totally different: right product, right price, and right label. Anything less would doom the company in the U.S. market.

After the Boston meeting with Deutsch, John took a quick sales tour of the States. One of his stops was Charlotte, North Carolina, where he still remembers going into a big wine store. Off in the distance he saw a bottle of Hardys wine from Australia with a yellow label and a large H. He also noticed the price: $5.99. It was an epiphanic moment: his new product for Deutsch was going to have a yellow label and cost $5.99.

Once back in Australia, Casella told Soutter he had to get the new wine quickly to Deutsch, but didn't want to present it in stages. It had to be a finished package—wine, name, and label.

Casella prides himself on being both a winemaker and a business man-ager; and he can look at those two crucial sides of the business. He knows the complexity of wine taste, but he also understands market demands.

John Casella the winemaker now turned his attention to the taste profile of the new wine. It was not going to be just a slightly tweaked Carramar. John says he often wished his father had started the winery in Australia's famed

McLaren Vale, home to some of the country's finest *terroir* and best wines. But John had to play the hand of Riverina grapes that nature dealt him. Wines from there are not for laying down and aging. Their advantages, however, are that they can be consumed early, are reliable, and offer unbeatable value because of their large harvests. The new wine should draw on those strengths.

It's become an urban legend that Casella tailored the taste of his new wine to the American palate, which was raised on Coca-Cola and likes drinks that are ever so slightly sweet, just as Jess Jackson had done with Kendall-Jackson Vintner's Reserve Chardonnay. John says the flavor profile he was after was actually influenced by an experience that took place when he was perhaps four years old. Since he lived in an Italian household that owned a winery, wine was always around. He remembers a particular local one that he found extremely offensive. It was so tannic and harsh that he never forgot it. He wanted to make a wine that would be attractive to uninitiated wine drinkers or people who drank wine only infrequently or on special occasions. He thought the wine had to appeal not only to the novice but also to the wine snob. Above all, it had to be a friendly wine. He wanted to use ripe fruit and very little, if any, oak. Immature fruit and wood result in tannins, which Casella assiduously wanted to minimize or avoid entirely. In addition, this new wine should have a *soupçon* of sweetness. "Just enough to make the wine friendlier," he says. "It was all about taking good wine and then making it a little easier to drink, a little bit more approachable, especially for people who didn't drink a lot of wine."

In developing the first two wines, Casella concentrated more on the Shiraz than on the Chardonnay, which pretty much took care of itself. Having long had a weakness for young reds and believing that Shiraz is the ultimate grape for Australia, he wanted it to be fresh, fruity, and ready to drink. The wine could be shipped six months after harvesting.

There could be no compromise, though, on the quality of grapes going into the wine. Casella maintains that many wineries buy cheap fruit and then try to cover up any problems with sugar. He wanted his wines to be made with quality grapes, mostly from Riverina but also from top-growing areas, including the McLaren Vale. David Littore, a longtime grower for Casella, confirms that, "John is hard on quality. He is a lot harder on quality than a lot of other wineries. If you don't make the color, they won't take the fruit. It is very simple."

With the price and taste profile in place, the next crucial element was the label. Barbara Harkness, a graphic designer in Adelaide, Australia, runs a company called Just Add Wine that provides labels and packaging for wineries around the world. Among her designs are successful labels such as Red Guitar from Spain and Monkey Bay from New Zealand. In the late 1990s Harkness had developed a label and packaging for a brand that showed a drawing of a long-tailed, leaping, yellow-footed rock wallaby, a member of the macropod family that also includes kangaroos and wallaroos. The brand name on the label looked right out of the dot-com age: [yellow tail]. The predominant colors were a bright, glossy yellow and black.

Timothy Boydell, the executive director of Angove, a producer of such premium Australian wines as Nine Vines, first bought the label from Harkness for AUD9,000 ($5,700). He owned it for only ninety days, though, before his boss told him he didn't like it because a kangaroo on an Australian wine was cliché. So Boydell resold the label to Harkness.

Shortly thereafter, John Soutter met Lorenzo Zanini, a sales representative for Harkness, at the Sydney Airport to look over a portfolio of labels that Casella Wines might purchase. Soutter found the [yellow tail] one interesting, but he brought back three to give John Casella a choice. The other two were Eight Mile Creek and Endeavour Bay. Casella also liked [yellow tail], although he didn't make a final decision that day. For a while, the wine's name was going to be either Yenda Vale or [yellow tail].

As part of the drive to make the new wine consumer-friendly, John Casella decided to put all the wine varieties in standard Bordeaux-style bottles. That was a gamble because Chardonnay, for example, no matter where it is made, has traditionally come in a rounder, Burgundy-style bottle. In fact, [yellow tail] would be the first major Chardonnay in a Bordeaux bottle. Casella also decided to launch the new brand with only two wines, for the sake of simplicity—Shiraz and Chardonnay, a red and a white. After the problems with Carramar's natural cork, this time he used plastic corks.

On September 15, 2000, John Soutter arrived at the Deutsch offices to present the new brand. Peter Deutsch was still a little apprehensive after the Carramar Estate disaster. As he remembers the visit, he and his father met Soutter in the company's conference room. Soutter carried with him two packages tied with string. He first opened one of the packages and pulled out two bottles with the bright [yellow tail] labels. The group first talked only about the packaging, one of the six P's. Peter was excited about the label, but at the same time had some nagging concerns. Wine is basically a conservative business, and American consumers look for familiarity rather than wild innovation. He also worried about selling Chardonnay in a Bordeaux bottle. Overall, though, Peter liked the look.

Bill Deutsch, on the other hand, loved the name, but he wasn't sure about that kangaroo. He said he couldn't think of any major wine brand with an animal on the label. Peter disagreed, saying, "Dad, you're crazy. It's beautiful; it's different; it's unique."

Then they tasted the wines. Deutsch father and son agreed that it was just right for the American market. Says Peter, "My initial reaction was that John Casella had a taste profile that I thought the American consumer would find appealing." Concurs Bill, "The wine was very easy to drink. It had a very pleasant taste in the mouth, and it had a fabulous finish."

After that, the group discussed price. They easily agreed on $5.99. Big Australian names such as Rosemount and Lindeman's were starting to increase the cost in the United States, and [yellow tail] was going to dramatically undercut them. The biggest American label then was Woodbridge by Mondavi, selling for $7.99, so [yellow tail] would also be lower than that.

Soutter finally took the string off his second package and pulled out some point-of-sales gifts that Casella was going to send to wine shops. These would be shipped in the same containers as the wine. The first thing was an iconic Akubra hat similar to the one Crocodile Dundee made famous. Bill Deutsch quickly put it on and hasn't given it back since. Then out came a long oilskin coat like the famous Driza-Bone. The goal was to make retail staffs not just [yellow tail] fans but [yellow tail] fanatics, and sell not just an Australian wine but also the laid-back Aussie lifestyle.

Soutter walked out of the meeting with an advance order for twenty-five thousand cases. Deutsch was committed, but the modest number indicated that the importer still had some reservations.

Back in Yenda, Casella began working on producing some cases to send to the United States so that Deutsch's staff could start preselling it just after the first of the year. On Christmas Eve 2000, the winery bottled one hundred fifty cases of [yellow tail] and air-shipped them to the United States. Deutsch at that time had only thirteen sales people, who began taking orders for a June launch. At each stop the Deutsch staffers held a tasting of the new wine, and the reactions were generally good. Retailers liked the wallaby, and also the wine. Says Bill Deutsch, "They all told us this was something very special, and at $5.99 to $6.99 for the consumer this was a very, very good buy." Sales came in stronger than expected, and Peter pushed the first order to fifty thousand cases. Eventually it went to seventy thousand. Things were starting to look up, and John Casella began feeling confident about the launch. Meanwhile, John Soutter was back in the United States once a month February through April to work with the distributors and retailers.

Casella marketing manager Libby Nutt says that from the beginning the winery's approach to promotion was to make everything simple. "Wine turns off many consumers because it's too complicated," she says. "If you give most people just a few sound bites, they're happy." Everything from the labels to glossy shipping cartons was color-coded: yellow for Shiraz and black for Chardonnay. The wine also came in only two sizes, the standard bottle and magnum, which cost $9. "In a store, it's easy to spot, pick up, and understand," Nutt says.

The initial promotion was heavy on what is known as "below-the-line marketing," such as in-store displays. Retailers received payments for placing stacks of [yellow tail] cartons as well as signs at the end of aisles so customers would see them more easily. In addition, the winery sent along those Australian hats and coats, all carrying the [yellow tail] logo. Those didn't cost much, but they won over the important people who recommend wines.

The marketing strategy was so unusual that it attracted the attention of academics. W. Chan Kim and Renée Mauborgne, professors at INSEAD, France's top business school, used the [yellow tail] launch in their best-selling book *Blue Ocean Strategy: How to Create Uncontested Market Space and Make Competition Irrelevant*. They wrote that it introduced a "fun and non-traditional wine that's easy to drink for everyone." That style pulled in many nontraditional wine drinkers who normally consume beer or cocktails. At the same time, [yellow tail] broke with standard wine marketing that stresses oak, complexity, and aging, to sell the product as "bold, laid back, fun, and adventurous." The authors concluded, "[yellow tail] is swimming in the clear blue waters of a new market space. It has made the competition irrelevant and is enjoying strong, profitable growth as a result."

John Casella's goal when [yellow tail] hit the American market was to get 10 percent of Rosemount's American sales, at that time about 1.5 million cases annually. "I thought if we could sell a hundred fifty thousand to two hundred thousand cases, I'd be happy," he recalls. He believed he had a chance because Rosemount was selling at a price then about 50 percent higher, and its popularity had been sliding even before its April 2001 merger with Southcorp, another giant winery. With little more than the right product and word-of-mouth promotion, [yellow tail] hit Casella's dream goal within six months. *Wine Business Monthly,* which closely tracks sales trends, soon reported that consumers were marching into wine stores and requesting "that wine with the yellow color" or "the wine with the kangaroo." The wine was available only under allocations for the first three years, and the first traditional advertising campaign in the United States did not appear until 2004.

After anxiously worrying about the success of a new brand and the future of his company if [yellow tail] failed as Carramar had, John now faced another set of problems that could just as easily have tanked his family business. Overnight success is a nightmare for a small company, which often cannot keep up with demand. The first thing that usually happens is that product quality collapses, as the business increases production too fast and lowers standards. The second is that the company raises prices, and customers revolt. The third is that the company hires people too fast, and often the wrong people. Many high-flying companies have crashed and burned on the tarmac of success.

John Casella was facing exactly those issues by late 2001. The bottling line, which was running two days when sale started, began running seven days a week. The company introduced two shifts a day, then three. Finally a massive second bottling line was installed. At one point, the whole of Australia had run out of magnum bottles, and Casella faced the loss of those attractive sales. He had to air-freight bottles from Italy to continue production. Could the company keep up with the almost insatiable demand from American consumers? It was a nice problem to have, but still a major challenge.

In the second half of 2001, the first seven months on the market, sales were 399,000 cases. In 2002, they reached 2.2 million. The following year the company hit 4.7 million, in 2004 6.5 million, and in 2005 8 million. During that spectacular growth, many Australian and American wineries off on the sidelines were saying that [yellow tail] would never last. It was going to be just another American fad, similar to earlier booms in Lambrusco and wine coolers.

One of the first steps Deutsch and Casella took was to control the roll-out across the United States. Instead of trying to supply the whole country with the suddenly popular wine and running out in some markets, they introduced it state by state. The last state to get [yellow tail] was California. That was the biggest state market, and Deutsch and Casella wanted to make sure they could properly supply it.

Another immediate challenge was to build more production facilities in Yenda. Casella at the time was still basically the family winery that Filippo had built. John had added a few things, such as the bottling line, but had nothing like the equipment needed to meet the American demand. He started a crash building program, pulling out some vineyards to expand the existing facilities around the old family home. In 2006, Filippo and Maria finally moved out of the house. In his office, John has behind his desk eight pictures showing the systematic Casella expansion over five years that turned a small winery into one of the world's biggest wine factories. A decade ago, Casella was a dot on the Australian landscape; today it is an industrial city. Prefab trailers were brought in and turned into offices, and the company built warehouses with corrugated steel walls that could hold 1 million cases. Casella ordered tanks that can hold 1.1 million liters (245,000 gallons) of wine. The structures were so big that they could not be moved into position and had to be built in place. A special feeder railroad line was constructed to carry wine to a nearby main rail line for the first leg of its voyage to America. Despite all the emergency construction, there was never enough room, and production still had to be done in other facilities. At one point, the company was bottling at five nearby locations.

Another problem that could have crippled the company was the simple issue of cash flow. Casella Wines was suddenly spending millions of dollars to buy grapes, bottles, plastic corks, and more. At one point, the company owed its printer alone AUD1 million ($900,000). As a small firm, Casella didn't have the cash reserves to cover the difference between the time it paid its bills and when it received payment for the wine. John desperately needed to increase the company's short-term borrowing power. Reluctantly he took the problem to Bill Deutsch, who offered to give him unusually generous seven-day payment terms, meaning that he would pay for the wine seven days after it was shipped, rather than the normal ninety days. Without this concession from Deutsch and patience from his vendors, John Casella might have had to take in outside investors and thus lose family control.

Staffing also had to ramp up in a hurry. Almost overnight, the company had to hire winemakers, warehouse workers, forklift drivers, export specialists, publicists, marketing gurus, and more. It was impossible to find all those people, especially with special professional skills, in Yenda (population one thousand), so new employees began working out of offices in Sydney and Melbourne. Casella's payroll went from 65 in 2001 to 230 in 2006. The time of harvest and winemaking is always a madhouse around a winery, but for several years the Casella staff was routinely working twelve-hour days; as one veteran employee told me, "We all lived on adrenaline."

The biggest challenge was getting enough grapes or bulk wine to keep up with demand, while still maintaining quality. Then and now, Casella grows only about 5 percent of the grapes that go into its wine. The majority comes from farmers in its local area in Riverina, but John also bought large quantities of grapes from the country's premium wine regions such as the Hunter Valley and Coonawarra. Luckily for Casella, Australia was in a period of oversupply in the grape and wine market, so there was plenty of both good fruit and good juice. The Rosemount and Southcorp merger in April 2001 also freed up grape supplies. Says John, "That was one bit of good fortune. We were able to go to the market and buy wine at reasonable prices." Thanks to his years of working in the bulk market at Riverina Estate, John knew the best growers and winemakers. Casella still buys grapes or juice from some 650 sources and has four people on staff dedicated to keeping the growers happy. None-theless, in those hectic days John still had to make some unusual deals, like buying back from Hardys a batch of wine that he had sold to it only a few months before.

John Casella took advantage of the overwhelming demand and in 2006 raised the suggested retail price of [yellow tail] from $5.99 to $6.99 for the standard bottle, with a corresponding increase for the magnum. Some retailers, though, still sell it for the original price. Consumers accepted the change, and sales stayed strong.

The totally crazy times at Casella Wines lasted from late 2001 until 2005. By the end of that period, new equipment and an expanded staff were in place to meet demand. All orders were filled in that hectic period, although sometimes only by costly, heroic measures such as air-freighting wine to the United States. There would be more challenges ahead, but John Casella had reached the end of the beginning.

The American press was generally slow to pick up on the market success of [yellow tail]. In fact, the brand has never gotten much ink. The month [yel-low tail] was released, *Wine Enthusiast* magazine reviewed the Chardonnay, giving it a solid 88. The reviewer wrote, "There are no complaints with this Chardonnay. Apple, pineapple, butter and toasted oak load the flavor package. The perfect balance and velvety mouth feel provide a solid back-ground. The producer recommends kangaroo tail soup with this one—but why not? You get to go to Australia, and kangaroo is low in fat and choles-terol." The magazine rated it a Best Buy.

In December 2002, eighteen months after the U.S. launch, *Forbes* published the first significant story about the wine. The flattering article quoted Robert Trone, owner of the large wine retail chain Total Wine & More, saying, "We taste it against sixteen California wines [in the same price range]; it's on top every time."

Robert Parker Jr. rated the 2002 vintage for five [yellow tail] wines. He scored them between 83 points for the Chardonnay and 87 for the Reserve Shiraz.

Wine Spectator first mentioned [yellow tail] in the September 30, 2004, issue, when it was lumped in with more than thirty Australian wines under the title "A Menagerie of Aussie Values." The 2003 Shiraz was the only [yellow tail] wine mentioned. It got 85 points and the comment "Smooth and round, with a sweet red pepper edge to the berry flavors, which persist nicely on the finish."

Leo McCloskey, president of Enologix, a Sonoma company that developed a controversial system that claims to help wineries garner high scores from reviewers by playing with wine components, analyzed the 2002 [yellow tail] Shiraz and gave it 85 or 86 points on a scale of 100. Given the price, he concluded, "It's a lot of value."

It didn't matter that the American wine press wasn't paying attention; the American wine consumer had fallen in love with [yellow tail].

The Yenda winery today has the latest equipment from around the world. The facility contains nine warehouses with a capacity to hold one million cases, enough for one month's deliveries. The main bottling line is the fastest in the world, handling thirty-six thousand bottles an hour, which works out to labeling and sealing one bottle per second. It operates twenty-four hours a day, five days a week, and shuts down only for short periods at Christmas and Easter. There is also another slower bottling line used for special shorter runs. A sign on a door in the bottling room sends a message to employees: "Think quality. If you don't, our competition will."

During harvest, the winery can crush 520 tons of grapes an hour. Towering over the whole winery like a hulking, giant Emerald City are one hundred wine-holding tanks that have a total capacity of sixty million gallons. All day long, forklifts fill cargo containers with cases before they are shipped out. Every working day between thirty-five and fifty containers are loaded with up to 1,176 cases each. Everything in the production area is color-coded by grape variety, so the cases of Chardonnay stand out quickly from those of Cabernet Sauvignon.

[yellow tail] now has eleven winemakers. The boss of them all is Australian Alan Kennett, who has the title winery manager. American Randy Herron is chief winemaker. He grew up in California's Central Valley, graduated from the Fresno State University wine program, and formerly worked for Gallo. Herron said his goal is to make wines with the balance an average drinker likes, though wine geeks may not. He added, "Average consumers don't like those hard Cabs. They're too bitter."

One day in Yenda, while I was sampling the entire line of [yellow tail] wines sold in the United States plus a few more, Kennett told me he likes having a boss who is a trained winemaker because he understands the constant trade-offs that must be made in any winery. Kennett explained that if one of his winemakers needs to buy more grapes from a premium region—the Clare Valley, for example—to improve the quality of a batch of Riesling, no accountant trying to keep down costs is going to tell him no. He said John Casella sometimes still shows up in the lab without warning to work on a private project.

Kennett says the greatest achievement of [yellow tail] is that the quality has gotten better since the wine was introduced a decade ago, despite the company's massive growth. Harvey Steiman, who follows Australian wines for *Wine Spectator,* confirmed that view in his blog. In a posting on March 29, 2010, he wrote: "I noticed a significant uptick in quality and style. Tasting blind, I once could distinguish a [yellow tail] sample by its sugary sweetness. Not any more. The wines are now nearly dry, close enough that they don't stand out from their peers. They also seem to have more transparency and detail to their flavors. In the past, the $7 price tag seemed too high for the quality, usually scoring in the low 80s. Now it seems about right as the wines do three to six points better."

Today [yellow tail] is sold in some fifty countries around the world. After the introduction in the United States, Casella took the wines to Canada and Britain. Then it moved into Asian markets and the rest of Europe. In every market, [yellow tail] is one of the top-selling wines, often in first place.

Australia was one of the last major markets to get [yellow tail] wines, and they became available there only in 2006. Management realized that the home turf was going to be perhaps the toughest because they were fighting for shelf space against wineries that had been there for decades. [yellow tail] is now Australia's third-best-selling wine. Casella Wine offers some products only in Australia, for example, a line of box wines. It has also started two new labels: Yendah, a line of six high-quality wines, and Mallee Point, which has eight entry-level ones.

The reputation of [yellow tail] at home is mixed. Some Australians are proud of its success and enjoy its wines. Many people in the wine business, though, criticize it in a manner that locals call "tall poppy syndrome." According to an old Aussie maxim, if someone gets too successful, you'd better knock him down, as you would a tall poppy. Many in the wine business worry that [yellow tail] is hurting the reputation of all Australian wines and driving down prices for their products. Timothy Boydell of Angove Family Winemakers told me, "[yellow tail] has been a poisoned chalice for the Australian wine industry. It has been good for exports, but it has reduced the reputation of our wines and made it more difficult to sell wines at a price higher than it charges." This argument belies the fact that before [yellow tail], Rosemount and Lindeman's were selling lots of inexpensive wine. Casella officials are particularly proud that [yellow tail] has captured Australia's two most prestigious wine prizes: the Jimmy Watson Memorial Trophy for its 2003 Wrattonbully Cabernet Sauvignon and the Stodart Trophy for the 2003 McLaren Vale Shiraz.

While [yellow tail] wines have the same taste around the world, there are some minor variations in the product from market to market. Bottles for the U.S. market are sealed with a plastic cork, while screw caps go on those in many other markets, including Britain and Australia. Reserve wines have a Diam stopper, a manufactured cork closure that is guaranteed taint-free. The grape varieties offered for sale also vary from country to country in response to local tastes. The most popular wine in the American market is Chardonnay, while the best seller in Australia is a blend of Sémillon and Sauvignon Blanc that is not sold in the United States.

[yellow tail] currently sells more than twenty wines in the United States, ranging from pure varieties such as Merlot and Riesling to blends such as Shiraz Cabernet and Shiraz Grenache. It also sells a Sparkling Rosé and a Sparkling White. When I met John Casella in Australia, he was excited about a new Chardonnay that was about to be offered in the United States that is not aged in oak and contains a small amount of New Zealand Sauvignon Blanc. He particularly liked the name, Tree-Free Chardonnay, which had come from a contest the company ran on Facebook. He described it as "lean, crisp, long—a fun wine" and predicted it would be a hit.

[yellow tail] continues introducing new wines and seeking new markets. John Casella is particularly interested in his reserve line. The reserves are aged in oak, with the wood coming from a wide range of suppliers, including French and American sources, and using both oak planks and barrels for aging. They sell for about $10, which is 30 percent more than the standard brand. Reserves now make up only about 2 percent of the company's sales, and John would like to see that increase to 10 percent. In May 2010, as part of a relaunch of the [yellow tail] reserves in the United States, John Casella and Doug Frost, an American Master of Wine and Master Sommelier, held blind tastings of those wines against some of the world's best in San Francisco, Los Angeles, Chicago, and New York City. No one kept score, but at least at the New York tasting that I attended, the [yellow tail] reserves stood up well against such famous and costly brands as d'Arenberg The Dead Arm.

John Casella plus William and Peter Deutsch have enjoyed an historic success in the American market, but can it last? All Australian exporters are currently facing a difficult challenge because of the increasing value of the Australian dollar in relation to the American one. When [yellow tail] was launched in 2001, the Australian currency was near a historic low: an Australian dollar equaled fifty American cents. At the end of 2010, the two currencies were at parity, which theoretically means that any Australian product should cost twice as much in the United States as it did in 2001. A few Australian wines have raised prices and seen sales slip away. [yellow tail] has raised its suggested retail price only once since the wine was launched, going from $5.99 to $6.99, and that was long before the recent currency troubles. But how long will the company be able to hold the price? And if it raises the cost, how many sales will it lose? Can a good-quality/good-value wine survive as a good-quality/expensive product? Those are the tough questions now facing [yellow tail].

CHAPTER NINE

The Next Giant of Bargain Wines

While living in enforced exile on the small, rocky island of St. Helena in the South Atlantic Ocean, Napoléon Bonaparte remained a keen student of world affairs. In 1816, Britain's Lord Amherst visited him on his way back home from a failed diplomatic mission to China. Napoléon naturally had views about that country, having read the French translation of the journals kept by Lord Macauley, the English ambassador to China in 1793–94. When Lord Amherst asked Napoléon for his opinion of the mysterious Middle Kingdom, Napoléon, with his quintessential gift for the dramatic, pointed to a spot on a map and said, "There is a sleeping giant. Let him sleep! If he wakes, he will shake the world."

China is now shaking the world as it undergoes history's most rapid economic growth. The country is modernizing at a breakneck rate. China today is a country of 1.3 billion people, who all seem to be speaking on cell phones at the same time. While most of the world has paid little attention to Chinese wines, the country will soon be a key player in that field. According to the International Organisation of Wine and Vine, in 2009 China was the sixth largest producer and the fifth largest consumer. Wine sales in China increased by more than 100 percent between 2005 and 2009, going from 46.9 million cases to 95.9 million. It is expected to grow an additional 20 percent by 2014. British wine merchant Berry Bros. & Rudd predicted in 2008 that in fifty years China would lead world wine. Jasper Morris, a Master of Wine, said in the company's report, "I absolutely think China will be a fine wine player rivaling the best wines from France."

China's new wealthy consumers are spending money lavishly to improve their lifestyles, with wine being only one of the products they conspicuously consume. Just like Americans in the 1950s and 1960s, when they were the world's nouveaux riches, and the Japanese, when they took over that role in the 1970s, the Chinese have discovered wine and are buying it with abandon. David Elswood of Christie's Wine Department says the two capitals of world wine auctions today are Bordeaux and Hong Kong, which has already eclipsed old centers such as London and New York City. Chinese nationals buy much of the wine sold at auctions, mostly for personal consumption, not as an investment. In addition, they are purchasing two-thirds of the premium wines the auction house sells in Europe and the United States. China has become the top market for Bordeaux wine outside Europe, buying half of wine futures for later delivery.

In 2010, China produced 100 million cases of wine; some 90 percent of that was red wine. One reason for the heavy concentration is that China's wine neophytes find white too acidic. Another more important explanation is that the Chinese believe that red brings good luck, prosperity, and health. If you're bringing a house gift to a Chinese friend, don't embarrass yourself by giving a bottle of white.

China has been so busy developing its domestic wine market that it has had no time for, or much interest in, developing export sales. Insiders in China told me that it might be a decade before the Chinese product is good enough to take on world markets, but no one doubts that eventually they will. At present only a few Chinese companies are venturing abroad, and those are mostly selling in Europe. A generation ago, Italian producers dramatically increased exports to the United States by selling inexpensive Chianti in straw-covered bottles at Italian restaurants. China's Dragon Seal winery tried to copy that strategy and get its wines into Chinese restaurants, but so far without much success. The reason is that, while wine has accompanied Italian food for generations, Chinese food with wine is still a new concept, even in China. Dragon Hollow, a winery located in the Helan mountain range in the north-central part of the country, is one of the few trying to break into the U.S. market. It sells for about $13 a bottle through California's Broadbent Selections, but distribution is weak.

A hint of things probably to come, though, was the December 2010 visit of Joe Gallo, the president of the family company, to Shanghai, where he met with a major trading company. The two sides talked about what was described as "future strategic cooperation." Napa Valley's Robert Morey has already named the inexpensive wine the Chinese will sell in the United States: One Buck Chang.

I traveled around China in May and June 2010, asking dozens of Chinese as well as foreign wine experts one question: Does China have the capacity to produce world-class wine? Whether the person I queried was French, American, British, or Chinese, the answer was always the same: Yes. Christie's Elswood predicted that in twenty years his company would be auctioning off five or six Chinese wines with a quality of Australia's famous Penfolds Grange. Michel Rolland, the superstar of international wine consultants, said that China is in its age of discovery, finding which grapes and which regions provide the raw materials for truly great wines. Rolland added, "China is such a big country that I am sure they will find the areas where the best grapes grow and will develop them. They just don't yet know where those areas will be."

Typical of the new Chinese wine consumer is Yang Bin, chairman of Beijing DSH Auto, a General Motors dealership in the Chinese capital. Bin told me that he started drinking wine about ten years ago, and now enjoys almost exclusively those from Bordeaux's right bank: Château Figeac, Château Pétrus, Château Cheval Blanc, and Château Ausone. The last two are the only Premiers Grands Crus from St.-Émilion. Two years ago, Yang Bin visited Pétrus, where he was a guest for a lunch, an honor offered only to its best customers. He said that the night before we met he had enjoyed a bottle of Château Ausone, although his daily wine is Château l'Évangile, a Pomerol that retails for about $200 a bottle. Yang Bin has collected six thousand bottles.

China's wine culture goes back some nine thousand years, having come to the country probably along the Silk Road that connected Europe and Asia. In 2004, Patrick E. McGovern, the leading archaeologist on ancient alcoholic beverages, and Chinese researchers with whom he worked found traces of a winelike substance that contained fruit, honey, and rice in pottery jars in the village of Jiahu in Henan province, northern China. China's most enduring and for many its most endearing product is rice wine, which tastes like an aged sherry. The Chinese call it yellow wine. Historians believe Chinese wine was first made in about the fourth century BC in Xinjliang in the far northwestern part of the country. Two centuries later, the emperor of China sent a delegation to Europe to study wine.

By the eighth century of the modern era, wine was an integral part of Chinese culture. Just as in Europe, it was integrated into religious ceremonies. A group of poets during the Tang Dynasty (AD 618 to 907) became known as the "eight immortals of the wine cup." In the early eighth century, Wang Han wrote this poem that I saw on the walls of several wineries:

Battlefront

Fine wine in a translucent jade cup
As I ponder another sip, a lute sounded from horseback summons
Please don't laugh at me lying drunk on a battlefield
From time immemorial, how many men returned from war?

Wine, though, eventually lost out to *baijiu,* a distilled grain alcohol with a high-octane of 100 proof or even higher. For centuries it has been consumed at banquets that included endless toasts, where guests say with gusto, *"Gan bei,"* then chug whatever is left in their glass. The expression means literally "empty the cup," but could be translated colloquially as "bottoms up." Many Americans first became familiar with the drinking ritual in February 1972, when Zhou Enlai hosted President Nixon at a dinner in Beijing's Great Hall of the People. The Chinese premier tried to get Nixon to *gan bei,* but the president took only tiny sips of *baijiu,* probably out of concern that it would diminish his negotiating skills. The Chinese find exquisite aroma and tastes in *baijiu,* but to Westerners the drink is raw and sharp.

In December 1978, Deng Xiaoping, the pragmatic successor to communist purist Mao Zedung, introduced economic reforms called Socialism with Chinese Characteristics. Deng summed up his economic philosophy once by saying, "It doesn't matter if a cat is black or white, so long as it catches mice." Part of Deng's program was to discourage the consumption of *baijiu* in favor of wine, for a variety of reasons. For starters, government leaders were concerned about the country's increasing alcoholism as it became more affluent. In addition, in 1987 China decided that grains should go to more productive uses such as food for both humans and animals rather than into alcohol. Finally, grapevines could be grown on hilly areas with poor soils, providing a more efficient use of farmland.

Baijiu is still sold in China and remains popular among the older generation. Wealthy and younger Chinese, however, increasingly have turned to wine. In 1996, the government outlawed drinking *baijiu* at government banquets, and toasts are now made with wine. Private parties, though, often still have the old drink. In another attempt to encourage wine consumption, taxes on imported wines were dramatically reduced and cut even more for domestic wine. In Hong Kong, a Special Administrative Region within China since the 1997 handover of the former British colony, the tax dropped to zero in 2008, and on the mainland it was also lowered. Not surprisingly, wine sales jumped.

The government's heavy-industry department initially controlled the wine business, but later it was moved to the light-industry bureaucracy. The government still keeps an active hand in the business, rewarding companies that are successful and quietly merging those that are not with better-run competitors. Winery operators privately grumble about the heavy hand of officials, while enjoying the financial support they receive.

With the government's blessing, wine sales took off. First, some old operations that the Communist government had restricted or shut down in the early years of its rule came back to life. In the late nineteenth century, Zhang Bishi, a Chinese trader known as China's Rockefeller, had built the first Western-style winery in the country with the help of Austrians in the town of Yantai, in Shandong province on the country's eastern coast. Zhang Bishi planted a half million European and American vines at the ChangYu winery.

The Communists in 1949 nationalized it and shifted it to brandy production, which the party elders liked. After Deng's national policy favored wine, ChangYu switched back to wine and grew rapidly. Beijing Dragon Seal Wines, which had opened its doors in 1910 when a French monk made wine in a church graveyard, also started up again, producing its first vintage in 1988.

Many new wineries also started, and today the country has about six hundred. Just three, though, control 60 percent of sales, and six have 90 percent. The Big Three are ChangYu, Great Wall, and Dynasty.

ChangYu, officially known as Yantai Changyu Pioneer Wine, claims to be the largest producer in the country. It has an impressive wine museum and a visitor center at its headquarters still in Yantai that harks back to its nineteenth-century heritage. ChangYu also owns a replica of a French château outside Beijing that has become a big draw for tourists.

In 1983, COFCO, a large food and vegetable company officially named the China National Cereals, Oils and Foodstuffs Corporation, launched the China Great Wall Wine Co. Although Great Wall's headquarters are in Hebei province, its showpiece winery, Chateau Junding, is located to the east in Shandong province in the interestingly named Nava Valley. The winery proudly displays pictures of such visitors as Henry Kissinger and Nobel Prize–winning economist Paul Krugman. Chateau Junding also has a golf course and a ninety-two-bedroom luxury hotel. Great Wall was the exclusive wine supplier to the 2008 Beijing Olympics. In November 2009, when President Obama visited China, Premier Wen Jiabao served him Chateau Sungod, a premium Great Wall label.

The Dynasty Fine Wines Group is based in Tianjin and annually produces about nine million cases. It is constructing a replica of a French château for its headquarters that will include a copy of I. M. Pei's pyramid at the Louvre museum in Paris. In May 2010, Dynasty announced that it would be investing $150 million to expand production nearly 50 percent by buying vineyards in Australia, Chile, New Zealand, and France. Company officials said they were making investments abroad because of the limited prospects for developing top vineyards at home. Dynasty exports only 1 percent of its production to a few European countries, Korea, and Japan, but hopes to increase that to 10 percent by 2015.

In their attempt to get wine operations going in a hurry, many Chinese companies looked abroad for help. Firms in France, Australia, Italy, and New Zealand responded enthusiastically. Today it's common to meet young Chinese winemakers who have studied at the University of Bordeaux or

Charles Sturt University in Australia. After their studies, they often work a few harvests abroad before returning home to good jobs.

Chinese companies hell-bent on growth looked above all to France, considering it the home of the world's best wine. The French were anxious to help and saw China as a deus ex machina at a time when they were trying to boost slumping sales at home and abroad. The two countries, which take great pride in their culture and cuisine, were natural partners. Several Chinese companies quickly set up joint ventures with French partners. In 1980, Rémy Martin, a maker of Cognac, signed a deal with Dynasty. ChangYu did a partnership with Castel, a company from Languedoc-Roussillon. Dragon Seal teamed up with Camus, the French Cognac company.

The Chinese generally only allowed minority foreign ownership, and the ventures have not worked out well. In 2001, for example, Camus and Dragon Seal announced plans to sell Chinese wine in airport duty-free shops around the world, but the agreement died quietly and quickly. Other French-Chinese deals have also had problems. French winemakers are reluctant to talk about what has gone wrong, but one insider told me that they have learned never to sign contracts with a Chinese partner for more than three years, and preferably not more than two, because Chinese companies often soak up the Western intellectual property in a short time and then move on. In an endless triumph of hope over experience, though, French corporations continue to sign agreements.

The French have supplied China with some key winemaking talent. Gérard Colin is today the emperor of wine in China and has handled some of the most successful ventures. Born in Madagascar to French civil servants stationed there, Colin grew up as something of a stranger both in his adopted country and his native one. That international background, though, made him an astute student of diverse cultures, which has helped him succeed in China. He adapted easily to the country, and the Chinese hold him in high esteem. Wearing a red silk Chinese morning coat at his country home, Colin resembles the foreign teachers, missionaries, and soldiers of fortune who in centuries past went to China and played major roles in the country's history.

After studying at the University of Bordeaux with the famed enologist Émile Peynaud and working at his family's winery in St.-Émilion, Colin was at Edmond de Rothschild, Château Clarke, and the Edmond et Benjamin de Rothschild company. Colin first traveled to China in 1997, staying for only three months. He returned the following year and has lived there ever since, although he visits France often.

His newest and potentially most historic undertaking is a joint venture between CITIC, China's largest state-owned investment company, and Domaines Barons de Rothschild, whose properties include Château Lafite-Rothschild and other wineries around the world. Under a deal signed in early 2009, the Rothschilds own 70 percent of the Chinese venture, and CITIC 30 percent. While not the first Chinese-French deal, this one has the most potential, given the deep pockets of the owners and the talent they've assembled.

The new company is developing twenty-five hectares (sixty-two acres) of vineyard not far from Colin's rural home in Shandong province. One Sunday morning, I walked with Colin and Jim Sun, the owner of winechina .com, the country's largest and best wine website, through the freshly terraced fields where vines would soon be planted. The night before it had rained heavily, and Colin was happy to see that the property had drained well. With a nod toward Chinese tradition and culture, Colin did not move any of the dozen tall granite tombstones on the property, following the dictates of feng shui, the ancient Chinese system of aesthetics that is believed to improve the quality of life. Colin later explained that Domaines Barons de Rothschild "doesn't really see this as an economic investment, but an investment for the ages." The goal is nothing short of making a Chinese wine that will stand tall among the world's best.

Another French winemaker in a key position in China is Jérôme Sabaté, who heads wine production at Beijing Dragon Seal Wines. Sabaté studied enology at Montpellier and first went to China for two years in the late 1990s on a French government program similar to the Peace Corps. He then made wine in Israel for two years before returning to China. Sabaté now hopes to spend the rest of his professional life there. Two of his Chinese deputies are French trained.

Dragon Seal produces 360,000 cases annually. Its winery in the heart of Beijing is slowly being turned into a wine museum and retail store, and new production facilities are being built some 150 miles northwest of the capital. The company already has most of its vineyards there and cultivates a dozen types of French-imported grapes.

Sabaté was pleased with his 2009 Cabernet Sauvignon that I tasted with him in the spring of 2010. He said he thought it was his best yet and showed the improving quality of Dragon Seal wines. The rich, mellow wine could have won a medal in an international competition. The winery has already picked up some awards, including a bronze from a competition in Bordeaux. Dragon Seal also made the first Chinese sparkling wine using the traditional Champagne process.

The French have profited from their early investment in China, and today virtually own the import market. At the trade show Vinexpo Asia-Pacific in May 2010, more than one hundred French wineries dominated the exhibit hall, while fifty California ones were lost in the crowd. The most popular imported wines in China today, both at the top of the market and at the bottom, are French. Château Lafite-Rothschild is the gold standard for wine in China. It is not only the best-selling luxury wine but also the favorite target for the country's many talented forgers, who turn out perhaps as many fake bottles as there are authentic ones. Counterfeiters will pay more than $400 for empty Lafite bottles on the black market. The Chinese love to buy both aged Lafites at auction and new ones as futures. In a gesture of appreciation for its market success, Lafite put on every bottle of 2008 Château Lafite-Rothschild the Chinese symbol for the number *8*, a sign of good luck. Château Mouton Rothschild responded by having a Chinese artist paint the picture on its 2008 label.

Castel, which has its headquarters in Southern France, rules the Chinese import market for less expensive imported wines, selling more than three million cases a year. Castel is also the biggest wine advertiser in the local media. As much as one-third of all Chinese wine contains some foreign juice bought in the international bulk market, which is added to beef up the quality of the local product. Castel is a favorite for blending.

Looking at the rapidly evolving Chinese wine market, Aubert de Villaine, the codirector of the Domaine de la Romanée-Conti, France's most famous vineyard, told me that he could probably sell two-thirds of his total production in China, but then would have to take it away from traditional markets in Europe and the United States. He, along with many others, has heard perhaps apocryphal stories about the Chinese mixing great wines such as Château Lafite-Rothschild with Coca-Cola to create a concoction that all but destroys both products. De Villaine said with a smile that he once heard those same tales about the Americans and Japanese. He dismisses them and sees an educational process at work. "At first people in new wine countries buy famous wines as gifts for their friends or business associates," he says. But over time, they drink the wines themselves and learn to appreciate them. De Villaine believes it will be only a matter of time before the Chinese, just as the Americans and the Japanese before them, are connoisseurs of top French wines.

Good-quality wine grapes grow in a narrow latitudinal band of the earth between 30° and 50° in both the Northern and Southern hemispheres. Bordeaux, for example, is located at 44.8°N, while Napa Valley is at 38.3°N. Mendoza, Argentina, is at 32.9°S, and Stellenbosch, South Africa, is at 33.9°S. As a country that occupies much of a continent, China has several potential wine areas in the northern hemisphere. Grapes are currently being grown in eight major regions of China, where viticulturists are searching for the best *terroir*. Ask a dozen winemakers to name the best, and you're likely to get nearly as many answers. The response is usually the place where that person works. Most of the areas are in the north-central and east-central parts of the country, which have four seasons a year, rather than in the hot, tropical south, where the climate is much less favorable to grape growing.

The most promising area is Shandong Province, which is on a peninsula with the same name that has the Yellow Sea on its south and the Bohai Sea on its north, about three hundred miles southeast of Beijing. This is where the Rothschild vineyard has been planted. The Germans occupied Shandong from 1897 to 1914, then lost it to the Japanese at the Versailles negotiations ending World War I. Shandong is China's Garden of Eden, where fruits and vegetables grow in abundance. Dotted across the countryside are endless orchards, which have made China the world's top apple exporter.

Shandong means "east mountain," and it is east of the Taihang Mountains. Confucius lived there in the sixth and fifth centuries BC, and reportedly enjoyed the local wines. Shandong has been a favorite place of Westerners looking for promising regions for viticulture, and Gérard Colin thinks it has the greatest potential. He told me that while some people worry that it gets too much rain in the early summer, total annual precipitation is about the same as Bordeaux's. The rains stop at the end of August, and then there is little until the end of November, after the harvest. There are already some sixty wineries in and around Penglai, a port town that is one of Shandong's major cities, and nearly half of all Chinese wines today come from the Shandong peninsula.

The ancient Yellow River Area, the birthplace of Chinese civilization, is a traditional table-grape area and now has about a dozen wineries. It is a hot location, however, and the high temperatures will make it difficult to make great wines there.

Hebei province, to the north of Shandong, shows a lot of wine potential. Changli, a county in Hebei, has been called China's Bordeaux, although there are other claimants to that moniker. The China Great Wall Wine Company has its headquarters in Shacheng, which is in Hebei. Rainfall there is light, growing conditions are good, and the soil is sandy. Some of China's biggest wineries are growing grapes there because of the abundant harvests. Both traditional Chinese grape varieties such as Dragon Eye and imported Western ones such as Cabernet Sauvignon and Merlot do well. The Great Wall Winery sources many of its grapes in Hebei.

The province, however, got a temporary black eye at the end of 2010, when six people were arrested on charges of adding sugar water, coloring agents, and artificial flavors to products claiming to be wine and putting forged labels on them. Some of the fake wines contained no grape juice at all. Authorities shut down thirty wineries and took their products off shelves all over the country.

Farther north and east, some Chinese vintners are trying to grow wine grapes, but the natural challenges are great. The regions are simply too cold. Though the soil is rich, farmers and winemakers face serious battles with nature.

Jim Sun of winechina.com thinks that the Helan Mountains region of the Ningxia Autonomous Region in the north-central part of the country may end up being the best area for wine. This is a high desert, irrigated region, and the Yellow River runs nearby. Growing conditions are similar to those found in winemaking areas of Chile and Argentina.

Farther to the west of the Helan Mountains is Wuwei, a small but blessed area that has sandy soil and a climate similar to Bordeaux. It is likely to be a good region for cool, early-ripening grapes that will have good acidity. Irrigated vines do well here, and there are fewer plant diseases than in other regions.

Yunnan, an area of mountains, rivers, and lakes, is China's southernmost wine region. It has long been a productive area for table grapes and only recently has gotten into those for wine. Some of the country's biggest producers have already planted vineyards there. Yunnan is subtropical and has a monsoon climate, but is cooled by winds from the Pacific and Indian oceans.

The most serious challenge facing Chinese vintners is the harsh weather. China's wine regions have a wide range of climates, and in many places temperatures can hit -30°C (-22°F) or even colder. In any other country, that would eliminate wine production, because freezing temperatures kill vines. The Chinese, though, are inventive and use their large reservoir of workers to solve the problem by covering vines with soil in autumn and then uncovering them in the spring.

The level of coverage varies from region to region. At Chateau Huadong-Parry, a winery in southern Shandong, winter temperatures can drop to -8°C (18°F). Winemaker Xin Zheng explained that each autumn workers cover the roots of vines to about six inches above the base. At a Dragon Seal vineyard seventy-five miles north of Beijing, the temperature in the winter of 2010 fell to -29°C (-20°F). Xu Lin, the winery's technical manager, told me that his workers bend each vine, which may be more than two meters (six feet six inches) in height, over into rows between the plants and cover the entire vine with forty centimeters (sixteen inches) of soil. Officials at both Chateau Huadong-Parry and Dragon Seal admitted that they lose some vines each year to the cold, but the vast majority of plants survive thanks to the winter cover. Northern Shandong province is the only region where temperatures never get below freezing, and covering vines is unnecessary. That's another reason the region looks promising.

Such heroic steps to protect vines would never be considered in any other wine region in the world, but China has an army of underemployed workers on call. Judy Leissner of Grace Vineyard has been quoted as saying, "I can have three thousand people in twenty-four hours [to do the work]."

One side benefit of the freezing temperatures is that they eliminate the danger of phylloxera, the nasty little bug that has been the scourge of winemakers since the middle of the nineteenth century. In Europe, winemakers had to plant bug-resistant American rootstock and then graft vines on top of it to eliminate the pests. Chinese grape growers don't worry about phylloxera, because freezing temperatures kill the insects. Only about 15 percent of Chinese vines grow on rootstock, while the rest have natural roots. Some winemakers are still worried that a phylloxera infestation might eventually cause trouble, especially in warmer areas. But for now, most ignore the problem.

Another major challenge facing Chinese winemakers is that they have little control over the most important raw material for their product: the grapes. Around most Chinese wineries are a few rows of grapes to impress tourists or visiting dignitaries, but those are only for show. The vast majority of the winery's grapes come from peasant farmers under contract. As Dragon Seal's Xu Lin and I were walking through a relatively small vineyard by Western standards, with perhaps forty rows of grape vines intermingled with a few rows of corn, he explained how the system works. The state owns all land in China, and citizens have the right to lease property for long periods, often decades. Peasants living in a nearby village work the land, and each family tends three or four rows of grapes. The Dragon Seal winery negotiates with villagers to grow its grapes. The peasants are ultimately responsible for the care of their rows of vines, although the winery manager can make recommendations.

Winemakers in other countries would find it impossible to work under those conditions, but no one expects change to come in China anytime soon. Chinese peasants for centuries have been a powerful force in the country's politics. Countries as diverse as Russia and the United States have learned all too well that land reform is a herculean undertaking anywhere. As a result, Chinese winemakers have no illusions that they will ever be able to enjoy the control over grape production that winemakers in France and the United States take for granted.

Chinese wine companies also have to transport grapes long distances to the facilities where crushing, fermentation, and aging take place. It's rare in the rest of the world for grapes or juice to be shipped miles and miles to winemaking and bottling complexes.

Despite its ancient wine tradition, strong government support, and abundant foreign assistance, the new Chinese wine business got off to a slow start. Western winemakers who traveled there in the 1980s still talk about primitive conditions and equipment that were common then. Tanks originally designed for making beer or grain alcohol were often used to age wine, with disastrous results. There were plenty of foreign experts to help, but simply not enough for such a big country. Visitors today can still find Chinese wines that are truly terrible. I went into a large Chinese grocery store in Shandong and bought three wines off the shelf that ranged in price from $1.50 to $5.50. The least expensive one had the brand name Dasen Red Tsing. It had no vintage date and sold for nine yuan. It was without a doubt the worst bottle of wine I have ever tried in my life. It tasted worse than vinegar, and I poured most of it down the drain. Others told me of similar experiences in China fifteen or twenty years ago, but not recently. I must also admit that during my stay in China, I tasted many outstanding wines and brought home some wonderful bottles.

Wine production, however, is changing fast. Jim Sun says the whole sector finally began taking off in the mid-1990s. With higher domestic consumption, wine quality became much better. Growth lately has been staggering. In 2009, Chinese wine sales jumped by 28.6 percent over the previous year. That same year, imports increased 50 percent. Growth is likely to continue.

Imported Western technology is one of the reasons quality has improved so quickly. Inside many Chinese wineries today you'll find the same equipment that you'd see in the Barossa Valley, Napa Valley, or Bordeaux. The Chinese have been putting money on the table to buy the best international presses, tanks, and barrels. Jim Sun admits candidly that it will take his country's wineries at least another decade to achieve parity with world standards, and Chinese winemakers privately agreed with his assessment.

Perhaps China's most beautiful and well-equipped winery is Chateau Huadong-Parry, which stands on Nine Dragon Hill above the large industrial town of Qingdao. Michael Parry, a Hong Kong wine merchant, started construction there in 1983 and completed it two years later. The winery was built in the style of an English country home, complete with large, majestic white buildings, a formal garden, a host of animals, including two black swans, and 200 hectares (494 acres) of vineyards in an area that used to be an apple and pear orchard. Pine trees and cedars grow abundantly in the hills above. Chateau Huadong-Parry also houses a private club that frequently hosts meetings of China's new business elite.

Parry died in the early 1990s, but his Chinese successors still fly the Union Jack over the property, and the current manager explained to me that he feels his job is to preserve Michael Parry's heritage. Part of that was the goal of making great white wines in a country where red wine is king, and Chateau Huadong-Parry today is most noted for its whites.

Each year the winery brings in enologists from France, Italy, Australia, and New Zealand to train its staff and improve the quality of its wines. Several of its winemakers were also trained aboard. Assistant winemaker Xin Zheng, who is twenty-seven, studied at Charles Sturt University in Australia and then interned at the Oyster Bay winery, where he made Sauvignon Blanc and Pinot Noir. He describes Parry's wines as Asian in style, with lower alcohol and softer tannins than their California counterparts. Xin Zheng considers all the wines, with the exception of an ice wine, to be dry, with less than four grams of sugar per liter.

Xin Zheng was particularly proud that Chateau Huadong-Parry today has some of the oldest vines in China, even though they were planted in the 1980s, which would not be old by French standards. He adds that the biggest challenge now facing Chinese wineries is to improve their vineyards, "We have all the best available international equipment and plenty of advice from abroad. But fruit needs time, patience, and love." Then he added, "Come back in twenty or thirty years, and you'll see that we have mastered everything about winemaking."

Conventional wisdom in the wine world is that the best products are usually not made by giant companies such as the ones now dominating the Chinese market but by small boutiques where winemakers labor over their products with love. I asked Jim Sun to predict a few wineries that will someday achieve international cult-wine status. His choices:

- Grace Vineyard is already the favorite Chinese wine with international critics, especially its Deep Blue, a Bordeaux blend served on business-class flights of Cathay Pacific. Jancis Robinson called Grace "the most successful producer of Chinese red wine to date." Cynics might say that is like being the tallest dwarf in Belgium, but kudos nonetheless. Deep Blue's first vintage was in 2001.

  The founders are Indonesian-born Chan Chun Keung, a Hong Kong business tycoon who spent time working as a mechanic in rural China during the Cultural Revolution, and France's Sylvain Janvier, who has worked for years in Asia. The president and pretty face out front is Judy Leissner, Chan's daughter, who worked for two years in the Hong Kong office of Goldman Sachs. Gérard Colin was behind its early success, but the company traded his French style for an international one by hiring Australian winemaker Ken Murchison.

- Silver Heights is the work of Emma Gao Yuan, who went to Bordeaux first as a translator for Chinese enology students, returned to study there, and married a French winemaker. Her first job back in China in 2004 was working for Spain's Miguel Torres. At the same time, she started a winery with her father. Silver Heights is located in the Ningxia Autonomous Region and produces just two Bordeaux-blend wines, Summit, which sells for HKD350 ($45), and Family Reserve, HKD230 ($30). Both are made in very small lots and are hard to find. Silver Heights has only two hectares (five acres) of land, but foreign investors are anxiously encouraging her to expand and offering to finance her venture.

- Treaty Port Vineyards is another winery launched by Gérard Colin. The owner is Chris Ruffle, who made a fortune in Hong Kong international finance. The name comes from its location between

Yantai and Penglai, two nineteenth-century treaty ports. Next to the vineyards, Ruffle built a huge Scottish-style castle that serves as a winery and offers guest quarters. The winemaker now is Mark Davidson, who previously made wine in Australia's Hunter Valley. The first vintage had not yet been released when I visited Treaty Port, but given its French heritage and location, it should succeed.

The Rothschild venture in China is too young to include in this list of wineries with the greatest potential, but undoubtedly it will be there one day. It has all the marks of success. Development money is no problem. Colin provides the technical expertise, and his knowledge of Chinese growing conditions is second to none. The wine is unlikely to hit the international market for a decade, but when it does, it may also shake the world.

The Chinese are creative and hardworking people, who over the past few years have entered many fields of business that were once new to them but where they soon became major players, usually selling quality products for attractive prices. China in a few years will be making not only world-class wines but also good inexpensive ones. The weather will remain a challenge, but Chinese business people in the past have conquered bigger ones than that.

On May 24, 2008, some forty Chinese wine lovers and a few foreigners gathered at the Badaling section of the Great Wall of China, not far from Beijing, for an evening with Robert Parker Jr. The man behind the event was Dominique Renard, a member of the Bordeaux wine establishment and an old friend of Parker. The wines were largely French, but a few others were included in the spirit of international cooperation. No Chinese wines were served. The price of admission for the seven-course, seven-wine dinner was $2,300. The bottles Parker chose and his scores for the wines:

Louis Jadot Corton-Charlemagne Grand Cru 2002 (94)
E. Guigal Côte-Rôtie La Turque 1999 (100)

Château Haut-Brîon 1989, Premier Grand Cru Classé (100)
Torbreck Run Rig 2003 (99)
Shafer Hillside Select Cabernet Sauvignon 2002 (100)
Alois Kracher Chardonnay No. 7 1999 (96)
Taylor's Port 2003 (98)

Parker's Great Wall dinner marked a milestone in China's coming of age in wine. The event was only the beginning, though. Much more is still to come.

Guides to Best Buys

Wine critics and snobs have taken much of the joy out of wine, and it's time for people to reclaim it. The current situation reminds me of a scene in George Orwell's *1984,* where wine was one of life's joys that Big Brother had taken away. The hero Winston Smith tastes it at a meeting of rebels like himself. "It is called wine," the leader of the group says as he hands Smith a glass, adding, "You have read about it in books, no doubt."

I suggest that you start your new education in wine with bottles costing less than $10. The supposed experts will say none exist, but don't believe them. Elliott Morss, blogger on wine and economic affairs, has written: "Ten years ago it was difficult to find a reasonably good wine for $10. This is not true anymore. Good $10 wines are available for every varietal."

In this guide I first list bargain wines and two splurge wines for thirty-four of the most popular wine varieties, then ten value brands from twelve regions around the world, and finally, my ten favorite box wines.

My Favorite Bargain Wines

When wine lovers are trying to decide which wines to select to have with dinner at home or at a restaurant, they will probably first choose the *type* of wine. So, here I will recommend some of my favorite bargain wines according to grape variety.

I hope that you now trust your own wine instincts. Don't let some so-called expert with a byline and a big reputation tell you what you should be drinking. Don't even let me tell you what wines are best for you. You alone know what you like, or with experience will learn what you like. It may not come the first day and your taste will undoubtedly evolve, but your taste hotspot will eventually show through.

The evolution of a person's wine appreciation is something similar to their changing taste in music. Growing up, I liked rock music and couldn't understand why anyone listened to classical. Over time, though, I tried a little here and a little there, and at some point I became a Bach fanatic. My ideal afternoon is listening to all six Brandenburg Concerti. I think the second concerto is as close to perfection as a human being can get, but I'm not about to tell anyone else in the world that he or she should join me for afternoons of Bach.

The same goes for the wines listed below. These are simply wines that I have tried and liked.

I'm not going to get into detailed discussions of food pairings, although I will give some general suggestions. Too many wine reviews get too complex. Gary Vaynerchuk, after all, can tell you the wine to drink with Cap'n Crunch. My basic recommendation, as Tim Hanni explained earlier, is light with light and heavy with heavy. Light food (chicken or fish) demands a corresponding light wine, usually a white or light red—for example, Sauvignon Blanc, light Chardonnay, or Pinot Noir. Lamb or pork goes with heavy whites or medium reds—Tempranillo, Chianti, or big Chardonnay. Heavy food (steak or roast beef) demands a bold red wine such as Cabernet Sauvignon, Shiraz, or Zinfandel. Those rules of thumb will take you a long way.

Most days you probably want to have a bargain wine that costs less than $10 a bottle with dinner. Many call those Wednesday wines since people drink them in the middle of the week. On weekends or for a special occasion, they might want to splurge a little and go for a higher-priced wine. So I have also included in each grape category two splurge wines selling for less than $25. Wines are listed according to price.

Every price in this chapter is the retail cost. If you are out at a restaurant, don't bother trying to find a wine on the list for $10. Unfortunately, they don't exist. In 2005, Bronco Wine's Fred Franzia tried to combat high mark-ups by restaurant owners, proposing to sell his Salmon Creek wines exclusively to eating establishments for $2.50, so they could charge $10 for it and still make a good profit. That $7.50, though, wasn't good enough. Markups vary from place to place, but the price on a wine list is usually double the retail cost and three times what a restaurant pays buying it wholesale. Wine is a major profit center, and dining establishments make more on costly bottles, since one at $60 retail goes to $120. Franzia's proposal was stillborn, and Salmon Creek is now sold in stores for about $5.

When you look at these recommendations, you'll notice there are almost no vineyard-specific wines. In order to increase the perceived value of their products, winemakers emphasize the importance of the land where the grapes are grown. The smaller the vineyard, the higher the wine price. That allows producers to create the illusion that there is something so special about that piece of land that the wine is worth whatever is charged. There's no doubt that some vineyards, such as To Kolan in Napa Valley or Château Figeac in Pomerol, are unique. But those are exceptions. Far too many winemakers stress the importance of their *terroir* to charge more. If you buy vineyard-specific wines, be prepared to pay a high price.

Writing about wine prices in the United States is difficult because cost varies greatly from state to state, thanks to American tax laws and distribution regulations. I have seen a bottle of Crane Lake Chardonnay selling for $3 in California and $8 in Rhode Island. According to the Tax Foundation, which tracks the numbers state by state, the levy on a gallon of table wine varies from eleven cents in Louisiana to $2.50 in Alaska. Distribution laws also stifle competition and drive up costs. In California, you can buy wine in all sorts of retail outlets—drugstores, supermarkets, even gas stations. However, in many states, including New York, wine cannot be purchased in a store where food is also sold. That unfortunately reduces competition. In Pennsylvania, New Hampshire, and a few other places, there are still state monopolies on liquor sales, reducing competition. They often have high prices and poor selection.

On the basis of my personal experience, the most competitive wine market in the United States is California, partly because the wineries are nearby and so transportation costs are low. In addition, wine is sold in many different stores. The California state tax is still only twenty cents per gallon, although politicians repeatedly threaten to raise it.

Wine reviews that recommend bottles not easily found irritate me, and I have tried hard to avoid that pitfall. I selected wines that have good distribution in most American states, but I can't promise that you'll find every wine in your corner liquor store.

I do not give vintages for these wines because that is not nearly as important for bargain wines as it for expensive ones. European producers, especially the French, have to deal with more difficult growing conditions than new-world ones. As a result, Europeans have a great variability in quality and price. A great vintage of a Bordeaux might sell for twice as much as a less attractive one. Wines from California, Australia, or South Africa have neither the variability in weather nor the swings in quality or price.

Although I have enjoyed many years of drinking wines and had tasted many of the wines discussed here, I decided to do a systematic study of inexpensive products for this book. Starting in early 2009, I began doing blind tastings of usually five or six wines of a certain variety. I normally had two such events a week. Most of the tastings were with bottled wines, but I also did similar comparisons of box products. While I waited in another room, my wife, Jean Taber, set up the wines. I knew the variety in the comparison, but not the order in which they were presented. I usually included one expensive bottle among the bargains just to see if I could spot it. Sometimes I could; sometimes I couldn't. In one round of six Cabernet Sauvignons, for example, there was also Chile's Don Melchor, which retails for about $70. In a Merlot sampling, I mixed in a $23 St. Francis from Sonoma County. Along the way, many wines fell out of contention.

All wines are listed by their basic brand names and do not include such repetitive additions as Domaine, Château, Finca, or Vineyards. Products are ranked by price and are in alphabetical order when several products cost the same.

So now, sit down and contemplate some wonderful wines that you will have tomorrow night or next month and then look at the wineries that you should seek out as you go about your quest for bargain wines. Your research should be great fun.

White Wines

Chardonnay

The world's most popular white wine, Chardonnay, is made in many countries and easily available at bargain prices. Its place of origin is Burgundy, a region with an often cold climate that makes growing it more challenging than in most new-world countries.

In recent times there has been a disagreement among wine drinkers about French-style Chardonnay versus California-style. The French version has more minerality and subtlety. Poorly made ones, though, can be a little tart. Most, but not all, new-world Chardonnays tend to be more oaky and buttery, although some producers in recent years have been toning down that style and trying to make them more in a Burgundian style.

Winemakers around the world appealing to bargain hunters tend to make Chardonnay in the California fashion on the grounds that the majority of wine drinkers prefer it. One ongoing disagreement among Chardonnay producers has been about sweetness. Many American wineries such as Kendall-Jackson have prospered by leaving just a touch of sweetness in the bottle. That's not an attribute the French admire.

Chardonnay goes well with shellfish; other seafood such as sole, salmon, and snapper; poultry; pasta with a white or light sauce; veal or pork; mild cheeses; cream-based dips. Some Chardonnay lovers maintain that the buttery-flavored wine even goes with popcorn! No wonder it is the world's most popular white wine.

My Favorite Bargain Chardonnay

Charles Shaw	California	$3
Oak Leaf	California	$3
"Down Under"	Australia	$5
Frontera	Chile	$5
HRM Rex-Goliath	California	$6

Oxford Landing	Australia	$7
[yellow tail]	Australia	$7
Cupcake	California	$8
Fat Bastard	France	$9
Red Bicyclette	France	$9

My Splurge Chardonnay

Errázuriz Wild Ferment	Chile	$16
Beaulieu Reserve Carneros	California	$25

Chenin Blanc

Chenin Blanc is perhaps the world's most versatile white wine. It can be sweet or dry. An unfamiliar bottle might be a pleasant surprise or a disaster, depending on what you were expecting. France's Loire Valley is the traditional home of this grape, but it also prospers in South Africa, where it is sometimes called Steen. In fact, South Africa now cultivates about three times more Chenin Blanc than France. Because of its versatility, this wine has become popular with winemakers in many other countries, including the United States, Argentina, and New Zealand.

Chenin Blanc is often used for sparkling wines, and bubbly Vouvray from the Loire Valley town of Vouvray can be outstanding.

Chenin Blanc goes well with appetizers, cream-based dips and dishes, most cheeses, shellfish, fish such as sole, poultry, baked ham, Asian food, and fruit or cream desserts.

My Favorite Bargain Dry Chenin Blanc

Indaba	South Africa	$8
Ken Forrester Petit	South Africa	$8
Herding Cats	South Africa	$9
Kanu	South Africa	$9
Spier	South Africa	$9
Bogle	California	$10
Dry Creek Dry	California	$10
Pine Ridge	California	$10
Raats	South Africa	$10
Roulerie Chenin Sec	France	$10

My Splurge Dry Chenin Blanc

Mulderbosch	South Africa	$16
Aubuisières Vouvray Cuvée de Silex	France	$20

My Favorite Bargain Off-Dry Chenin Blanc

Beringer	California	$6
Sea Ridge	California	$6
Messina Hof	Texas	$7
Sutter Home	California	$7
ForestVille	California	$8
Barton & Guestier Vouvray	France	$9
Bougrier Vouvray	France	$9
Pacific Rim	Washington	$10
Sauvion Vouvray	France	$10
Vaufuget Vouvray	France	$10

My Splurge Off-Dry Chenin Blanc

Simonsig	South Africa	$12
François Pinon Vouvray	France	$20

Gewürztraminer

People love it or hate it. The key to understanding this wine is that the German word *gewürtz* means "spice," so this is a rich, spicy wine. The aroma and taste should be full of flavors, much like a ginger snap straight out of the oven.

Gewürztraminer grapes were first grown in about the year 1000 in the Tyrol area of Austria and Italy. The vines then migrated to Germany and Alsace, where it is the second most planted grape after Riesling. Many experts think the best examples of it are made today in Alsace, but those have become very expensive and many are late-harvest dessert wines. Gewürztraminer also grows well on the American West Coast. This wine is often a little sweet.

This spicy wine goes well with spicy food. In Alsace people often drink Gewürztraminer with foie gras, quiche, and even *choucroute garnie*. It also pairs well with mild blue cheeses such as Gorgonzola.

My Favorite Bargain Gewürztraminer

Crane Lake	California	$5
Coastal Ridge	California	$6
Sutter Home	California	$6
Covey Run	Washington State	$7
Alexander Valley	California	$8
Columbia Crest	Washington State	$8
Hogue	Washington State	$8
Fetzer	California	$9
Ste. Michelle	Washington State	$9
Columbia	Washington State	$10

My Splurge Gewürztraminer

Pierre Sparr	France	$19
Hugel	France	$25

Italian White

Although Italian winemakers are turning more and more to the popular international grape varieties, which is seen most clearly in the growth and success of the Super Tuscans that use Bordeaux grapes, most Italian wines are made from indigenous varieties that have been cultivated locally for centuries. An estimated two thousand grape varieties are grown in the country. Italy also has a long tradition of blending wines from several types to make the final product.

Many of the white wines are identified by their regions, and I have indicated that area below. While Italians like many wines, all of these are dry or semi-dry. Italian sweet wines are included in the listing on page 203.

Italians do a wonderful job of matching their local foods with the wines produced in that area. Italian whites pair well with fish and other seafood, light summer dishes, and veal.

My Favorite Bargain Italian White

Citra	Trebbiano d'Abruzzo	$8 (magnum)
Bolla Soave	Soave	$8
Monte Porzio Catone	Frascati	$8
Ruffino Orvieto	Orvieto	$8
Bigi Orvieto	Orvieto	$9
Fontana Candida Orvieto	Orvieto	$9
Terrale Catarratto	Sicily	$9
Banfi Centine Bianco	Excelus Sant'Antonio	$10
Conti Speroni	Gavi	$10
Pietro Vernacchia	San Gimignano	$10

My Splurge Italian White

Argiolas Costamolino Vermentino	Sardinia	$13
Pietrafitta Vernacchia	San Gimignano	$16

Pinot Grigio

The grape that the French call Pinot Gris goes by the name Pinot Grigio in Italy. The name *grigio,* or "gray," comes from the grayish-blue color of the fruit just before harvest. It was first grown in Burgundy, but adapted easily to other areas. The Burgundians stopped growing it in the eighteenth or nineteenth century. Pinot Grigio is made today in several regions of Italy, but it does best in the country's far north, where cold weather gives it a pleasant acidity. Italians escaping poverty at home by immigrating to other countries took Pinot Grigio with them. As a result, today the wine is made in California, Australia, Chile, and Argentina.

Pinot Grigio pairs well with shellfish and light fish such as sole or salmon, poultry, pork chops and veal, salami and other sausages, mild cheeses, pasta with butter-and-cheese sauce, and fresh green vegetables.

My Favorite Bargain Pinot Grigio

Crane Lake	California	$5
Frontera	Chile	$5
Ca' Donini	Italy	$6
Cavit	Italy	$6
Sutter Home	California	$6
Bolla	Italy	$7
Lindeman's Bin 85	Australia	$7
[yellow tail]	Australia	$7
Forest Glen	California	$8
Santa Julia	Argentina	$8

My Splurge Pinot Grigio

Banfi San Angelo	Italy	$18
Santa Margherita	Italy	$23

Portuguese White

Because of the strength of the euro in recent years, the traditional European favorites of many American wine drinkers have become too expensive. Portugal is a fortunate exception. Its wines can still be enjoyed for a fraction of what you would pay for a top French, Italian, or German counterpart. In order to appreciate them properly, you will have to learn about Portugal's wines beyond Port.

In the past decade or so, Portuguese winemakers have increasingly turned away from Port because its global market has been declining. The English used to be the premier Port client, a tradition that goes back to the 1703 Methuen Treaty, when it became inexpensive to import. Even the British, though, are not drinking as much Port as they once did, so Portuguese winemakers are making more table wines even in the Douro, the home of Port. One of the challenges for consumers is to understand the grapes that go into Portuguese white wines. Instead of Chardonnay, how about Alvarinho, Malvasia Fina, or Loureira? The Portuguese word for white is *branco,* so look for that on the label.

Portugal was once a world seafaring power because of its long shoreline, and you can find many excellent white wines to go with fish. The country's best wines, though, are reds. As a result, the Portuguese don't stand on the tradition of drinking only white with fish.

Portuguese whites, because of their freshness and low alcohol content, are wonderful in the summer with light foods or by themselves.

My Favorite Bargain Portuguese White

Gazela Vinho Verde	Minho	$6
Cabriz	Dão	$7
Casal Garcia Vinho Verde	Minho	$8
Fado	Alentejo	$8
Famega Vinho Verde	Minho	$8
Adega de Pegões	Terras do Sado	$9
Esporão Monte Velho	Alentejo	$9
Grão Vasco	Dão	$9
J. Portugal Ramos Loios	Alentejo	$9
Porta da Ravessa	Alentejo	$9

My Splurge Portuguese White

Periquita	Terras do Sado	$12
Évora Cartuxa	Alentejo	$13

Riesling

Many Americans dislike Riesling because they had a bad experience in their early wine-drinking days with Blue Nun or another sickly sweet German Riesling. Its fans, though, claim this is the best white variety of all. Its home is Alsace in eastern France and the Rhine and Mosel regions of Germany. French Rieslings tends to be a littler dryer than German ones. The grape in recent decades has spread widely, and today good examples of it come out of France, California, Washington, and Australia. Outside Alsace and Germany, I think the best Riesling today is made in Australia's Eden Valley.

The trick with German Riesling is to learn how to read the labels, which admittedly can be complicated. You can find dry German Riesling, but it must have the word *trocken,* or "dry," on the label. It shouldn't have any adjective before the word such as *halb trocken,* which means "half-dry." If *trocken* is not on the bottle, you will be getting a wine that has at least some sweetness, and perhaps a lot of it.

Riesling is very adaptable and pairs well with all sorts of different foods. It generally goes with baked ham; crab and other shellfish; turkey; chicken, squab and duck; sausages; sushi; spicy Asian dishes; and most cheeses.

Sweet Riesling goes well with foie gras, rich cheeses, and avocado.

My Favorite Bargain Dry Riesling

Alverdi	Italy	$7
Jacob's Creek	Australia	$7
Covey Run Dry	Washington	$8
Ste. Michelle Dry	Washington	$8
McWilliams Hardwood Estate	Australia	$9
Pacific Rim Dry	Washington	$9
Blue Fish Original	Germany	$10
Selbach Riesling.Incline	Germany	$10
Willm	France	$10
Yalumba Y Series	Australia	$10

My Splurge Dry Riesling

Pewsey Vale	Australia	$15
Zind-Humbrecht	France	$25

My Favorite Bargain Off Dry/Sweet Riesling

Alice White	Australia	$6
Turning Leaf Johannisberg	California	$7
Blue Fish Sweet	Germany	$8
Dr. Beckermann Piesporter Michelsberg	Germany	$8
Blüfeld	Germany	$9
Hogue Late Harvest	Washington	$9
Ste. Michelle Harvest Select	Washington	$9
Pacific Rim Sweet	Washington	$9
Clean Slate	Germany	$10
Yalumba Y Series	Australia	$10

My Splurge Off Dry/Sweet Riesling

S.A. Prüm Essence	Germany	$14
St. Urbans-Hof Ockfener Bockstein	Germany	$20

Rhône-Style White Blend

The Rhône Valley has a rich and separate tradition from other French wine-growing areas such as Burgundy and Bordeaux, as well as a distinct collection of grapes. The white Rhône-style blends are dry and often have bold floral flavors. The classical Côtes-du-Rhône white blend includes Clairette, Grenache Blanc, Marsanne, Rousanne, Bourboulenc, and Viognier grapes. California winemakers in the Paso Robles area copy the French style so closely that they were nicknamed the Rhône Rangers. Beaucastel, one of the Rhône's most prestigious wineries, has a California outpost named Tablas Creek Vineyard.

Rhône-style white blends go with fish and shellfish, roasted or grilled vegetables, and foods cooked with garlic and olive oil.

My Favorite Bargain Rhône-Style White Blend

La Vieille Ferme	France	$7
La Châsse du Pape	France	$8
Goats do Roam	South Africa	$8
Jean-Luc Colombo Les Abeilles	France	$8
Big House	California	$9
Mommessin	France	$9
Parallèle 45	France	$9
Les Deux Rives	France	$10
Ferraton et Fils	France	$10
Michel Gassier Cercius	France	$10

My Splurge Rhône-Style White Blend

d'Arenberg Hermit Crab	Australia	$14
Le Cigare	California	$22

Sauvignon Blanc

Sauvignon Blanc is a wine of many names. The French made it first, and in Bordeaux they often blend it with Sémillon and call it simply Bordeaux Blanc. In France's Loire Valley it is called Sancerre and Pouilly-Fumé. In the United States it is sometimes called Fumé Blanc. Whatever you call it, it is a light wine that is generally a little less acidic than Pinot Grigio and not as big as Chardonnay.

A decade ago, a new-style Sauvignon Blanc came roaring out of New Zealand that was fresh and grassy. The softer, rounder Bordeaux version still has its fans. This is the wine you'll get in and around Bordeaux if you walk into a café and ask for a glass of *vin blanc*. British Tommies did that in France during World War I, but they couldn't pronounce it correctly, and the closest they got to it was "plonk," hence the generic name for low-quality wine.

Sauvignon Blanc pairs well with most kinds of seafood; shrimp, including shrimp cocktail, and shellfish; fresh green vegetables; cream or cheese sauces; sushi; and mild cheeses.

My Favorite Bargain Sauvignon Blanc

Vendange	California	$10 (magnum)
Barefoot	California	$6
Bogle	California	$8
Chalone Monterey	California	$8
Cono Sur	Chile	$8
Fetzer	California	$8
Réserve St. Martin	France	$8
Monkey Bay	New Zealand	$9
Redcliffe	New Zealand	$9
Urban Uco/Copete	Argentina	$9

My Splurge Sauvignon Blanc

Robert Mondavi Fumé Blanc	California	$15
Cloudy Bay	New Zealand	$25

Spanish White

The Spanish claim to grow some two hundred grapes, with most of them going back to ancient history. In reality, though, only about twenty of them are prominently used. Spanish wine regulators now also allow the use of some international white-wine grapes such as Chardonnay. Given the country's mainly hot, dry climate, red grapes do better than white and are more widely planted. Spain drinks a lot of dry whites, especially during the summer. These wines are meant for early consumption and not to be laid down. In the last few years, Spain finally got its big international hit in white wines with Albariño, which unfortunately has driven up the price. Good bargains, though, can still be found among the traditional Spanish whites.

Spanish whites pair well with oysters, lightly fried white fish, and roast chicken.

My Favorite Bargain Spanish White

René Barbier Mediterranean	Penedès	$6
Paso a Paso Verdejo	La Mancha	$8
Conde de Alicante	Alicante	$9
El Coto	Rioja	$9
Marqués de Cáceres	Rioja	$9
Marqués de Riscal Rueda	Castilla-León	$9
Protocolo	La Mancha	$9
Torres Sol	Penedès	$9
Vega Sindao Viura-Chardonnay	Navarra	$9
Pirineos Mesache	Catalonia	$10

My Splurge Spanish White

Burgáns Albariño	Rias Baixas	$14
Muga	Rioja	$15

Torrontés

Torrontés hit the international scene only recently, and I still remember the first bottle I bought, about four years ago. It was made by Lurton and cost about $4. I bought it because I figured it was so inexpensive, I had little to lose. Ever since, I've been buying Lurton Torrontés whenever I can get it, even though the price has gone up. Torrontés is called the white wine of Argentina, and it remains a good value. Its origins are lost in the history of Spanish wines, and this variety was seemingly brought to Argentina from Galicia, in northwestern Spain. It has some relationship to the Muscat grape. My first sip reminded me of a good Viognier, since both have lots of floral aroma and taste. Torrontés does particularly well in northern Argentina. This is a wine to enjoy in its youth.

Torrontés goes well with smoked meats, both mild and strong cheeses, and seafood. It is also a good partner for spicy food such as Thai cuisine.

My Favorite Bargain Torrontés

Astica	Cuyo	$5
Trapiche	Mendoza	$6
Lurton	Mendoza	$7
Santa Julia	Mendoza	$8
Alamos	Salta	$9
Los Cowboys	Mendoza	$9
Norton	Mendoza	$9
Zuccardi	Mendoza	$9
Trivento	Cuyo	$10
Urban Uco/Copete	Salta	$10

My Splurge Torrontés

Crios	Mendoza	$15
Michel Torino Don David	Salta	$16

Viognier

In the past decade, this once obscure wine has become the chic thing to order, especially by the glass, if you can pronounce the name correctly. It's a word made for the French mouth and tongue and sounds something like *vee-own-yeh*. It originally came from the Rhône Valley. Château Grillet, which Thomas Jefferson once visited, today makes one of the most expensive. Viognier is now planted in other places, particularly California and Australia. The non-French versions have all the floral and big-wine experience that you expect from a Rhône product.

Viognier pairs well with mild cheeses, fish, spicy dishes such as Thai food or curry.

My Favorite Bargain Viognier

Cono Sur	Chile	$7
Altas Cumbres	Argentina	$8
Loredona	California	$8
Oak Grove	California	$8
Oxford Landing	Australia	$8
De Gournier	France	$9
Smoking Loon	California	$9
Cline	California	$10
Santa Julia	Argentina	$10
Yalumba Y Series	Australia	$10

My Splurge Viognier

Calera Central Coast	California	$16
Triennes	France	$18

Red Wines

Beaujolais

This is France's daily wine, which they drink with abandon. When in Paris and in doubt about what wine to order, ask for a glass of Beaujolais. Part of its great appeal is the light taste, low price, and that it can be drunk young.

Beaujolais is technically part of Burgundy, but today has little to do with the Burgundians. Beaujolais got its big break in 1395, when Philip the Bold outlawed growing Gamay, the grape that goes into Beaujolais, in the heart of Burgundy and relegated it to the region around the town of Beaujeu. No other wine in the world is so identified with one man as Beaujolais is with Georges Duboeuf, who made Beaujolais famous outside France and now controls a big part of the business. Duboeuf popularized Beaujolais Nouveau, the first wine of the year, coming out in late November. In order to sell the wine quickly and help his cash flow, he began shipping it around the world and plastered signs proclaiming, *Le Beaujolais Nouveau est arrivé!* ("The New Beaujolais has arrived!"). It was perhaps the most successful promotion in wine history. Better-quality Beaujolais carries names such as Brouilly or Morgon. A small amount of white Beaujolais is made with Chardonnay grapes.

Attempts have been made to grow Beaujolais in other areas, including California, where Robert Mondavi made a stab at producing it and called it Napa Gamay.

Beaujolais matches well with ham, pork, and sausage; roast turkey; hamburgers and picnic fare; Chinese food; shellfish and salmon; strong cheeses; and pasta with red sauce. It's a good match for turkey on Thanksgiving.

My Favorite Bargain Beaujolais

Barton & Guestier Beaujolais	$8
Georges Duboeuf Beaujolais Nouveau	$8
Labouré-Roi Beaujolais Nouveau	$8
Mommessin Beaujolais Nouveau	$9
Barton & Guestier Beaujolais-Villages	$10
Georges Duboeuf Beaujolais-Villages	$10
Joseph Drouhin Beaujolais Nouveau	$10
Louis Jadot Beaujolais-Villages	$10
Louis Latour Beaujolais-Villages	$10
Mommessin Beaujolais-Villages	$10

My Splurge Beaujolais

Chaize Brouilly	$15
Marcel Lapierre Morgon	$25

Cabernet Sauvignon/Bordeaux Blend

The world's favorite red-wine grape was first grown in Bordeaux. For centuries, the French loved and cared for Cabernet Sauvignon, and winemakers starting in the 1970s spread it around the globe. Cabernet Sauvignon is now made just about everywhere grapes are grown. Bordelais winemakers usually blended it with other grapes such as Cabernet Franc. Vintners in California often produce 100 percent Cabernet Sauvignon, while Australians blend it with Shiraz. Cabernet Sauvignon also played a starring role in the development of Italy's Super Tuscans.

Cabernet Sauvignon is a big wine that goes well with big food such as beef, lamb, game, duck; strong cheeses; pasta with tomato sauce; chocolate; and grilled mushrooms.

My Favorite Bargain Cabernet Sauvignon/Bordeaux Blend

Charles Shaw	California	$3
Oak Leaf	California	$3
Frontera	Chile	$5
Columbia Crest	Washington State	$7
Finca Flichman	Chile	$7
Hacienda	California	$7
Lindeman's Bin 45	Australia	$7
Santa Rita 120	Chile	$8
Alamos	Argentina	$9
Fortant de France	France	$10

My Splurge Cabernet Sauvignon

St. Francis	California	$22
Camensac	France	$25

Carménère

Before the phylloxera insect devastated French vineyards in the late nine-teenth century, Carménère was a popular blending wine in Bordeaux, where it was often used to add ruby color to Cabernet Sauvignon. French Carménère, though, never recovered from that disaster and virtually van-ished. By then, thousands of Carménère cuttings had been sent to Chile, where the pest never hit and vines prospered. As a result of its similarity to Merlot, it was often accidently planted in Merlot vineyards. In 1994, a French researcher determined that perhaps half of Chile's Merlot was actually Carménère. The country's vineyard managers adopted the grape as their own and planted it widely.

Chilean Carménère today is a great value. A little is planted in Califor-nia and Washington, but Chile dominates the market. If you're looking for a bargain red, consider Carménère.

Carménère goes well with lamb, beef, dishes with tomato sauce, and strong cheeses.

My Favorite Bargain Carménère

Frontera	Chile	$5
Santa Rita	Chile	$7
Xplorador	Chile	$7
Cono Sur	Chile	$8
Gato Negro	Chile	$8
Terra Andina	Chile	$8
Calina	Chile	$9
Root: 1	Chile	$9
Casillero del Diablo	Chile	$10
Viu Manent	Chile	$10

My Splurge Carménère

Lapostelle	Chile	$15
Errázuriz Single Vineyard	Chile	$19

Chianti

Chianti is the mother's milk of Italy. The country might make other wines that have greater prestige and sell for much more, but nothing else touches an Italian heart like Chianti. In 1773, Grand Duke Cosimo III de' Medici issued an edict designating three villages as the Chianti region. The area has since been expanded and changed many times. Baron Bettino Ricasoli, a statesman and wine expert, in 1872 led the movement to have Sangiovese declared the cornerstone grape for Chianti wines. The baron argued that Sangiovese grew particularly well in the region, claiming it had more aroma and "vigor of taste" than other red grapes.

Italian immigrants in the twentieth century introduced Sangiovese to the world, where it often grew well, particularly in California. Millions of Americans in the post–World War II years had their first wine experience with a straw-covered bottle of Chianti that they later turned into a candleholder.

Naturally Chianti is perfect with most Italian food, but also with pork roast, full-flavored veal dishes, vegetarian meals featuring beans and cheese, roast chicken, pasta with tangy tomato sauce, and strong cheeses.

My Favorite Bargain Chianti

Carlo Rossi	California	$7 (magnum)
Livingston Cellars	California	$7 (magnum)
Crane Lake Sangiovese	California	$5
Il Bastardo	Italy	$7
Folonari	Italy	$8
Norton Sangiovese	Argentina	$8
Piccini	Italy	$8
Ruffino Fonte al Sole	Italy	$8
Gabbiano	Italy	$9
Melini	Italy	$9

My Splurge Chianti

Albola Chianti Classico	Italy	$15
Antinori Peppoli Chianti Classico	Italy	$25

Malbec

Malbec originally was a supporting player in world wine. Small amounts were used for blending with Bordeaux's Cabernet Sauvignon to give it deeper color and more complexity. British merchants used to call it black wine. Malbec is known for its hard tannins, which can produce a rough feel in the mouth. It is grown in France in Cahors, a region east of Bordeaux, where it is known as Côt Noir. Malbec must make up at least 70 percent Cahors wine.

The wine really flourished, however, in Argentina, where it became the country's most popular export since the tango. When the Argentine Malbec boom hit, many California winemakers planted the grape, and it does well in the Central Valley. Napa's Francis Ford Coppola is now making Malbec.

This is another big wine that will overwhelm mild food, so pair Malbec with beef, lamb, chili, spare ribs; strongly flavored game dishes such as wild duck or wild boar; strong and mature cheeses.

My Favorite Bargain Malbec

Astica	Argentina	$6
Falling Star	Argentina	$6
Marcus James	Argentina	$7
Trapiche	Argentina	$7
Flichman	Argentina	$8
Gato Negro	Argentina	$8
Alamos	Argentina	$9
Casillero del Diablo	Chile	$9
Clos La Coutale	France	$10
Tilia	Argentina	$10

My Splurge Malbec

Clos de los Siete	Argentina	$18
Achaval Ferrer	Argentina	$25

Merlot

Despite being out of fashion since the movie *Sideways*, Merlot remains a wonderful grape and now is also a good value. It grows well in many countries, so competition is strong and keeps prices down. No matter where it comes from, Merlot is usually softer and easier to drink than its comrade in blends, Cabernet Sauvignon. In its native homeland of Bordeaux, Merlot does better on the right bank of the Gironde estuary, while Cabernet Sauvignon is the master of the left bank. Some of the most expensive reds in the world, such as Château Pétrus and Château Le Pin, are made with predominantly Merlot grapes. Merlot has done very well in California, in part because of its softness.

Merlot is a perfect match for Chinese food, cheddar and mild yellow cheeses, roast chicken and duck breast, pork roast, and full-flavored veal dishes.

My Favorite Bargain Merlot

CK Mondavi	California	$6 (magnum)
Forest Glen	California	$5
Pacific Peak	California	$5
Foxhorn	California	$6
Santa Rita 120	Chile	$6
Little Penguin	Australia	$7
Beringer	California	$8
Blackstone	California	$8
Norton	Argentina	$8
Les Jamelles	France	$10

My Splurge Merlot

Casa Lapostolle	Chile	$17
Ferrari-Carano	California	$20

Pinot Noir

This has been called the heartbreak grape, because it is so difficult to produce well. Pinot Noir first flourished in Burgundy but because of inheritance laws the region today is dominated by many small, family-run, artisanal domains. Burgundy's most famous vineyards have multiple owners, with people often cultivating only a few rows of grapes. As a result, two Burgundy Pinot Noirs from the same property can taste dramatically different and prices can range widely. To its fans, and there are millions of them, there is nothing like a Pinot Noir. This soft, elegant, and aromatic wine is often compared to a beautiful lady. The best Pinot Noirs, such as Domaine de la Romanée-Conti, sell for thousands of dollars a bottle, and wealthy consumers around the world fight over them. Pinot Noir made outside Burgundy is much less expensive, and some people think that New Zealand may eventually produce the best.

Although it is a light and soft wine, Pinot is still a good match for game dishes and roast duck, steak or roast beef, roast leg of lamb, pâté, mushrooms, and any cheeses. I often serve Pinot Noir with fish that have a lot of flavor, such as salmon.

My Favorite Bargain Pinot Noir

Forest Glen	California	$6
Beringer	California	$7
[yellow tail]	Australia	$7
Barton & Guestier Bistro	France	$8
Beaulieu Coastal Estates	California	$8
Cavit	Italy	$8
Nicolas	France	$8
Trapiche	Argentina	$8
Les Jamelles	France	$9
Montes	Chile	$10

My Splurge Pinot Noir

Calera	California	$20
Mt Difficult Roaring Meg	New Zealand	$22

Portuguese Red

The declining popularity of Port has been a boon for Portuguese reds. Winemakers had to find something to sell, and turned to making dry red wines from excellent grapes such as Touriga Nacional, which used to go into Port. Quality is up, and prices are still relatively low. The grape varieties are probably unknown unless you live in Portugal or are married to a Portuguese, but don't let that stop you. The reds are rich in color and flavor. The best-quality wines come from the Douro Valley, the home of Port. The best prices come from other areas.

Portuguese reds are big and masculine, so they go with the same foods that you would pair with Cabernet Sauvignon: steak, roast beef, and strong cheeses.

My Favorite Bargain Portuguese Red

Berço do Infante Reserva	Estremadura	$7
Cabriz	Dão	$7
Palestra	Douro	$7
Vasco da Gama	Dão	$7
Charamba	Douro	$8
Grão Vasco	Dão	$8
Monte Velho	Alentejo	$8
Porca de Murça	Douro	$8
Alianca	Dão	$10
Periquita	Terras do Sado	$10

My Splurge Portuguese Red

Vallado	Dão	$18
Meandro do Vale Meão	Douro	$22

Rhône-Style Red Blend

Rhône winemakers are masters of blending and making creative use of their region's distinctive grapes. Going into the region's most famous wine, Châteauneuf-du-Pape, can be as many as thirteen different grape varieties, including reds such as Syrah or Cinsaut, as well as whites, including Roussanne and Grenache Blanc. White grapes in a red wine? It works for Châteauneuf-du-Pape.

The Côtes-du-Rhône red has been called a mini-Châteauneuf with fewer grapes. Usually, but not always, Grenache Noir, Syrah, Carignane, Counoise, and Mourvèdre go into the blend. Wineries in other countries rarely use as many varieties as the French, although they might put two or three into their own Rhône wines.

A Rhône-style red blend is fine with roast duck and venison, hamburgers and picnic food, liver and country pâté, salami and other hearty sausages.

My Favorite Bargain Rhône-Style Red Blend

La Vieille Ferme	France	$7
[yellow tail] Shiraz-Grenache	Australia	$7
Big House Red	California	$8
Oxford Landing GSM	Australia	$8
d'Arenberg Stump Jump GSM	Australia	$9
Goats do Roam Red	South Africa	$9
Rasteau Côtes-du-Rhône	France	$9
The Wolftrap	South Africa	$9
Parallèle 45 Côtes-du-Rhône	France	$10
Red Truck California Red	California	$10

My Splurge Rhône-Style Red Blend

Guigal Côtes-du-Rhône	France	$16
Tablas Creek Côtes de Tablas	California	$25

Spanish Red

Until recently, Garnacha, a big red, was Spain's most widely planted grape. It is considered a cult wine in the Catalonia region, where it goes into making expensive Priorat, and also does well in Navarra, Rioja, and Aragón. The grape is one of the most widely planted in the world, and is elsewhere called Grenache. Tempranillo, a lighter red, is now the most popular Spanish grape. It does particularly well in Rioja. Some call it Spain's noble variety, and it is also grown in many other countries.

Spain has a strict system of aging red wines. The youngest and least expensive are called Crianza, which means they have been aged for two years, with six months in oak. A Reserva is three years old, and has had twelve months in wood. A Gran Reserva has had five years of aging, with eighteen months in barrel and a minimum of thirty-six in bottle. If you see the terms *vino joven* or *sin crianza* on a bottle, it means the wine has had little, if any, aging in wood. Those wines are not commonly exported. I find young Spanish wines easy to drink and often a good deal. With one exception, all the selections in this section are *crianza.*

Argentina also makes good Tempranillo, which is usually less expensive than the Spanish original. Among the bargain Argentine labels are Santa Julia and Trapiche, selling generally for less than $10. The recommended wines in this section do not include non-Spanish brands.

The Spanish rival the Italians as masters of wine-food pairings, and their menus carry a lot more fish than one might expect from the land of the bulls. Garnacha, Tempranillo, and a blend of the two go well with tapas; dishes made with tomato sauce, lamb chops, Spanish omelets, and roasted meat or chicken.

My Favorite Bargain Spanish Red

Campos Reales Tempranillo	La Mancha	$6
René Barbier Mediterranean	Penedès	$6
Fontana Mesta Tempranillo	La Mancha	$7
Garnacha de Fuego	Calatayud	$7

Borsao Garnacha	Campo de Borja	$8
Monte Oton Garnacha	Campo de Borja	$8
Venta Morales Tempranillo	La Mancha	$8
Riscal Tempranillo	Castilla y León	$9
Tapeña Garnacha	Tierra de Castilla	$9
Cortijo III Tempranillo	Rioja	$10

My Splurge Spanish Red

R. Lopez de Heredia Cubillo	Rioja	$25
Ysios	Rioja	$25

Syrah/Shiraz

You say Syrah; I say Shiraz. This popular grape is known by both names and does best in hot climates. In France it's called Syrah, and is grown in the Rhône Valley. In Australia it goes by Shiraz, and is found all over the country. Australia seems an ideal place to make this wine, and they have some expensive ones such as Penfolds Grange and Henschke Hill of Grace. Dozens of good Australian producers make many inexpensive ones.

Syrah/Shiraz is generally a spicy wine, so with this you should serve games, lamb, duck, roast beef or steak, strong cheeses, or barbecued ribs.

My Favorite Bargain Syrah/Shiraz

Banrock Station	Australia	$6
Gato Negro	Chile	$6
Rosemount	Australia	$7
[yellow tail]	Australia	$7
Astica	Argentina	$8
Excelsior Paddock	South Africa	$8
Pepperwood Grove	California	$8
d'Arenberg Stump Jump	Australia	$9
Lurton Les Bateaux	France	$9
Penfolds Koonunga Hill	Australia	$10

My Splurge Syrah/Shiraz

Peter Lehmann	Australia	$15
Mollydooker The Boxer	Australia	$25

Zinfandel

This is America's native wine. Well, not exactly. Some version of Zinfandel probably came to this country from Croatia, but since the nineteenth century it has prospered in California. The wine has gathered a cult following among consumers who endorsed the slogan of California's Ravenswood Winery, a big Zinfandel producer: No Wimpy Wines. Australia makes some Zinfandel, but by and large it is a California specialty.

This is a spicy wine and also tends to have high levels of alcohol, which is part of the reason Zinfandel fanatics like it. With this wine, think big and pair with strong cheeses; dishes with red sauce; hamburgers and picnic fare; ham; hearty vegetarian bean-and-cheese dishes. Zinfandel is often an ideal wine for a barbecue.

My Favorite Bargain Zinfandel

Glen Ellen Old Vine	California	$7 (magnum)
ForestVille	California	$6
Sutter Home	California	$6
Canyon Oaks	California	$7
Woodbridge	California	$8
Cellar No. 8	California	$9
Fetzer	California	$9
Gnarly Head Old Vine	California	$9
Ravenswood	California	$9
Smoking Loon	California	$10

My Splurge Zinfandel

Rosenblum North Coast	California	$17
Ridge Three Valleys	California	$20

Rosé Wines

During the summer in Southern France, Spain, and Portugal, you'll see plenty of people drinking rosé. Winemakers in those countries make it with all sorts of different red grapes. Name a red grape, and someone will be making it into rosé simply by letting the juice stay in contact with the grape skins for less time than a vintner would to make a red wine. A good dry rosé should be crisp.

One of life's truly great pleasures is to enjoy a glass of the local rosé in Europe, while playing *pétanque, boules, bocce,* or whatever the locals call the sport. Alcohol levels in rosé are a little lower, so it won't hurt your game. Americans haven't generally caught on to either the wine or the game, but this is the drink for when they do.

Dry rosés go with quiche and other egg dishes, salads such as *salade niçoise* but NOT if it has a vinegary dressing, mild cheese, Mediterranean food in general, and salty finger foods.

There are two other types of rosés in addition to dry rosés. The first are slightly sweet ones. They are called demi-sec, the French term for half-dry, or off-dry. The distinction is based on the amount of sugar in the bottle, but that difference is lost on most consumers. The third rosé category is sweet, and includes White Zinfandel and White Merlot. Both are made in the same way and are pink or rosé despite the word *white* in their names. Some people hate them; some people love them. For a while, White Zin was the most popular wine in America.

Either slightly or really sweet wines go with spicy foods, poultry, mild cheeses, creamy dips or desserts, and fruit.

My Favorite Bargain Dry Rosé

Frontera	Chile	$5
Borsao	Spain	$7

Garcia Casal Vinho Verde	Portugal	$7
Goats do Roam	South Africa	$7
La Vieille Ferme	France	$7
Forest Glen Magenta	California	$8
Jacob's Creek Shiraz	Australia	$9
Marqués de Cáceres	Spain	$9
Fat Bastard	France	$10
Parallèle 45	France	$10

My Splurge Dry Rosé

Muga	Spain	$12
Tablas Creek	California	$25

Off-Dry Rosé

My Favorite Bargain Off-Dry Rosé

Livingston Blush Chablis	California	$8 (magnum)
Lancers	Portugal	$7
[yellow tail]	Australia	$7
Big House Pink	California	$8
Ironstone Xpression	California	$8
Robertson	South Africa	$8
Barton & Guestier Rosé d'Anjou	France	$9
Bougrier Rosé d'Anjou	France	$10
Ménage à Trois	California	$10
Sauvion Rosé d'Anjou	France	$10

My Splurge Off-Dry Rosé

Maysara Roseena	Oregon	$14
Terrebrune Bandol Rosé	France	$25

White Zinfandel/White Merlot

My Favorite Bargain White Zinfandel/White Merlot

Oak Leaf White Zinfandel	California	$3
Forest Glen White Merlot	California	$5
Beringer White Merlot	California	$6
Beringer White Zinfandel	California	$6
Canyon Oaks White Zinfandel	California	$6
Gallo Twin Valley White Merlot	California	$6
Riunite Strawberry White Merlot	Italy	$6
Glen Ellen White Zinfandel	California	$7
Vendange White Zinfandel	California	$7
Woodbridge White Zinfandel	California	$7

My Splurge White Zinfandel/White Merlot

No White Zinfandel or White Merlot should cost more than $10.

Sparkling Wines

Only sparkling wines that come from the Champagne region of northern France can use that name, which has, alas, gotten too expensive for most people. Fortunately, many alternative bubbly wines are now available all over the world. These have names such as *cava, crémant, prosecco,* or simply sparkling wine, and more and more people are drinking them. Whether it's the real thing or a substitute, let no one repeat the mistake of the great British economist John Maynard Keynes, who said on his deathbed, "My only regret is that I did not drink more Champagne."

Since sparkling wine is usually more expensive than still wine, I have increased my top price for these wines to $15, although the splurge stays at $25. Terminology on sparkling wine labels can be deceptive. All of the dry whites below are *brut,* which is the French term for "dry." Some other bubblies calling themselves *brut* are slightly sweet.

Champagne or sparkling wine goes with anything. There's no meal that won't be improved by a few bubbles. To be more specific, it goes well with Asian food, moderately hot and spicy dishes, omelets, lobster and other shellfish, seafood such as sole, dishes with a cream sauce, and chocolate.

Dry Sparkling Wine

My Favorite Bargain Sparkling Dry White

Cupcake Prosecco	Italy	$9
Cristalino	Spain	$9
Korbel	California	$10
Codorníu	Spain	$11
Freixenet	Spain	$11
Willm Crémant d'Alsace	France	$12
Yellowglen Yellow	Australia	$12

Ste. Michelle	Washington	$13
Mionetto Prosecco	Italy	$14
Chandon Classic	California	$15

My Splurge Sparkling Dry White

Simonnet-Febvre Crémant	France	$20
Roederer Estate	California	$25

Sweet Sparkling Wine

The next time someone turns up his nose at sweet sparkling wine, remind them that for most of history, people drank sweet Champagne. No need to be ashamed of it. An added benefit is that because sweet sparkling wine is out of fashion, prices are good. These are usually low in alcohol, mostly at about 10 percent.

Sweet sparkling wines go well with just about any dessert you name, especially one with lots of cream. It also is a good match for chocolate.

My Favorite Bargain Sweet Sparkling Wine

Cook's Spumante	California	$6
Verdi Spumante	Italy	$6
Ballatore Spumante	Italy	$9
Barefoot Moscato Spumante	California	$9
Beringer White Zinfandel	California	$9
Cinzano Asti	Italy	$10
Korbel Sweet Rosé	California	$11
St.-Hilaire Blanquette de Limoux	France	$12
Martini & Rossi Prosecco	Italy	$13
Mumm Napa Cuvée M	California	$15

My Splurge Sweet Sparkling Wine

Graham Beck Bliss	South Africa	$17
Banfi Rosa Regalie	Italy	$20

Sweet Wines

Sweet wines generally fall into two categories. The first group is meant to be enjoyed just as one might drink a dry wine as an aperitif or with meals. These can be sweet Riesling or Chenin Blanc, which I have listed earlier, or Moscato and sweet reds, listed here. The second type are dessert wines that are consumed in small amounts, usually at the end of the meal. It's comparable to having a chocolate truffle as you linger over a meal that you wish would never end. Dessert wines have been popular for centuries and are made around the world. Hungary's Tokaji was first made in the late 1500s, and the most famous is France's Château d'Yquem. On December 18, 1787, Thomas Jefferson ordered 250 bottles of its 1784 vintage directly from the winery in order to "be sure it is genuine, good and sound," as he wrote in a letter.

Sweet wines are often sold in half bottles (375ml), because people consume so little as an after-dinner drink. As with sparkling wines, I had to increase the maximum price for dessert wines.

Some of history's tough guys liked sweet wines. Julius Caesar's favorite was Mamertino, a sweet wine made in Sicily. On his deathbed, Napoléon asked for a bottle of sweet Constantia from South Africa. Stalin's favorite was Khvanchkara, a sweet wine from the republic of Georgia, where he was born.

Since sweet wines are not trendy, no matter what the category, they offer the best wine values around. Sweet table wines go well with foie gras, spicy food of all kinds, mild cheeses, and cream-based dips.

My Favorite Bargain Moscato

Alice White Lexia	Australia	$6
Barefoot	California	$7
Beringer	California	$7
FishEye	California	$7

Jacob's Creek	Australia	$7
Lindeman's Bin 90	Australia	$7
Sutter Home	California	$7
Woodbridge	California	$7
Bartenura	Italy	$10
Il Conti d'Alba	Italy	$10

My Splurge Moscato

| Fratelli d'Asti | Italy | $13 |
| St. Supéry | California | $20 |

My Favorite Bargain Sweet Red Table Wine

Crane Lake	California	$5
Riunite Lambrusco	Italy	$5
Sutter Home	California	$5
Tilsdale	California	$5
Fünf	Germany	$6
Georgian Royal Estates Velvet	Georgia	$8
Robertson	South Africa	$9
Carl Sittmann Dornfelder	Germany	$10
Jam Jar Shiraz	South Africa	$10
Twisted River Dornfelder	Germany	$10

My Splurge Sweet Red Table Wine

| Adesso Cagnina di Romagna | Italy | $12 |
| Bruno Verdi Sangue di Giuda | Italy | $17 |

My Favorite Bargain Sweet Dessert Wine

Taylor Tawny Port	New York	$7
Florio Marsala	Italy	$12
Graham Six Grapes Port	Portugal	$18
Barton & Guestier Sauternes	France	$20
Fonseca Bin No. 27 Port	Portugal	$20
Broadbent Rainwater Madeira	Portugal	$13*
Haut Charmes Sauternes	France	$15*
Pacific Rim Vin de Glacière	Washington	$15*
Rosenblum Désirée	California	$17*

My Splurge Sweet Dessert Wine

Sigalas Rabaud Sauternes	France	$25*
Badia a Coltibuono Vin Santo	Italy	$40*

* Half bottles.

My Favorite Bargain Brands

Wineries usually determine the market strategy they want to follow and then make products with that goal in mind. Do they want to be a low-volume, high-price shop that tailors its wines to a small clientele? There's certainly a market for that. On the other hand, wineries can also conclude that they might be better off going after a broader market by offering value-oriented wines. Fortunately for consumers, many follow the second business strategy and turn out excellent, inexpensive wines.

I'm not guaranteeing that you will love every wine made by every producer listed in this section, but I can promise you will find that these brands offer many good wines at good prices. One of the starting points in my search for bargain brands was my belief that good wineries tend to produce good products across the board. If a place makes an outstanding Chardonnay, it probably has a top technical team and can repeat its success when it comes to Pinot Grigio or Cabernet Sauvignon.

The most glamorous regions, such as California's Napa Valley or Bordeaux's left bank, are not the places where you find many wineries going after the masses. Don't expect to see in the listings below many wines from those areas. I have found some, but not many. Real estate there is expensive, so producers have to push up their prices to make money. Demand for wines from those areas is naturally strong, and that makes them more expensive.

In general, the new world is the best place to look for bargains. Argentina, Australia, Chile, New Zealand, South Africa, and the United States all offer wonderful wines at equally wonderful prices. The global wine surplus causes problems for producers, but it's great for consumers and exists in all markets from France to New Zealand.

The most important development in international wine during the last half century, as the new world eclipsed the old, has been the increased quality of daily wines. These are both better and cost less than the ones Europeans drank for centuries. An ordinary new-world wine today is far superior to the old world's traditional *vin ordinaire*.

An additional advantage for American consumers is that many of those wineries are now tailoring their products to the American palate, because the United States is the most attractive market for exporters. Winemakers today are constantly tinkering with their enology to make products similar to those that the marketplace has shown Americans like. Given the competitive nature of the wine world, if there is a hot new product out there, you can be certain that some winemaker in the Southern Hemisphere is trying to produce an inexpensive version of it.

One of the clearest examples of that was the boom in New Zealand–style Sauvignon Blanc. The Kiwis in the mid-1980s introduced a new version of that traditional Bordeaux wine that is fresher than the old French version, which was often flat and boring. Soon winemakers from California to Chile were making Sauvignon Blanc in the New Zealand style. One of those was Chile's Cono Sur, which sells in the United States for about $8, as compared with more than $20 for its top-of-the-line New Zealand counterparts.

The following lists center on brand names rather than wineries because that is what consumers find in stores. Often wineries have more than one bargain label. I have generally given the top-selling brand from that winery, but in some cases have separate listings for another from the same winery. Brands are in alphabetical order, and no attempt has been made to rank them by quality. All have many good bargain wines.

Ten Argentine Bargain Brands

Argentina is both old and new to wine. Though wines have been made there for centuries, the Spanish having first introduced viticulture and Italian immigrants at the beginning of the twentieth century bringing with them their enology skills, few Argentine wines were exported until Argentina began producing Malbec. It was a great value, and the grapes did better in Argentina than they did in their native France. In more recent years, Argentina has given the world Torrontés, an interesting white wine.

Alamos

Nicolás Catena is the father of modern Argentine wine. His father, Nicola Catena, came to Argentina from Italy in 1898 to escape a famine and got into wine because that was his heritage. He made the low-quality wines he had back home. His son Nicolás took over the business in the mid-1960s with plans to do things differently. Nicolás went to California on a teaching scholarship in economics at the University of California–Berkeley. In his free time he traveled to the Napa Valley, where a wine renaissance was getting under way, and spent many hours with Robert Mondavi.

Nicolás arrived back in Argentina and put what he had learned into practice, but the going was tough. His country suffered recurring political and economic crises, which slowed him down. Gradually, though, Nicolás built Argentina's first winery that could hold its own with those of California and Europe. Today Catena Zapata is recognized as one of the world's top-tier wineries. In 2009, Nicolás was named Man of the Year by Britain's *Decanter* magazine. His daughter Laura Catena is now on track to take over the winery and already has her own brand, Luca Wines.

Catena has several product lines at different price points. The expensive wines carry the name Catena Zapata. Alamos is his less expensive label, offering a host of products in the $7 to $10 range. It offers twelve still wines and one sparkling. The table wines include all the major international varieties plus two Malbecs, a pure version and a blend. Alamos also offers a Torrontés and a Malbec Rosé.

Altos Las Hormigas

Normally I recommend wineries that offer many varieties on the grounds that everyone will find something he or she likes. This is the exception. Altos Las Hormigas specializes in Malbec, offering two versions, the entry-level wine and the Reserva. It also makes Bonarda, an Italian grape, but that sells under the Colonia Las Liebres label.

Wine Spectator gave the 2005 Altos Las Hormigas Reserva 92 points and the #27 position on its Top 100 list for 2007. *The Wine Advocate* awarded the basic wine of the same vintage 89 points. Altos Las Hormigas is one of the most frequently ordered wines in American restaurants. One of the secrets behind the brand is Alberto Antonini, an Italian "flying winemaker" who consults there and brings his friends along.

The Altos Las Hormigas Malbec Reserva sells for about $25. The basic Malbec goes for some $10, and with luck you can find it on sale for $8. The Colonia Las Liebres generally runs about $8.

Los Cardos

Doña Paula is a relatively new winery, founded only in 1997, that offers expensive and bargain products. It had its first vintage two years later, and has recently been getting high-level attention. Ricardo Claro, a well-known Latin American entrepreneur, founded the winery, and its target is exports, which means it cultivates a taste that Americans like. *The Wine Advocate* has reviewed its wines regularly, giving some scores in the 90s.

Los Cardos is Doña Paula's bargain brand and offers Chardonnay, Sauvignon Blanc, Cabernet Sauvignon, Malbec, Merlot, and Shiraz. They all cost around $8, which is a good price for better-than-average quality. It's possible that the winery is pricing its goods at a low level in order to grab a foothold in the U.S. market. The cost may go up once it's established, but the wines are attractive.

Crios

A bottle of Crios wine is eye-catching. The label's image of three overlapping hands was inspired by an ancient Mayan artifact. Susana Balbo, one of the rare women winemakers in Argentina, has been making Crios wines for more than two decades. She's also an international consulting winemaker. Balbo puts her own name on the better wines she makes, and those run $13 to $15. The entry-level Crios wines are nearly as good, and less expensive. The line includes Cabernet Sauvignon, Chardonnay, Malbec, Rosé of Malbec, Syrah/Bonarda, and Torrontés.

The standard Crios wines cost $8 to $10. Keep an eye out, though, for the wines bearing Susana Balbo's name. I have often seen them on sale for $10.

Norton

So what's a winery in Argentina doing with an English name like Norton? In 1895, James Palmer Norton, an English engineer, was helping build a railroad line in Mendoza to connect the area to Chile, no easy task given the Andes Mountains, which separate the two countries. Norton took a liking to Mendoza and planted some French grapes. Argentines now run the totally modern, efficient operation. Some of Norton's expensive wines have received more than 90 points from *Wine Spectator.*

Norton's young varietals provide good value. Twelve wines make up this category, with a natural emphasis on red wines, which do well in Mendoza's hot climate. Beyond the standard Cabernet Sauvignon and Merlot, Norton has also ventured into less common varietals such as Sangiovese, Tempranillo, Bonarda, and Barbera. Among its whites are Chardonnay, Sauvignon Blanc, and Torrontés. Norton also produces a Malbec Rosé. The average price for the wines in the United States is just $9.

Santa Julia

Familia Zuccardi has built a major wine operation in Mendoza that includes a popular restaurant, where you can watch your meal being prepared on an open-air grill. Alberto Zuccardi, an engineer, believed that he could bring irrigation into Mendoza's desertlike area and make great wines there. He planted his first vineyard in 1963, and his son José now runs the winery.

Santa Julia is the bargain line of Zuccardi wines. When José puts his own name on its products, they tend to be in the $20 range. At the top end of the Santa Julia line, they cost about $15. But the lower, nonreserve prices become very attractive. There's a great selection of varieties in this range, including Malbec and Torrontés. Some wines in the Santa Julia line are organically grown, which is unusual among bargain wines.

Tierra de Luna

Jacques and François Lurton are the sons of André Lurton, one of the power brokers of Bordeaux. At last count, seventeen members of the clan were working somewhere in wine. François has invested heavily in wine ventures in Argentina, partnering in some of them with his brother Jacques.

Lurton in Argentina operates under a maddening number of brands, including Land of Fire, Bodega Jacques & François Lurton, Chacayes, and Gran Lurton. Its best bargain is Tierra de Luna, which is available in some stores for less than $6 a bottle. It offers a generic red and white. Lurton delivers a lot of value in Argentine wines for less than $10.

Tilia

Sometimes you can tell the quality of a wine by the distributor who has decided to handle it. Tilia is imported by Winebow, a New Jersey–based company that represents some of the best wineries in the world. Tilia is made at Bodegas Esmeralda, another of the Catena family's properties. That's also a good sign. The winemakers have strong academic backgrounds and are letting nature do its thing as much as possible. Tilia was started only in 2006, but it already has a strong track record.

The prices for Tilia are usually in the $7 to $9 range, sometimes even less. The company does a big business in magnum bottles. The varieties, though, are somewhat limited. It now offers just two whites, Chardonnay and Torrontés, and four reds, Malbec, Merlot, Cabernet Sauvignon, and Malbec-Syrah. Try Tilia wines before the crowds get there.

Trapiche

Trapiche is a major exporter of premium Argentine brands that also has a strong line of popular-priced products. It buys most of its grapes from more than two hundred growers, which it claims gives its wines great diversity. Trapiche specializes in vineyard-specific wines, in particular Malbecs. It brags that it has a Malbec for every price level and its offerings include Pinot Noir, which is unusual for an Argentine winery. The average price is $7. In addition, there are Trapiche Oak Cask wines, which age twelve months in oak barrels and cost about $9.

Trapiche also sells Astica wines, which are in the $6 to $8 range with a variety of products, including Cabernet Sauvignon, Chardonnay, Malbec, Sauvignon Blanc, Syrah, and Torrontés. Trapiche offers good value for both Astica and Oak Cask.

Urban Uco/Copete

José Manuel Ortega Gil-Fournier gives new meaning to the term *worldly*. He was born in Spain, went to high school in Mobile, Alabama, college at Notre Dame and the University of Pennsylvania, worked for Goldman Sachs in London, and now owns wineries in Argentina, Portugal, and Spain. A businessman by training and entrepreneur by nature, he has hired his winemakers with care and attention. His Argentine products sell at four levels of price and quality from expensive to bargain: O. Fournier, Alfa Crux, B Crux, and Urban Uco.

Urban Uco, the bargain wines, have already garnered a host of international praise. *Wine Spectator* has given them scores from 87 to 90 points. The brand does particularly well with Argentine and Spanish grapes: Malbec, Tempranillo, and Torrontés. It also offers Chardonnay and Sauvignon Blanc. Wines are in the range of $7 to $9.

In some states O. Fournier's bargain wines sell under the brand Finca Copete and sell at the same price range as Urban Uco. The varieties include Chardonnay, Malbec, Malbec-Tempranillo, Sauvignon Blanc, and Torrontés.

Ten Australian Bargain Brands

Nature blessed Australia with many fertile regions and climates that seem designed for grape growing. From the beginning, though, it has been primarily a mass producer. As wine expert André Simon wrote in 1909: "Winemaking in Australia is less of an art but more of a scientifically conducted industry than in Europe." Most Australia wineries today produce large quantities of good wines that sell at inexpensive prices. Government incentive programs stimulated the country's large wine glut.

Alice White

Now owned by Constellation, the large American company, Alice White got started in 1996 with a kangaroo on the label and a $7 price tag. Sound familiar? It was and is a good wine, but it didn't enjoy the runaway success of [yellow tail]. Nevertheless, Alice White's wines provide quality at attractive price. The wines come from South Eastern Australia, the home of many leading wineries.

Alice White offers six wines, including two from what may be a new grape for you: Lexia. It's also called Muscat of Alexandria and dates from ancient Egypt. If you like White Zinfandel, but want to drink a white rather than a rosé, give it a try. The other wines in Alice White's portfolio are Riesling, Chardonnay, Cabernet Sauvignon, Shiraz, Pinot Noir, and Merlot.

Prices tend to be in the $7 to $8 range for standard bottles. I've often seen Alice White in wine shops in magnum bottles, which brings down the cost per glass.

Black Swan

Black Swan is one of the international ventures of California's Gallo. It is made with Australian juice and sells for between $5 and $7. It comes in several Shirazes, plus popular whites including Chardonnay and Pinot Grigio. The wines have an American taste with lots of fruit up front. Do not confuse Gallo's Black Swan with the Black Swan Winery and Restaurant in Henley Brook, Washington.

Hardys

Thomas Hardy, the winemaker not the writer, was only twenty years old in 1850, when he landed on the shores of South Australia. He worked as a farmer, gold miner, and cowboy, and by 1853 had saved enough money to buy a farm and plant a vineyard. The business slowly but steadily expanded until it became a major player in the country's wine trade. The company Thomas Hardy & Sons bought up many Australian wineries, but in 2003, America's Constellation took it over.

Somewhere along the way, Hardy became Hardys, and now Hardys Stamp offers bargains in both bottles and boxes. The wines come in four varieties: Cabernet Sauvignon, Chardonnay, Merlot, and Shiraz. Standard bottles retail for about $7, while three-liter boxes go for $18 or so.

Hardys also has a line of wines selling at around $10. It's called Hardys Nottage Hill but is not as widely distributed as Hardys Stamp wines. Nottage Hill has some other varieties such as Pinot Noir.

Jacob's Creek

In 1847, the young Bavarian immigrant Johann Gramp planted the first commercial vineyard on the banks of Jacob's Creek in the Barossa Valley, today Australia's most prestigious wine region. Gramp made a sweet German-style wine, and the first year he produced only twelve bottles. Jacob's Creek is now owned by Orlando Wines, an Australian company that is a subsidiary of Pernod Ricard, the French wine and liquor giant.

Jacob's Creek is best known for its eleven standard wines, which it calls classics, and two sparkling wines. My favorites are the three Shirazes: Shiraz, Shiraz Cabernet, and Shiraz Grenache. The Sparkling Rosé, which is made with Chardonnay and Pinot Noir grapes, is pleasant and a good value.

Jacob's Creek is one of the most widely distributed Australian wines in the United States, and the retail prices are among the best, starting at about $7 a bottle and rarely going above $10, even in tax-heavy states.

Lindeman's

In 1840, Henry Lindeman left Britain for Australia with his new bride. Two years later, he bought land in Hunter Valley, New South Wales, and the following year planted his first vineyard with Riesling, Shiraz, and Verdelho grapes. He called his company Cawarra Wines and was soon shipping bottles to England. The company almost failed during the Depression, but came back to enjoy great success after World War II.

Lindeman's is part of the monumental corporate mess known as the Foster's Group. Misguided managers attempted to turn a beer company ("Foster's, Australian for Beer" may ring a bell) into a wine-beer superpower. New managers are trying to sell off the wine holdings, but have had a hard time finding buyers.

Lindeman's had great success in the United States with its Bin 65 Chardonnay, which was both a good price and a good wine. For a time it was Australia's top export. Today the company has a whole line of Bin wines in addition to Bin 65. There is Bin 45 Cabernet Sauvignon, Bin 50 Shiraz, Bin 85 Pinot Grigio, Bin 99 Pinot Noir, and on and on. All of them sell in the $7 to $9 range.

Little Penguin

Little Penguin was part of the critter craze that hit the wine business following the success of [yellow tail]. The critters all came into the market with labels showing cute animals and implicitly promising to be just as good as [yellow tail] at about the same price. Perhaps the worst example of copycat winemaking and marketing was California's Yellow Bird. Few of the critters are as good as [yellow tail], but Little Penguin delivers an acceptable product at a decent price.

Little Penguin undersells even [yellow tail] in most U.S. markets, going for $5 to $6 for a standard bottle and $10 for a magnum. It's often the least expensive Aussie wine in the store.

McWilliam's

McWilliam's has been making top-quality wines for six generations, yet at the same time produces some good bargain ones. At a time when big Australian companies have all but wiped out the family producers, it carries on that tradition.

Founded in 1877, McWilliam's claims to be the oldest family-run winery in Australia. It has vineyards in all the country's important grape-growing regions. In the U.S. market it concentrates most of its attention on Chardonnay and Shiraz. It's good at both, and they sell for $8 to $10.

Oxford Landing

Although now owned by Australia's Yalumba, Oxford Landing started out in 1958 as a vineyard with that name on the banks of the Murray River in South Australia. The Australian guide *Quaff* in 2011 gave Oxford Landing its award for the Best Wines in Australia Under AUD15 ($15).

Oxford Landing has a full line of the standard Australian wines, including Chardonnay, Sauvignon Blanc, Pinot Grigio, Viognier, Cabernet Sauvignon, Shiraz, Cabernet-Shiraz, Cabernet Rosé, and Merlot. As would be expected from an Aussie winery, its Shiraz is particularly good. *Quaff* wrote of the 2007 Oxford Landing Shiraz, "You can't ask for more at the price." It also has some special wines such as a blend of Grenache, Shiraz, and Mourvèdre, in the Rhône style. Oxford Landing wines retail in the United States for between $7 and $9 for a standard bottle.

Rosemount

In 1969, Bob Oatley founded Rosemount in South Australia's Hunter Valley. He had previously been in the coffee business and had a solid background in agriculture, which was a good foundation for wine. Oatley paid close attention to his vineyards and soon hired Chris Hancock, a former Penfolds winemaker. Among Rosemount's first commercial products was a Chardonnay-Sémillon called Pinot Riesling that reflected the company's rugged independence and its homage to Hunter Valley tradition, where Sémillon is called Hunter Riesling. Rosemount became famous in the 1970s with its Chardonnay, which was copied by winemakers in many countries.

Since 2001, however, Rosemount has been bounced around among owners as the Australian wine business consolidated. Quality and individual style seem to decline whenever family ownership gives way to large corporate management. Mega-wineries seldom show the kind of independence that sparked Rosemount.

While it had higher ambitions as an independent, Rosemount today is largely a bargain winery. Its Diamond series provides good value at about $8 a bottle for all the standard varieties plus a few interesting ones like Grenache Shiraz. It offers the favorite Aussie blend of Cabernet Sauvignon and Shiraz. Rosemount has several wines in the $20 range that are worth a try when you want to splurge.

Yalumba

England's Samuel Smith, who had been a brewer in his native country, in 1849 started the Yalumba vineyard and winery just outside the town of Angston in the Barossa Valley, South Australia. The name came from the local native language and means "all the land around." Today Yalumba is the largest privately held winery in the country, producing a staggering number of wines at all price points, from supervalue to superpremium. Robert Hill-Smith, a descendent of Samuel, now runs the company.

While Yalumba sells $100 bottles, its average price in the United States is only $13, and it has plenty of products at $8 and $10. Bargain seekers are probably most familiar with the ten wines in the Y Series that includes not only the standard varieties but also some unusual ones such as a Sangiovese Rosé. For those who want a touch of sweetness, Yalumba offers an off-dry Riesling. I'm a big fan of the Yalumba Shiraz Viognier. I still remember my first bottle.

[yellow tail]

Chapter Eight, "John Casella Grabs the World by the [yellow tail]," recounts the [yellow tail] story in detail. Having achieved a dominant market position among bargain wines in a brief time, the company is likely to keep selling its standard-size bottles at the suggested retail price of $6.99. It is often on sale for less. Owner John Casella would also like to build sales of the [yellow tail] reserve wines, which are now about $10.

Ten California Bargain Brands

When it comes to producing good wines at a good value, no one in the world can beat California. Chile and Argentina get close, but they have expensive shipping costs, which force their prices up. Bronco Wine, Gallo, and The Wine Group are all turning out many options that cost less than $5 a bottle. In addition, many other California wineries are competing in the under $10 market. The result is a buyer's heaven. And no matter what the critics say, the quality of many of the California wines is amazingly good.

Barefoot Cellars

Barefoot Cellars is the best-selling American bargain wine. In 1965, David Bynum, a reporter for the *San Francisco Chronicle* and self-taught wine-maker, started his own winery. He had great success with a product called Barefoot Bynum Burgundy, which had a drawing of a footprint on the label. Bynum, though, wanted to make boutique wines and produced the first single-vineyard Pinot Noir in the Russian River Valley. The Barefoot brand had been dormant for a decade when Michael Houlihan and Bonnie Harvey took it over in 1986 and turned it into the hot product in the bargain market. Barefoot's sales quickly rose to nearly one million cases a year. In 2005, Gallo bought the brand and used its marketing and distribution power to make Barefoot a wine superpower and its best-selling product.

Barefoot now has nearly two dozen offerings. All the standard varieties have a suggested retail price of $6.99, but usually cost a dollar or so less in stores. Sparkling wines are $10.99.

Beaulieu

Beaulieu is one of the oldest wineries in the Napa Valley, tracing its heritage back to Frenchman Georges de Latour, who started it in 1900. The winery survived Prohibition by becoming a top provider of wines to the Catholic Church for religious services. Beaulieu reached its peak of fame and quality from the 1940s to the 1970s under the stewardship of legendary winemaker André Tchelistcheff. The liquor company Heublein took over Beaulieu in 1969, expanded production, and began introducing less expensive wines. Diageo, the London-based global beverage company, bought Beaulieu in 1997, but in June 2010 sold it to a San Diego real estate firm that immediately leased it back under a twenty-year agreement. Beaulieu still makes icon wines such as the Georges de Latour Cabernet Sauvignon, but the bulk of its business is less expensive products.

The main attraction at Beaulieu for bargain hunters is its Coastal Estates line, which includes seven varieties selling generally for less than $10: Chardonnay, Pinot Grigio, Pinot Noir, Riesling, Sauvignon Blanc, Shiraz, and Zinfandel. Across the board, they offer good value for the money and are proof of the winery's deep technical talent. The Pinot Noir is made with French grapes grown in Languedoc-Roussillon.

Beringer

Beringer, which has a German winemaking heritage, is another historic Napa Valley producer. In 1876, Jacob and Frederick Beringer, natives of the Rhine wine region, started the winery. It has since been owned by Nestlé and by the Australian company Foster's.

Beringer has long had an impressive line of bargain wines selling for about $7 a bottle. Those are called the California Collection, and they come from grapes often grown in the Central Valley. The Beringer Stone Cellars wines are also a good value. The winery has had great success selling sweet wines such as Moscato, White Merlot, White Zinfandel, White Zinfandel sparkling wine, and White Zinfandel–Chardonnay. In addition, it sells two California Collection whites, Chenin Blanc and Pinot Grigio, but no reds. Beringer has some Napa Valley wines for less than $20, but the bulk of its products from Napa grapes cost much more.

Charles Shaw

The history of the Bronco Wine Company is presented in Chapter Seven, "The Rebel from San Joaquin Valley." Charles Shaw, which is sold exclusively at Trader Joe's, is Bronco's best-known brand. Bronco CEO Fred Franzia summed up his philosophy succinctly when he said, "We choose to sell good-quality wines at two dollars a bottle because we think it's a fair price. We think the other people are charging too much."

Not all of Bronco's wines sell for $2, but most are less than $10. The company sells wines under close to fifty labels and is constantly adding new brands. The name *Bronco* appears nowhere on the labels, but some of the most popular are Black Mountain, Crane Lake, "Down Under," Forest Glen, Montpellier, Napa Creek, Rutherford Vintners, and Santa Barbara Crossing.

The company's distribution is best on the West Coast and in states with Trader Joe's stores, as long as there is not a state law that prohibits the sale of wine in the same location as food. Crane Lake is Bronco's most widely sold wine after Charles Shaw.

Delicato

Gaspare Indelicato landed in America from Sicily in 1919, and the following year became part of the Central Valley's Italian community, where he grew grapes, as he had in Italy. After the end of Prohibition, Indelicato and Sebastiano Luppino started the SamJasper winery, which got its moniker from their two American nicknames. The winery prospered selling bulk wine to more famous brands.

In 1974, the name was changed to Delicato Family Vineyards, and the company began concentrating more on its own brands. Napa Valley's André Tchelistcheff became a consultant and improved Delicato's quality. The company has been slowly pushing its brand upmarket, but it still sells five varieties in the $6 to $8 range—Cabernet Sauvignon, Chardonnay, Merlot, Shiraz, and White Zinfandel. Delicato has other bargain brands, such as Gnarly Head and King Fish. In addition, it has the three-liter Bota Box wines and a half-liter Tetra Pak.

Fetzer

Mendocino County, north of Sonoma, is a historic wine region but not a fashionable one. Its climate near the coast is favorable to producing quality wines, and it offers great values. In the 1950s, Bernard and Kathleen Fetzer bought a large old ranch there and began growing grapes that they sold to wineries, and in 1968 Bernie started making his own wine. He was a fan of Chardonnay and Gewürztraminer, which both do well in Mendocino. Fetzer was an environmentalist long before that was fashionable, making a commitment in 1984 to sustainable farming. In 1992, the family sold the winery to Brown-Forman, a liquor company, that in 2011 sold it to Chile's Concha y Toro.

Fetzer has a broad range of varieties and concentrates on the less expensive part of the market, although it sells some more costly wines. The bargains are five whites, five reds, and one rosé (White Zinfandel). In style they run the gamut from sweet (Johannesberg Riesling) to dry (Pinot Grigio). The company is a major exporter and sells wines abroad tailored to national tastes. Fetzer is one of the few inexpensive wineries to produce vineyard-specific wines under its Valley Oaks label, but it doesn't excessively jack up their prices. Most of its products retail in the $6 to $8 range.

Gallo

Gallo is the longtime American master of selling bottles of wine for $10 and less. It has some sixty brands under its own name and a host of others. Originally the company started all of its own brands, but in recent years it has become a major buyer of wineries, including the prestigious Louis M. Martini.

The family ones include Gallo Family Vineyard, Gallo Twin Valley, and E. & J. Gallo brandies. The company also has other big sellers, including Carlo Rossi, Livingston Cellars, Redwood Creek, Rancho Zabaco, Turning Leaf, and Tisdale Vineyards.

In recent years, Gallo has also launched several brands made with grapes grown abroad. They usually carry foreign-sounding names like Red Bicyclette (France), Pölka Dot (Germany), Sebeke (South Africa), and Ecco Domani (Italy).

The third generation of Gallos since the company's founding in 1933 is trying to go upmarket with the Gallo Family Sonoma Reserve line, which sells for slightly more than the company's other brands but generally still less than $15. Gallo keeps a low public profile, and lets its wines sell mainly on price and strategic advertising.

Oak Leaf

As an answer to Bronco's Charles Shaw, The Wine Group, a major player in inexpensive wines, developed the Oak Leaf brand, selling at supervalue prices of $3 or $4 a bottle. Oak Leaf is available at Walmart stores in states where food and wine can be sold at the same establishment.

The Wine Group focuses almost exclusively on low-cost wines, and is now the second largest wine company in the world after Gallo. Franzia box wines are The Wine Group's cash cow, and it would be a giant business even if that were the only brand it owned. The Wine Group claims Franzia is "the world's most popular wine."

The Wine Group also owns many other brands such as Concannon, Corbett Canyon, FishEye, Foxhorn, Glen Ellen, Almaden, and Paul Masson. In 2006, The Wine Group bought the Cardinal Zin and Big House brands from Randall Graham's Bonny Doon Vineyard. In 2010, The Wine Group's Cupcake wines, which generally go for just under $10, were among the hottest brands. It has a broad array of products often made with both domestic and foreign-grown grapes.

The Wine Group's wines may not be the best, but many of them are among the least expensive. Franzia's five-liter box wine sometimes costs only a little more than $1 a liter. That price is hard to beat.

Sutter Home

Tracing its heritage back to 1874, Sutter Home is located in the heart of Napa Valley. It closed its doors during Prohibition and didn't reopen them until 1947, when the Trinchero family bought the property and concentrated on the bargain market. As late as the 1960s, it sold a gallon jug of Zinfandel at the winery for $1.78. Trinchero in the 1960s hired Darrell Corti, a Sacramento-based merchant, as part of a program to improve quality. Sutter Home is perhaps most famous, or infamous, for having invented White Zinfandel. Originally the wine was going to be called Oeil de Perdrix after a Swiss rosé, but federal officials wanted an English name for the new variety, so the winery named it White Zinfandel, even though it is pink. Sutter Home also played a major role during the Fighting Varietals era in the 1980s. At his annual state-of-the-business speech to the Unified Wine & Grape Symposium in 2010, Jon Fredrikson named Sutter Home his winery of the year because of its runaway success with Moscato.

Trinchero has gone upmarket in recent years. It bought the Folie à Deux winery in 2004, which gave it a prestige location on the Napa Valley's Route 29, to promote its high-end Trinchero Family Estates wines. Trinchero then successfully turned the Folie à Deux and Ménage à Trois brands into two of California's best-selling wines, at about $8.

Sutter Home has an extensive portfolio of inexpensive products, competing with the likes of Bronco, Gallo, and The Wine Group. It sells sixteen wines priced between $4 and $10 under the Sutter Home brand. It is not ashamed of sweet wines and has one called Sweet Red.

Three Thieves

Three Thieves likes to call itself the "liberators of world class wine." Founders Joel Gott, Roger Scommegna, and Charles Bieler come from widely different backgrounds, and Gott was the only one who grew up in the business. They operate what is loosely called a *négociant* firm, owning no vineyards but buying bulk grapes or juice and handling the winemaking and marketing. The French started the practice, and *négociants* are particularly strong in Burgundy.

The first year in business, sales of Three Thieves went from zero to one hundred thousand cases thanks to the success of a product called Jug Wine. It came in liter jugs with a handle and a screw cap. The product debuted in 2004, only ninety days after the three founders first met. Three Thieves was growing so fast that the men concluded they needed some outside help and made a deal with Trinchero.

Three Thieves now also makes a Tetra Pak product called Bandit that comes in a one-liter container. The slogan: "It's what's inside the bottle that counts. So we got rid of the bottle." The Bandit liter sells for about $9. The company also has a line of bottled wines selling for around $13 under labels such as Cowboy and The Show made with surplus wine from around the world. In addition, Three Thieves produces Newman's Own wines, which generally retail for about $10. Gott says his sweet spot in pricing is between $8 and $12, adding, "There will always be a market for Harlan Estate and Château Margaux, but there are too many wineries making $100 bottles, and a lot of the wines are not that good."

Woodbridge by Robert Mondavi

Robert Mondavi became a giant of the California wine business in the 1960s when he opened the first new major winery in the Napa Valley since Prohibition. Patriarch Cesare Mondavi had two sons, Robert and Peter. Cesare died in 1959, and six year later Robert's mother and brother threw him out of the Charles Krug Winery, the family's prized property. So, the following year, Robert started a new winery down the road that carried his name. He built a broad line of products in all price ranges. Constellation bought the Robert Mondavi Winery in 2004.

A staggering number of wines are sold with the Mondavi name on the label, which has led to some consumer confusion and diminished its reputation. Prices for Robert Mondavi Reserve and Spotlight wines go up to $250 a bottle. At the other end of the market, there are eight Private Selection wines with a list price of $10 to $13, but often selling in stores for less than $10.

In 1979, Mondavi started the Woodbridge by Robert Mondavi brand to be the center of his bargain-wine ventures. It's located east of Napa in Lodi, which for decades was the place where the Napa elite made bulk wines. Lodi today is better than its reputation. Thanks to cool San Francisco Bay breezes that blow through the hot area, it has the climate to make excellent wines. Many of the old bulk producers have been starting their own labels and increasing their quality. The least expensive wines bearing the Mondavi name are the more than thirty Woodbridges that generally sell for less than $10. The most interesting part of the portfolio is the line of fourteen Winemaker's Selection wines that include such unusual Mediterranean varieties as Verdelho, Vermentino, and Portacinco.

Ten Chilean Bargain Brands

The history of Chile's wine development is similar to that of Argentina. The Spanish introduced wines there, but for centuries the country was a distant, low-quality producer. Until the last few years, Chile was known for inexpensive but not necessarily good wine. Though in Argentina Malbec was the wine that captured world attention, in Chile it was Carménère, another Bordeaux grape that did better abroad than at home. Quality has dramatically improved in the last decade, while prices remain bargains.

Caliterra

In 1996, Chile's Eduardo Chadwick and California's Robert Mondavi did a fifty-fifty joint venture similar to the one that Mondavi had previously formed with Baron Philippe de Rothschild that resulted in the prestige winery Opus One. With Chadwick, Mondavi wanted to make wines in Chile by marrying California technology with Chilean *terroir*, hence the name Caliterra. In 2004, when Mondavi sold his company to Constellation, Chadwick acquired Mondavi's 50 percent share in Caliterra. Chadwick now owns both Caliterra and his family's historic winery Errázuriz.

Caliterra has an extensive portfolio of wines, selling in the range of $6 to $8, and rarely going above $10. Its wines won four medals at the 2010 *Decanter* magazine World Wine Awards.

Cono Sur

Cono Sur has been making some interesting wines since it was founded in 1993 with a mandate to concentrate on export markets. The brand name, in addition to being a play on the word *connoisseur,* is also a tribute to South America's Southern Cone, a geographic region with Chile as its western edge. The company has been innovative, making the first Chilean Viognier and the first Riesling in the Bio Bio Valley, and is already the biggest Pinot Noir producer in South America. Its white wines are perhaps better than its reds, which is unusual for Chile, a predominantly red-wine country. I particularly like the Cono Sur Sauvignon Blanc. Others sing the praise of the Pinot Noir. Peter Richards in his book *The Wines of Chile* wrote: "Cono Sur is, for my money, one of Chile's best wine producers, exemplary not only in its quality but also value, diversity, and ambition." I totally agree.

Cono Sur sells wines at every price point, but few of the expensive ones get to the American market. Bargain hunters should look for the Bicycle Series of eleven wines, which range from such standard varieties as Cabernet Sauvignon and Chardonnay to the Chilean specialty Carménère and a popular Merlot Rosé. Prices start at about $6 and shouldn't go above $10.

Cousiño Macul

Cousiño Macul has been going through a rebirth in recent years as it abandoned its historic vineyard in greater Santiago, where the sprawl of the capital was overrunning its grapevines. The company planted new vineyards south of the city near the town of Buin in the Maipo Valley. As a result, for a while Cousiño Macul wines seemed to be a little unstable, as if the grapes didn't like the move. They are now back to their former quality levels and are some of the best wines in the low-priced range. Cousiño Macul also produces expensive wines.

Cousiño Macul's bargain wines are called varietals, and there are only five: Chardonnay, Sauvignon Blanc, Cabernet Sauvignon, Merlot, and a dry Riesling, which is called Doña Isidora and is particularly nice. They are in the $8 to $10 range.

Errázuriz

In 1870, Don Maximiano Errázuriz, who made a fortune in copper, went to France to buy vines for a winery he was about to start. In the mid-1980s, Eduardo Chadwick, the fifth generation of family winemakers, followed tradition and went to Bordeaux for his wine education. Since then, he has become a visionary in Chilean wines, pushing not only his own company but also other Chilean wineries to do better—much better.

Errázuriz makes some of Chile's most outstanding wines. His icon brands are Don Maximiano Founder's Reserve, a Cabernet Sauvignon; Kai, a Carménère; and La Cumbre, a Syrah. All have captured international acclaim. Among the winery's least expensive offerings are its Estate series, selling for between $7 and $10. The five offerings include Chardonnay, both oaked and unoaked, Sauvignon Blanc, Fumé Blanc, and Cabernet Sauvignon Rosé.

Frontera

Concha y Toro, Chile's biggest wine company, offers products for every budget from inexpensive (Frontera) to costly (Don Melchor) and has been the backbone of Chilean wines for decades. In 1883, Don Melchor Concha y Toro, a politician-businessman, brought Bordeaux grape cuttings to the Maipo and Pirque regions of Central Chile. The country had its own version of Prohibition in the 1930s, when no new grape plantings were permitted. Winemaking declined, and by the 1950s, Chile was turning out only low-quality products. Eventually, new managers took control of Concha y Toro and started a comeback. That had barely begun when the political troubles of the 1960s and 1970s culminated in the coup d'état that toppled the government of Salvador Allende and put General Augusto Pinochet in power. As a result, Chile for several years was politically and economically isolated from world trade, and many foreigners refused to drink its wines. In the 1980s, the wine business reemerged, with a new emphasis on exports and Concha y Toro the market leader.

Concha y Toro's large portfolio includes several bargain labels. Frontera, which starts at about $5 a bottle and does big business in magnums selling for about $7, has excellent distribution. There are also the Xplorador and Sunrise brands, which do not seem to be as widely sold, at about the same price. Still more expensive are Casillero del Diablo wines. Depending on the state and local competition, those sometimes cost less than $10. There is no doubt that Casillero del Diablo is better for the few extra dollars. The wines offered under all those labels are extensive and include all of the major varieties plus such exotics as Merlot Rosé and Cabernet Blush, another rosé. Casillero also makes a sparkling wine.

Gato Negro

Viña San Pedro, one of Chile's three largest producers, makes the popular brand Gato Negro, which was first made in the 1960s. The name means "black cat" in Spanish, and there's a cat on most of the labels. San Pedro was started in the middle of the nineteenth century, but was struggling a decade ago under new ownership that had trouble controlling the business. New managers eventually came in and stabilized operations. Fortunately there was no change in the winemaking. Irene Paiva remained at the helm, and it is a pleasant surprise to have a woman winemaker in a land of *macho*.

Gato Negro is a great buy, and you can often find it on sale for less than $5. San Pedro also sells a top-end Cabernet Sauvignon for some $40, a tribute to Irene Paiva's abilities.

Montes

Bodega Casa Montes has been growing at a rapid pace and has garnered a stellar international reputation. In 1988, two top mangers from Viña San Pedro, production manager Aurelio Montes and exporter manager Douglas Murray, started Montes with the dream of making better wine. Montes has become strongly implanted at the expensive part of the business with brands such as Alpha M, a Bordeaux blend; Purple Angel, a Carménère; and Folly, a Syrah. At the same time, it has several less expensive wines for consumers working their way up to the premium-priced products. Aurelio Montes is considered one of the best winemakers in Chile and keeps an eye on even the bargain wines, although his heart is in Alpha M and the other icons.

The Montes Classic wines are the place for bargain hunters. It makes only five varieties: Sauvignon Blanc, Chardonnay, Cabernet Sauvignon, Merlot, and Malbec. You should be able to find those for between $7 and $10 in most states.

Santa Rita

Founded in 1880, Santa Rita has long been a major producer of inexpensive wines and is just behind Concha y Toro as Chile's biggest winery.

Industrialist Ricardo Claro bought Santa Rita in 1990 and expanded its operation by picking up several wineries, including Carmen, an inexpensive label. Santa Rita's upper-level wines include Medalla Real, an excellent product for about $15.

The big seller among Santa Rita's bargain wines is the 120 line, which got its name from 120 soldiers fighting in 1814 for Chile's independence who took refuge in the cellars where Santa Rita wine is made today. The 120 wines in red, white, and rosé sell in the range of $6 to $8, and I regularly find them for even less. In 2010, *Wine & Spirits* named Santa Rita the Value Winery of the Year.

Los Vascos

In 1988, Domaines Barons de Rothschild bought controlling interest in Los Vascos and quickly put a Bordeaux stamp on the wines. Gilbert Rokvam, Château Lafite-Rothschild's technical director, undertook a vineyard restructuring and replanting program. Cabernet Sauvignon, which had been a pure variety, soon became a Bordeaux blend. The winery now makes several Cabs plus Sauvignon Blanc, Chardonnay, and a Cabernet Rosé.

Los Vascos wines sell in the $7 to $10 range.

Veramonte

Veramonte seems like a California winery dropped into the eastern end of the Casablanca Valley just outside Santiago. It could be straight out of Napa, and some 80 percent of its sales are exports to the United States. All that is not surprising, as Agustín Huneeus, the man behind Veramonte, also played key roles in Napa Valley's Franciscan and Quintessa wineries.

Veramonte offers a broad range of California-style wines at Chilean prices. The bargain reserves come in six varieties: Cabernet Sauvignon, Chardonnay, Merlot, Pinot Noir, Rosé Syrah, and Sauvignon Blanc. I've always liked Chilean Sauvignon Blanc, which does well in the cool climate of Casablanca. If you want to splurge a little, try Veramonte's Primus, a blend of Cabernet Sauvignon, Merlot, and Carménère. It's a great value at about $17.

Ten French Bargain Brands

The best place in France to find inexpensive wines is Languedoc-Roussillon, in the southern part of the country on the western Mediterranean coast. France's *vin de table* has long been made there. In 1979, the French established a new wine classification called *Vins de Pays*, which now has six regions. Languedoc-Roussillon wines are designated *Vins de Pays d'Oc*. Another source of French bargains are *négociant* wines made and marketed by companies that buy grapes and juice from small producers.

Barton & Guestier

The Barton and Guestier families have been in the wine business in Bordeaux since the eighteenth century. The Bartons were Irish, and the Guestiers were French. In 1802, Hugh Barton and Daniel Guestier formed the *négociant* firm Barton & Guestier. The Canadian liquor company Seagram owned it for many years, but in 2010 Castel, a major wine company in Southern France, bought it. Over the years and through multiple owners, Barton & Guestier expanded its horizons far beyond Bordeaux and now sells wines from all over France.

B&G, as the company is generally known in the wine business and often on its label, sells many wines in the $6 to $10 range. You can be fairly confident that you will get a solid wine at a good price, although perhaps not an exciting one. B&G Bistro is a good label to seek out.

Georges Duboeuf

A 2007 biography of Georges Duboeuf by Rudolph Chelminski had the subtitle "Beaujolais and the French peasant who made it the world's most popular wine." Duboeuf did that by offering the world a good wine, Beaujolais, at a good price. He has since moved beyond that one product into other regions of France with the same underlying philosophy. There's a lot to like about Duboeuf wines. They are attractively packaged, and his worldwide distribution is awesome.

Duboeuf's Beaujolais starts at about $7 a bottle, and it's one of the best buys among French wines. He also sells some excellent Pays d'Oc wines that are slightly more expensive, but generally still less than $10. He recently launched the Patch Block line of wines, which come in five varieties and sell in the same price range as the Beaujolais. According to Duboeuf, the name "refers to a select patch of land within a vineyard called a block, where the grapes exude distinct characteristics and quality resulting from exceptional soil conditions." Patch Block Pinot Noir is particularly interesting at $8 to $10.

Les Jamelles

Les Jamelles is a bargain producer of Pays d'Oc wines. The winemakers since 1991 have been Catherine and Laurent Delaunay, who hail from an old winemaking family in Burgundy. They worked in California before landing in Languedoc-Roussillon. *Wine Advocate* critic David Schild-knecht wrote in his review of their 2008 Sauvignon Blanc: "Les Jamelles's wines continue to be well-sourced from throughout the greater Languedoc and include some notable values."

The winery makes Rhône-style wines as well as Chardonnay and Pinot Noir that cost between $8 and $10. Unfortunately, their distribution is not great, but they are worth the search.

J. P. Chenet

J. P. Chenet has become known in the wine world for its funky bottles with slightly curved necks that makes them look a bit tipsy. This is the brand of the *négociant* Grands Chais de France, which works largely in the less famous wine regions of France. Chenet was launched in 1996 and claims to be the best-selling French wine in the world. It makes both still and sparkling wines from the Pays d'Oc and Côtes de Gascogne regions. Its best sellers in the United States are such unusual blends as Chardonnay-Colombard and Cabernet Sauvignon–Syrah.

J. P. Chenet's products are mostly in the range of $8 to $10.

Lurton

In addition to making wine in Argentina, Chile, Portugal, and Spain, brothers François and Jacques Lurton have been active in their native France. François, who now runs the company, has been particularly interested in Languedoc-Roussillon, where he has more than a half dozen operations. The brothers have three labels: Les Salices, which comes in Viognier, Chardonnay, and Pinot Noir; Les Fumées Blanches, a Sauvignon Blanc; and Terra Sana, an organic wine in red, white, and rosé. In 2009, François produced an interesting new Côtes de Roussillon white, Mas Janiel Traou de l'Oillue, which is made from forty-year-old Grenache and Macabeu vines.

André Lurton, the father of François and Jacques, has a brand that sells just over the $10 cut-off. It's called Château Bonnet—Blanc, Rouge, and Rosé. These are good Bordeaux-style blends that generally sell for about $13, but sometimes you can find them on sale for $10.

Maison Nicolas

Nicolas has been a chain of specialty wine stores in France since 1822 and now has shops all around the world. It claims to have been the first store to sell wine in a bottle. In addition to stocking major brands, the company also carries a long line of French wines with the Maison Nicolas label. These are sold at their stores, but also at other wine outlets outside France. Nicolas is now part of the large Castel wine group.

The range of Maison Nicolas products goes from the very expensive to the very modest. It has a 2006 Maison Nicolas Potel Chambertin Clos-de-Bèze Grand Cru Pinot Noir selling for $250 as well as a Maison Nicolas Merlot for $5.99.

Mouton Cadet

Baron Philippe de Rothschild spent most of his time working on his beloved Château Mouton Rothschild. He achieved the unthinkable in 1973, when he got the French government to promote the wine from a Second Growth to a prized First Growth in the 1855 Bordeaux Classification. That was the first change in the ranking since 1855, and will probably be the last. Rothschild was a good businessman, who wanted to sell wine to people who couldn't afford his First Growth price. That product was Mouton Cadet, which he launched in 1930. It comes in Bordeaux Blanc, Rouge, and Rosé.

Mouton Cadet is one of the most widely distributed French wines in the United States and sells generally for between $8 and $10. The wines are also available in magnum.

Parallèle 45

Maison Paul Jaboulet Aîné traces its roots in the Rhône Valley back to 1834, when Antoine Jaboulet was working vineyards on the hillside of Hermitage. There is still a Jaboulet at the company as export director, but in 2006 the Frey family, which makes wine in Champagne and Bordeaux, acquired the firm. Jaboulet produces Rhône wines, including such famous ones as Hermitage and Châteauneuf-du-Pape. In addition, it has a strong line of inexpensive wines.

Parallèle 45 is the best-selling Jaboulet wine in the States. Parallèle Rouge is a blend of 60 percent Grenache and 40 percent Syrah. Parallèle Blanc is 50 percent Grenache Blanc, 20 percent Marsanne, 20 percent Viognier, and 10 percent Bourboulenc. Parallèle Rosé is 50 percent Grenache, 40 percent Cinsault, and 10 percent Syrah. All sell for between $8 and $10. The next time you are looking for a bargain Rhône blend, check these out.

Red Bicyclette

Red Bicyclette is the brand for Gallo's French wine venture, and since 2003, the company has been buying the wine for it in Languedoc-Roussillon. At present Gallo is making five varieties: Chardonnay, Merlot, Pinot Noir, Rosé, and Syrah. The wines are typical Gallo: technically well produced and reliable.

Red Bicyclette sells for as low as $6 in some markets, but in most areas is in the $8 range.

La Vieille Ferme

Château Beaucastel is one of the most famous wineries in the Rhône Valley, and critics around the world praise its Châteauneuf-du-Pape, which sells for about $100. Beaucastel also sells inexpensive wines. The Perrin family has owned Château Beaucastel since the early twentieth century and also produces two bargain wines, Vieille Ferme and Réserve Perrin. Vieille Ferme has three products that are perhaps the best value in French wines today. Vieille Ferme Rouge Côtes du Ventoux is a blend of 50 percent Grenache, 20 percent Syrah, 15 percent Carignan, and 15 percent Cinsault. Vieille Ferme Blanc Côtes du Luberon is 30 percent Grenache Blanc, 30 percent Bourboulenc, 30 percent Ugni Blanc, and 10 percent Roussanne. Vieille Ferme Côtes du Ventoux Rosé is 50 percent Cinsault, 40 percent Grenache, and 10 percent Syrah. Trader Joe's has an exclusive arrangement to sell the red, white, and rosé as La Ferme Julien. These appear to be the same as the Vieille Ferme products.

All Vieille Ferme wines are in the $6 to $8 range and are also sold in magnum. Réserve Perrin has a good variety of Rhône wines, and many are between $10 and $20, but sometimes you can find them on sale for less than $10.

Ten German Bargain Brands

It helps to know at least a smattering of German to navigate the country's wines. Bargain hunters don't need to understand terms such as *Spätlese* and *Trockenbeerenauslese* because they are used only for expensive wines. The bulk of German wines are white and are made with Riesling grapes, although there are a few other whites and even some reds. Many German wines are sweet, and that turns some people off. If you're looking for a dry wine, make sure the word *trocken* (dry) is on the label.

Black Tower

Black Tower was launched in 1967 and soon became the largest-selling German wine brand in the world. Surprisingly, less than 5 percent of its sales are in Germany. Much bigger markets are the United States, Britain, Sweden, and Norway. Reh Kendermann, originally a Mosel wine producer but now a beverage company that exports German wines around the world, currently owns the brand. It bought the label from Allied Domecq in 1992. Black Tower sells several varieties in the United States. Among them are not only standard German wines such as Riesling but also Dornfelder, a red wine created in 1955 and now the country's second most popular red after Pinot Noir, which Germans call *Spätburgunder*. Black Tower also sells international varieties including Pinot Grigio. All Black Tower wines are sweet.

Black Tower sells in the United States for between $7 and $10, with magnums starting at about $13.

Blue Fish

Blue Fish Riesling is a new wine on the market, introduced only in 2005. It is made by a cooperative of wine growers from the town of Niederkirchen in the Pfalz region of Germany. Expensive wines generally come from the Rhine and

Mosel areas. Those from the Pfalz, which is due west of the Rhine and near the French border, generally cost less. The cooperative that makes this wine has been operating for a century and has more than four hundred members. Blue Fish comes in two styles, sweet and dry. The dry one is called Original Riesling on the label and has almost no sugar. The other is called Sweet. In addition to the two Rieslings, Blue Fish makes a Pinot Grigio.

Blue Fish wines sell in the $8 to $10 range.

Clean Slate

Clean Slate is the result of a project between Moselland, the largest vineyard grower in the Mosel area, and Winebow, an American wine importer. The steep vineyards leading up from the Mosel River are covered with slate, which gives German wines their minerality and this one its name. The alcohol level is a low 10.5 percent, which is typical of Mosel wines. It is also sweet, with sugar weighing in at 26.2 grams per liter. If you like sweet Riesling, this is for you. If you don't, look for something else, such as Blue Fish Original.

Clean Slate sells for $8 to $10.

Dr. Beckermann

The Germans have great respect for academic degrees. If someone has two doctorates, the person is called Doctor Doctor. Not surprisingly, many German wineries have a Doctor in their names. The most famous vineyard in the Mosel, located in the quaint town of Bernkastel, is named Bernkasteler Doktor. The Dr. Beckermann winery has products from both the Rhine and Mosel areas. One of its biggest sellers is Liebfraumilch, which means "beloved lady's milk." It's made from Riesling, Müller-Thurgau, Silvaner, and Kerner grapes. In the eighteenth century, the wine was first made from grapes grown in the Church of Our Lady, in the town of Worms. Dr. Beckermann's Liebfraumilch has the classification *Qualitätswein bestimmter Anbaugebiete (QbA)*, meaning it is a quality wine from a specific region. It must also have between eighteen and forty grams of residual sugar per liter to be a *QbA*. Most of the Dr. Beckermann wines are inexpensive, low in alcohol, and sweet. The Liebfraumilch has only 9 percent alcohol.

Dr. Beckermann wines start at about $5 and go to nearly $20 for a specialty wine such as its Piesporter Michelsberg Riesling Spätlese.

Dr. Loosen

Dr. Loosen is a step up in quality from Dr. Beckermann. Since 1988 Ernst Loosen, the *Decanter* magazine Man of the Year in 2005, has run the winery that has been in his family for two centuries. The winery is excited about its new Red Slate Riesling, which they call dry, meaning it should have less than four grams of residual sugar. It's very difficult to get a truly dry wine in the Mosel because of the naturally long and difficult fermentation because the area's cool weather during the fall harvest.

Dr. Loosen has introduced the Dr. L Riesling, which is made with grapes not grown in its own vineyards. *Wine Spectator* gave the 2008 Dr. L 90 points and put it on its Top 100 for 2009. It has about twenty grams of sugar per liter, making it medium-sweet. The wine can sometimes be found for $8 a bottle, but is more often $10.

Leonard Kreusch

Leonard Kreusch has its headquarters in Trier. It has a few quality wines such as its Rheingau Riesling, Rheinhessen sweet wines, and vineyard-specific wines from the Rhine and Mosel. The company's bread-and-butter products, though, are its five *Qualitatswein*: Liebfraumilch, Piesporter Michelsberg, Zeller Schwarze Katz, Moselblümchen, and Maywine. They are usually sold in magnums. Leonard Kreusch also has four wines under the Twisted River label that are popular with a younger crowd thanks to a modern bottle design. It comes in Riesling, Gewürztraminer, Late Harvest Riesling, and Dornfelder.

Most of the Kreusch wines sell for between $8 and $10 and are often available in magnums.

St. Urbans-Hof

Nicolaus Weis founded St. Urbans-Hof winery in 1947 in the Mosel town of Leiwen. The prices are generally outside our range. The basic St. Urbans-

Hof Riesling QbA sells for about $10 and can be hard to find. Many of its other wines cost $40 and more.

The founder's grandson Nik Weis is now running the winery and maintaining the tradition of quality wine. He has started a new label called Nik. Weis Selection, made with grapes he buys from neighboring growers. So far he is making just one wine, Urban Riesling. The alcohol level is 9.5 percent, and it's medium-sweet. *The Wine Advocate* gave the 2007 87 points, while *Wine Spectator* gave the 2008 vintage 89 points. In most areas Urban Riesling sells for $9, but sometimes it's going for $12 or $13. St. Urbans-Hof wines have excellent U.S. distribution.

Schmitt Söhne

The Schmitt Söhne winery is located in the village of Longuich on the Mosel River near Trier, where it has been for two hundred years. Since German wines have those tongue-twisting words on the label, it's not surprising that Schmitt Söhne has been introducing some with English monikers such as Relax, Superstition, and Anything Goes. Fünf, which means "five," comes in both Riesling and Sweet Red. Both were designed to be aperitifs and drunk at 5:00 p.m. The mainstays of Schmitt Söhne's business remain sweet Riesling and Liebfraumilch.

Prices for Schmitt Söhne wines start at about $5 and go up very slowly. If you like sweet, they are great values, especially in magnums.

Selbach

Johannes Selbach is a well-known maker of Rieslings sold under the brand Selbach-Oster. It makes excellent wine from such famous vineyards as Wehlener Sonnenuhr, Zeltinger Sonnenuhr, and Graacher Domprobst. *Wine Spectator* gave 99 points to the 2001 Selbach-Oster Bernkasteler Badstube Eiswein. Selbach also owns the *négociant* firm J. & H. Selbach, which has its own line of wines. The winery brags that "long-term partnerships with quality-oriented producers are the basis for J. & H. Selbach's grapes, juice, and wine purchases, ensuring consistency and quality for these wines."

J. & H. Selbach has a wine called Riesling.Incline, which it brought into the United States selling for $9.99. If you like great German Riesling, take the time and effort to seek out Selbach Riesing.Incline.

Villa Wolf

The J. L. Wolf winery is in Rheinhessen, which is the reason its wines are less costly than those from the Rheingau area, where real estate is more expensive. Wolf was founded in 1756, but was floundering in 1996, when Ernst Loosen of the Mosel's Dr. Loosen took over the vineyards. The winery's products for bargain hunters are the Villa Wolf and Wolf Erben brands and include Riesling, Gewürztraminer, Pinot Gris, Pinot Noir, and Rosé varieties. They are made with grapes from both the J. L. Wolf estate and outside growers.

Villa Wolf wines sell for between $8 and $10.

Ten Italian Bargain Brands

Many Americans first learned about wine by enjoying inexpensive *vino* at an Italian restaurant, and none is better suited to go with the national cuisine. Unfortunately, the days of a wide choice of Italian bargains have ended. Now one has to look hard to find them. Just as it's a challenge to find a Bordeaux or a Burgundy costing less than $10, it is hard to get a bargain from Tuscany, Italy's most famous wine region and the home of Chianti and Chianti Classico. But elsewhere there remain Italian bargains.

Antinori

The logo of the Antinori wine proudly boasts that the family has been in the business for twenty-six generations, stretching back more than six hundred years. During that time the family has made good wine and offered leadership in Italian winemaking. Rather than just repeat the status quo in its vineyards and cellars, Antinori was pushing in new directions. In recent times, it has also gotten into international ventures. While best known for its top-dollar wines such as Solaia, the winery has not forgotten about the rest of us who may never drink a drop of that gift from the gods.

Antinori makes wine in two Italian regions: Tuscany in central Italy and Umbria slightly to the south and east. Bargain Antinori wines are found among the whites, since even the least expensive reds start at about $25. My favorite is Toscano Bianco, which has 40 percent Trebbiano, 30 percent Malvasia, 15 percent Pinot Bianco, and 15 percent Pinot Grigio. It usually costs $9. Another favorite is Santa Crista Orvietto Classico, which is about $10. That's a blend of 40 percent Procanico, 27 percent Grechetto, 15 percent Chardonnay, 15 percent Verdello, and 3 percent of both Drupeggio and Malvasia.

Banfi

Banfi was originally an American wine distributor and then returned to its Italian roots to make wine at the historic Castello Banfi in Tuscany. Owners John and Harry Mariani began their career as importers in the business their father started, but now they produce a broad range of wines at various prices. For the wealthy there is Poggio all'Oro Brunello di Montalcino Riserva, which is one of the best wines Italy turns out and ranks with the Super Tuscans.

Banfi also sells several labels of bargain wines. Le Rime is an interesting Pinot Grigio–Chardonnay blend at $8. Centine offers red, white, and rosé wines at about $8. Col di Sasso is a Cabernet Sauvignon–Sangiovese for the same price. Principessa Gavia, a classic white that reminds me of an Alberiño, is excellent at $10.

Bolla

In the late nineteenth century, Abele Bolla owned the Al Gambero Inn in the old northern Italian town of Soave, southeast of Verona. The restaurant was famous for its house wines, and in 1883 Bolla started producing Soave, a local dry white wine made with Garganega grapes. Soon Bolla was winning medals and shipping his products to the United States, where they found a big audience among Italian-Americans. Today Bolla makes both classic northern Italian wines such as Amarone, Bardolino, Soave, and Valpolicella, and international wines from Pinot Noir to Chardonnay.

The Bolla mass-market wines start at about $7 a bottle and $11 for a magnum. Its prestigious red wines are more expensive. Bardolino, for example, is about $15, while Amarone is $40.

Cavit

In the late 1970s, Cavit introduced Americans to Pinot Grigio, and the company now sells three million cases a year, making it the top Italian wine in the United States. Cavit is a newcomer in a country where wineries chart their histories in generations. In 1977, David Taub, founder of Palm Bay International, a Florida-based distributor, was looking for a white Italian wine to import to compete with Soave. He traveled to Trentino in northeastern Italy, where he met with representatives of the Cantina Viticoltori del Trentino, a wine cooperative with the nickname Ca' Vit. That became Cavit, an easy name to pronounce in English. (Palm Bay salesmen told customers it was just like talk-show host Dick Cavett's name.) Cavit became the house wine for Olive Garden restaurants, which sells more wine than any other U.S. chain.

Cavit now makes five wines: Chardonnay, Pinot Grigio, Riesling, Cabernet Sauvignon, and Merlot. It also has sparkling wines under the Lunetta label. All generally sell in the $7 to $12 range.

Corvo

Sicily is a good place to find Italian bargain wines, and Corvo is one of the best brands. Giuseppe Alliata, the seventh prince of Villafranca, started the winery in 1824. Illva Saronno, the holding company of the Reina family, which markets Disaronno Amaretto, now owns Corvo. The best deals are the basic Corvo Rosso and Corvo Bianco. Rosso is made with Nero d'Avola, Pignatello, and Nerello Mascalese grapes and is aged in Slavonian oak barrels. Bianco is made from Inzolia, Catarratto, and Grecanico grapes.

Those two wines can be easily found in the $8 to $10 range.

Falesco Est! Est!! Est!!!

Since its first vintage in 1993, Falesco, a winery located on the border of Umbria and Latium, has attracted attention by turning out high-quality wines at bargain prices. Brothers Riccardo and Renzo Cotarella, who are big-time wine consultants, run it when they're not working for others. Their first big hit was a white with the interesting name Est! Est!! Est!!! In the twelfth century, England's Henry V showed his enthusiasm for the local wine by writing *Est!* (Latin for "it is") on the door wherever he found a good one. When he tasted the wines in Montefiascone, a town about seventy miles northwest of Rome, he wrote the word three times for emphasis.

Falesco makes two styles that have minor variations, Est! Est!! Est!!! Poggio dei Gelsi and Est! Est!! Est!!! de Montefiascone. Both are blends of Trebbiano, Malvasia, and Roscetto grapes. There is another wine with a similar name and price, Bigi Est! Est!! Est!!!, but I think Falesco is better.

Falesco also makes Vitiano Red, a blend of 33 percent each of Sangiovese, Merlot, and Cabernet Sauvignon, as well as Vitiano White, which is half Vermentino and half Verdicchio. People as diverse as the Internet's Wine Curmudgeon and Antonio Galloni, the Italian reviewer for *The Wine Advocate,* have trouble keeping in check their enthusiasm for Vitiano Red, which sells for about $9. The Wine Curmudgeon wrote that he is "not the fawning type, yet I sound like a gushing school girl whenever I write about these wines." Galloni hit a similar note, giving the 2009 Vitiano Red 89 points and writing: "The full-throttle style verges on over ripeness and is on the edge of being over the top, but readers who enjoy this type of wine will find much to admire, especially for what remains an exceedingly modest price."

Falesco makes a $90 Merlot called Montiano, but Est! Est!! Est!!! and Vitiano sell for between $8 and $10. As Henry V might have written on the door, Great Value! Great Value!! Great Value!!!

Folonari

The Folonari family started making wines in the Veneto region of northern Italy in the late eighteenth century and soon was selling it around the world. The family is particularly well known for its Folonari Soave, a favorite wine of the area and in the United States. In 1912, the company bought the Ruffino winery in Tuscany, an area famous for Chianti. Folonari has always been focused on the everyday-wine market, leaving the expensive products to others. It now exports thirteen wines to the United States, ranging from such Italian classics as Soave and Chianti to the international Cabernet Sauvignon.

Prices for all the Folonari wines are in the $8 range. The company doesn't have as good a distribution network as some other Italian wineries, but the quality and price are worth going an extra mile to find. The Valpolicella received an 86 from *The Wine Advocate.*

Fontana Candida

Fontana Candida is always associated first with Frascati, an inexpensive, light white wine made near Rome that is the most popular white in Roman cafés. It's been called the wine of the popes. According to legend, Frascati spouted in Roman fountains from the nostrils of Marcus Aurelius's marble horse. The wine is a blend of predominantly Trebbiano and Malvasia grapes. The next time you are about to order a glass of Pinot Grigio, ask for a Fontana Candida Frascati. It's full of refreshing floral flavors.

Fontana Candida was only established in 1958, and also makes Pinot Grigio from the Veneto region and Orvieto from Umbria. Fontana Candida prices are in the range of $7 to $9.

Gabbiano

The Castello di Gabbiano has been a fixture of the Tuscan landscape since the twelfth century, so it's a natural name for a Tuscan wine. The castle was the refuge for distinguished Florentine families, and its role in Tuscan intrigue could easily fill pages of a history book. Castello di Gabbiano is now owned by the Arcaini family, which in 1981 began restoring the castle.

Gabbiano makes just five wines, and two of them are priced much higher than the $10 limit. Its Chianti, Chianti Classico, and Pinot Grigio, however, come in just under that.

Riunite

In 1950, nine wine producers in the rich agricultural area of Emilia-Romagna region in northern Italy got together to start the Cantine Cooperative Riunite. Banfi, Riunite's importer, directed the wine's great commercial success in the United States, when it was the top-selling import, at only $2. One can debate about the wine's quality, but no one can doubt the enthusiasm of its loyal customers. Riunite now sells many different wines, including a sparkling Spumante in addition to the still-popular Lambrusco red and white.

Price depends on the state, but all the Riunite wines sell for less than $8 and in some places for less than $5.

Ruffino

Ruffino has an impressive offering of eleven red, six white, and two rosé wines. The company is proud of its long Tuscan history, and many of its wines come in its patented Florentine bottle. Ruffino is best known to wine magazines for Vino Nobile di Montepulciano, Brunello di Montalcino, and the Super Tuscan Urio. All of those are well above the $10 limit, but at the same time it has several inexpensive wines from both traditional Tuscan varieties and international grapes. The average price of its offerings in the United States is $10. The most popular of Ruffino's Italian varieties are Orvieto, Chianti, and Pinot Grigio.

Ten New Zealand Bargain Brands

New Zealand hit the radar of American wine drinkers in the late 1970s with its Sauvignon Blanc. In those days, they were mostly less than $10, but prices have steadily gone up. Kiwi winemakers have been worried about following their neighbor Australia and getting labeled as making cheap wine. I have been able to find ten good bargains that also show off the high quality of the country's products. The Central Otago area of the country makes excellent Pinot Noir, but the price for those wines is generally more than $25.

Brancott

Montana was the first modern New Zealand wine company, and the first to get into exports. It chose Brancott as the brand name for the products it shipped to the United States in honor of the Brancott Vineyard in Marlborough, which was planted in 1973 and showed the world the new grassy-style New Zealand Sauvignon Blanc. In addition to that breakthrough wine, Brancott today also makes Pinot Noir and Pinot Grigio. Pernod Ricard New Zealand owns Montana and Brancott.

Prices for the whites are in the $8 range, and the Pinot Noir is about $10.

The Crossings

The Crossings owns 143 hectares (353 acres) in three vineyards of the Awatere Valley of Marlborough. The founders planted the first vineyard in 1996 and made their initial vintage in 2001. The winery now produces Sauvignon Blanc, Chardonnay, and Pinot Noir. The Crossings quickly became one of the best-selling New Zealand wines in the American market. *Decanter* magazine named The Crossings one of its Top Ten New World Sauvignon Blancs selling for less than £10 ($16).

Prices for the white wines are in the $8 to $9 range, while the Pinot Noir is $15.

Dashwood

Dashwood is one of six labels of Vavasour Wines in Marlborough. Under the Dashwood brand it makes Sauvignon Blanc, Chardonnay, and Pinot Noir. The winery tried its hand at Cabernet Sauvignon, but then quietly gave it up. Glenn Thomas, a longtime winemaker who joined the company in 1988, started the Dashwood brand for wines that can be consumed earlier than the Vavasour line, which is also sold in the United States. Dashwood is made with fruit from both the Awatere and Wairau regions of Marlborough. It has often won best of show at New Zealand wine competitions.

Dashwood prices are generally in the $8 and $9 range. Both the Vavasour and Dashwood Pinot Noirs start at $13.

Giesen

Giesen is one of the senior citizens of New Zealand wineries, having planted its first grapes in 1981. Just to show how long ago that was in New Zealand wine history, that vineyard did not include Sauvignon Blanc, the grape that would make the country famous. The three Giesen brothers, Theo, Alex and Marcel, planted their first grapevines on uncultivated land near Christchurch on New Zealand's South Island.

Three years later, though, Giesen was making Sauvignon Blanc, but didn't begin exporting it until 1997. Giesen today also produces Chardonnay, Riesling, Pinot Gris, and Pinot Noir.

The white wines tend to be around $9, while the Pinot Noir goes as high as $20.

Matua Valley

Brothers Ross and Bill Spence come from a winemaking family. Ross studied enology at Fresno State University, while Bill majored in agriculture at Massey University in New Zealand. Their first winery was in Auckland, the nation's capital but not much of a place to make wine.

Its initial products in 1974 were Chardonnay, Sauvignon Blanc, Pinot Noir, and an unusual variety called Gamay Teinturier. They made their Sauvignon Blanc, which also happened to be the first in New Zealand, in a tin shed in West Auckland. The winery's headquarters are still in the capital, although Matua Valley gets most of its grapes from Hawke's Bay, Marlborough, and Gisborne. That gives its wines a slightly different taste than those from other New Zealand wineries. Both its Sauvignon Blanc and Pinot Noir are popular.

Matua prices are generally in the $10 range for the whites and a couple dollars more for the Pinot Noir.

Monkey Bay

Cloudy Bay was the New Zealand Sauvignon Blanc that made the world take notice. Alas, it now costs about $25. Kiwi wineries tried to emulate its success by putting the words *cloudy* or *bay* in their names, for example, Cloudy Cape and this one, Monkey Bay. There is actually a piece of New Zealand geography called Monkey Bay, so it has some legitimacy. This winery is today part of Constellation.

Monkey Bay Sauvignon Blanc in many markets sells for as little as $8. The wine is also available in a magnum, which brings down the price per glass. Monkey Bay is still building brand recognition, and the price will be going up. So buy it soon.

Nobilo

Nobilo Vintners is one of several New Zealand wineries that traces its roots to the wave of Croatian immigrants who arrived in the country in the early and mid-twentieth century. Winemaking skills were one of the few things they had when they left Europe. In 1998, Nobilo became one of New Zealand's biggest wine companies, when it took over Selak, another winery built by Croatians. Nobilo was sold in 2000 to the Australian company BRL Hardy, which Constellation bought three years later. Nobilo sources its grapes from all around the country: Sauvignon Blanc from Marlborough, Chardonnay from Gisborne, Pinot Gris and Merlot from Hawke's Bay. The Sauvignon Blanc and Pinot Noir have excellent U.S. distribution.

Nobilo seems to be more price aggressive than other New Zealand brands. Its wines sell a little below the others, starting at $8.

Redcliffe

Redcliffe, a winery legally named De Redcliffe, started out making Cabernet Sauvignon and Merlot, but has had more success with Sauvignon Blanc. It has a vineyard in Marlborough for the white grape, while its red wines are made elsewhere in New Zealand. Palm Bay, a Florida distributor, handles sales in the United States. The Sauvignon Blanc can be found in many stores selling for about $8. Redcliffe is not as famous as many of the others making that variety, but it has the same distinctive taste that consumers have learned to love.

Redcliffe is available in magnums, which makes it a still better value.

Sacred Hill

In 1986, brothers David and Mark Mason founded Sacred Hill Winery. They came from a farming family in the Hawke's Bay area of the country's North Island, where their father first recognized the potential for growing grapes. Initially the family sold the fruit to established wineries but soon started Sacred Hill, building a winery in 1995. Sacred Hill's upper-end wines have received high marks from Neal Martin in *The Wine Advocate*. The 2006 Sacred Hill Rifleman's received 93 points and the comment "This is rightly feted as one of New Zealand's finest Chardonnays." The winery makes a long line of wines from the expected Sauvignon Blanc to the unexpected Syrah.

Sacred Hill's less prestigious wines sell for $10.

Wither Hills

In the 1980s, Owen Glover owned a dairy in Marlborough, but milking two hundred cows at 5:00 in the morning was too much work. So in 1994, Glover started the Wither Hills winery, with Brent Marris of Oyster Bay as the winemaker. Owen's son Ben earned a degree in winemaking, and then honed his craft working short stints at wineries in Sonoma, Margaret

River in Western Australia, Burgundy, and Puglia, Italy. When Marris left in 2007, Ben Glover took over the job as chief winemaker.

Wither Hills makes two Sauvignon Blancs, Pinot Noir, Pinot Gris, and Chardonnay. Neal Martin of *The Wine Advocate* was blown away by the 2006 Chardonnay, giving it 92 points and writing: "Given that this is not a boutique Chardonnay, I cannot recommend it highly enough."

Prices are at the $10 mark. That highly praised Chardonnay is hard to find in the United States and usually costs about $25.

Ten Portuguese Bargain Brands

Portugal today provides the best bargain wine selection in Europe. The country is still coming back from decades of political and economic isolation, and its wines are often unfamiliar even to knowledgeable wine people. That handicap, though, helps make Portugal the go-to country for inexpensive wines. You will have to learn about some new grapes, but it's worth the time. Douro, the home of Port, is the place for costly Portuguese wine. Better prices are easier to find in the Alentejo and Dão regions.

Aliança

Caves Aliança produces a broad range of wines that have good American distribution. The winery started in 1927 and is located in the Bairrada region of northern Portugal. Aliança Floral Dão wines are particularly good, as are its rosés. Along with many other wineries, Aliança also produces interesting white wines.

Prices range from $6 to $8 in most states.

Berço do Infante

Some of Portugal's best inexpensive wines come from Estremadura, a region north of Lisbon. It's one of the country's largest wine producers. Berço do Infante is a quality product, a deep red with lots of fruit and light tannins. The wine became popular in the United States after *Wine Enthusiast* labeled it "one of Europe's best values" and gave it scores in the mid 80s.

The publicity unfortunately seems to have pushed up the price, but you should still be able to find it for $8, which is a good price for a reserve wine.

Cabriz

British wine critic Jamie Goode has called Dão Sul, the parent company of Quinta de Cabriz "one of Portugal's most dynamic wine companies." It was founded by four partners, who started making wine in the Dão region but have since expanded to the Douro, Bairrada, and Estremadura regions. You might also want to check out its other label, Quinta do Gradil Cortello.

To my taste, Cabriz is the best of the lot. It makes red, white, and rosé. All of them are relatively easy to find and priced in the $6 to $10 range.

Casal Garcia

Many wineries in Portugal make Vinho Verde, a light white wine with a bit of effervescence. In Portugal they pronounce it something like *vin-yo ver-che*. But they'll still understand you when you say the name as its looks: *vino ver-de*. If you like a high-alcohol wine, this is not the drink for you. All the Vinho Verdes come in at only about 8.5 to 11 percent. To my mind that makes it a perfect wine for a summer afternoon or evening. The little bit of sparkle also adds a festive note. At its best, Vinho Verde has a nice lemony taste. At its worst, it is as tasteless as dishwater. Fortunately for consumers, most of them are quite good.

I've tried many Vinho Verdes and like Casal Garcia the best. Many Vinho Verdes start at about $5, and you're being ripped off if a store demands $10.

EA

In case anyone ever asks the official name of this wine, it is Fundaçao Eugénio de Almeida Adega de Cartuxa Branco EA. The EA stands for Eugénio de Almeida, who is from a famous Portuguese family that has now spread to Brazil. If you buy a bottle of this wine, you will see only the letters *EA* on the label. The wine comes from the hot Alentejo part of the country. The red version is made from Aragonez (Aragonês), Trincadeira, Alfrocheiro Preto, Castelão, and Moreto grapes, which is probably more than you ever wanted to know about Portuguese grapes. EA also comes in white and rosé.

EA Red is a great value at about $7.

Grão Vasco

Grão Vasco is part of Sogrape, a prominent producer of both Port and dry wines, which gives Grão Vasco good distribution. It is one of the best-selling wines in Portugal. In 1990, the winery opened the state-of-the-art Quinta dos Carvalhais Winemaking Center, which will put the company in the forefront of wine research.

At first Grão Vasco made wine just in the Dão region in both red and white, but in 2005 the company expanded the operation to include red wines from the Alentejo and Douro regions. The labels simply call them Dão red and white, Alentejo red, and Douro red. All the wines are made with the traditional Portuguese grape varieties. The Alentejo wine is slightly higher in alcohol, but the Dão has always been my favorite. I've been drinking Grão Vasco Dão for years.

Prices range from $5 to $8; magnums are also available.

Loios

João Portugal Ramos has been called the country's first superstar wine-maker. He is also one of the best. One of his favorite lines explains his philosophy: "Rarely is a good wine the result of chance." His best wine to date is the Marquês de Borba Reserva, which comes in both red and white. The reds generally get higher scores from critics. Robert M. Parker Jr. gave the 1999 red 91 points in *The Wine Advocate* and wrote: "Readers who have not yet tried some of the exciting wines emerging from Portugal need to search out this offering from João Portugal Ramos. This offering represents an excellent value." That wine costs about $40.

Ramos's midprice wine at about $15 is Vila Santa, and it gets in the high 80 points from *The Wine Advocate*. His bargain product is Loios, which comes in both a red and a white. It's from the Alentejo region, which is rich in wines and where many cork trees grow. The red has a hefty 14 percent alcohol. It gets in the mid-80 range from the *Advocate,* but it's unusual for the newsletter to even review a wine that costs $6 or $7. Mark Squires in the *Advocate* gave the 2008 an 85 and called it "bright and charming, friendly and fun."

Monte Velho

This wine is made by an Australian. So what is an Aussie winemaker doing in Portugal? His name is David Baverstock, and he's making wine at Esporão, located 120 miles south of Lisbon. He was one of the first "flying winemakers" doing consulting internationally, but decided to settle down in Portugal. The Australian brought his new-world wine talents to the Old World and is making excellent wines that sell at good prices. Baverstock likes American oak, which tells you something about his style. From my experience, Monte Velho is the most easily available brand in the United States, but sometimes Baverstock's wines are also under the names Esporão or Alandra.

Monte Velho is in the Alentejo region, and prices start at $6 and rarely go above $10. Whether the label says Monte Velho or Esporão, the prices will be similar, and they come in both red and white.

Periquita

The official name of this wine is José Maria da Fonseca Periquita, and it has nothing to do with the famous Fonseca Port. Even in the dark days of the twentieth century, when Portugal was ruled by dictators, this was considered one of its best wines and was a hit abroad. It hails from near Lisbon, which helped make it popular in the capital. The company also makes Lancers White and Rosé. Periquita comes in both red and white, but the red is easier to find. The wine is proudly unfiltered.

Periquita sells for about $8 to $10, a little high for a Portuguese wine but worth it.

Porco de Murça

Real Companhia Velha is an ancient Douro Port company that now also makes inexpensive table wines. Because it is the home of Port, Douro wines tend to be more expensive, and you may have to go right up to the $10 per bottle limit. Jerry Luper, a Napa Valley winemaking legend who for years worked at Freemark Abbey, directed production for Real Companhia Velha. He's now retired, but he trained his staff well, and the wines are holding up without the master's touch.

Real Companhia Velha's best bargain table wines are sold under two labels: Porca de Murça and Evel. Both are in the price range of about $10, and they come in red as well as white.

Ten South African Bargain Brands

South African wines are some of the oldest, with records going back to the seventeenth century. At the same time, they are some of the youngest and therefore the most interesting. The country was isolated for decades, and the world took out its contempt for South Africa's racial policies by boycotting its products and refusing to sell it winemaking equipment. The new South Africa is less than two decades old, and the young winemakers are still mastering new skills. There are promises of great things still to come.

Brampton

This wine follows my strategy of looking for outstanding wineries making a line of bargain wines under another brand name. Brampton is the low-end label of Rustenberg, one of South Africa's most historic and honored wineries. The flagship brand has wonderful Cabernet Sauvignon, Chardonnay, Roussanne, and Syrah. The next time you win the lottery, buy a bottle each of Rustenberg Five Soldiers Chardonnay, Peter Barlow Cabernet Sauvignon, and John X Merriman, a blend of Bordeaux grapes. They are among the world's best in all three categories.

Until then, you can be happy with inexpensive Brampton wines. The prices are right around $10, and the company has a broad range of the popular varieties and also some interesting offerings, such as the Unoaked Chardonnay.

Excelsior Wine Estate

Excelsior in the Beede River Valley delivers a lot of value for the money. The de Wet family has owned the property since 1870. Its best wine is the Cabernet Sauvignon, which is rich and deep in color. Excelsior also produces a Merlot and a Shiraz on the red side, and a Sauvignon Blanc, Chardonnay, and Viognier on the white. The wine has gotten consistent scores in the mid-80s from Parker and also good marks from *Wine Enthusiast*. Excelsior tends to get lost in the pack of South African wines, but it's better than most and a good value. While picking up a bottle of the Cabernet Sauvignon, don't ignore the Chardonnay. It's classic Cape in style . . . elegant, fruity, and natural.

Excelsior is in the $8 to $10 range.

Goats do Roam

Located in Paarl, next to the more famous Stellenbosch wine region, near the bottom of the African continent, Fairview is home to Charles Back, one of South Africa's most creative wine people. His winery attracts lots of tourists, in part because of his small herd of goats that help promote his Goats do Roam wines. A lover of puns, Back's other labels include Goat Door and Bored Doe. His wine bottles tell the apocryphal story of how some animals broke away from the goat tower on his property and got into the vineyard, where they ate "the best and tastiest fruit." He concludes, "Their choice serves as our inspiration for this wine."

Back makes wines at all price levels, but his best sellers are the Goats do Roam, which come in red, white, and rosé. All are Rhône-style blends and much less expensive than you would pay for the equivalent French wine. They sell in the United States at an average price of $9.

Indaba

Indaba is a Zulu word that means "a meeting of the minds." Started in 1996, just after apartheid ended, the brand was developed primarily for the U.S. market. Bruwer Raats, a famous winemaker who watches over the highly regarded Raats Family wines, has been a consultant. The wines come from the new and less-famous South African wine regions of Robertson, Wellington, and Breede River Valley.

Indaba sells generally for between $6 and $8. Its offerings include all the major international varieties plus Pinotage. Cape Classics, the distributor that handles many of South Africa's top wines, has Indaba on its list, which gives it good U.S. distribution. *Wine Enthusiast* regularly cites Indaba as one of its Best Buy selections, while *The Wine Advocate* has called the wines "truly mind-boggling values."

Ken Forrester

In 1993, Ken Forrester, who had previously worked in the hotel industry, bought a vineyard and house in need of repairs in the foothills of Helderberg Mountain in the Stellenbosch region. He concentrated his attention on Chenin Blanc, a grape that grows widely and well in the Loire Valley of France and does even better in South Africa. His top-of-the-market FMC Chenin Blanc, which sells for about $50, is one of the best examples of that wine in the world. In addition, he has a midprice line that carries just his name.

Forrester's bargain wines have the word *Petit* in big letters on the label. These are Petit Chenin, Petit Pinotage, and Petit Cabernet Sauvignon Merlot. The Chenin (Blanc) stands up against some of the Loire's best but costs much less. The Pinotage is South Africa's showpiece grape, a hybrid of France's Pinot Noir and Hermitage. The Cabernet Sauvignon Merlot is a Bordeaux blend. They all generally sell for $8 or $9.

KWV

KWV is a leftover from the era when the government's heavy hand controlled the South African wine business. The organization was known by its initials rather than its full name, Koöperatieve Wijnbouwers Vereniging van Zuid-Afrika Bpkt. In the bad old days, the KWV's nickname among winemakers was KGB. But now it is a wine cooperative that sells at good prices a wide selection of wines, ports, and brandies. It's located in the wine region of Paarl. KWV's best wines are Steen, a local name for Chenin Blanc, and Pinotage. Those are the country's best traditional wines, and there's plenty of expertise on how to make them. KWV has good distribution in the United States.

KWV wines sell for less than $4 a bottle in Texas, and prices rarely get over $10 elsewhere. It's a less known brand that offers real value, and the wines are fine.

Nederburg

Nederburg sells a good lineup of wines, many of them starting at about $6. Another of the country's old wineries, dating back to German immigrants in 1791, it is also home to the famed Nederburg Auction, South Africa's biggest wine show. Nederburg's proudest possession is the Manor House, a Cape Dutch thatched-roof structure that was completed in 1800 and is now a national monument.

Among its wines are six Chenin Blancs, five Chardonnays, and five Sauvignon Blancs plus several unexpected wines such as a white called Stein that is a blend of Chenin Blanc, Gewürztraminer, Muscadelle, and Riesling. Nederburg also has an equally good lineup of reds that includes traditional varieties such as Cabernet Sauvignon and, naturally, lots of the country's showpiece, Pinotage. The winery has developed excellent distribution in the United States for wines selling at between $7 and $10.

Spier

Dick Enthoven, a white politician who for years fought apartheid in South Africa, left the country for Britain after losing many political battles, but came back after the fall of apartheid and founded the Spier Wine Estate near Stellenbosch. It is one of the leaders of South Africa's wine tourism and also makes some value products that are widely distributed in the United States. The historic winery dates back to 1712.

Spier's Discover red, a Shiraz-Pinotage blend, sells for only about $6, the same price as its basic Spier Chenin Blanc. The wines come in a wide range of grape varieties and also include Chardonnay, Sauvignon Blanc, and Merlot costing between $6 and $8.

Two Oceans

This new winery is creating buzz for offering solid wines at good prices. *Wine Enthusiast* recommended it as a Best Buy in September 2010, and blogger Natalie MacLean called it a Good Value Pick.

The Wine Advocate gave Two Oceans scores in the 80s for both its Sauvignon Blanc and Shiraz. Reviewer David Schildknecht called the 2009 Sauvignon Blanc "an amazing value as well as a delightful 'refrigerator white' for the coming 9–12 months."

Two Oceans has all the leading wine varieties, with the prices starting at about $6 and rarely going over $10. South Africa does very well with Chenin Blanc, and that would be a good place to start your education in Two Oceans wines.

The Wolftrap

The Wolftrap is a wonderful wine made by Boekenhoutskloof. If that was the name of your winery, you'd probably also be looking for something easier to pronounce and remember on the label. Boekenhoutskloof wines hail from the Franschoek part of South Africa, which is not far from the more famous Stellenbosch. French Protestants who were run out of their country originally settled Franschoek, and the Dutch gave it that name. The French brought with them winemaking traditions that continue today.

The wine got its name from the traps pioneers laid out to capture wolves. The Wolftrap red is a blend of Syrah, Mourvèdre, and Viognier. The white has Viognier, Chenin Blanc, and Grenache Blanc. If you like wines with some strength and boldness, you'll like these. They sell in the $6 to $8 range. The winery also makes Porcupine Ridge, which comes in Syrah, Cabernet Sauvignon, and Sauvignon Blanc. Those are usually a little more expensive.

Along with a lot of other wineries in South Africa, this one opened in 1996 after the end of apartheid. Winemaker Marc Kent started out training to be an air force pilot, but soon turned to wine. British wine critic Jamie Goode is particularly high on Kent's work. He called the Porcupine Ridge Syrah "possibly the best value £6 [$9] wine." Kent is adventurous and also works with less common grapes such as Clairette and Grenache Blanc.

Ten Spanish Bargain Brands

Spanish wines have come a long way since the 1930s, when Ernest Hemingway was waxing poetic about the joys of drinking the local wine out of a bota bag. As he wrote in *For Whom the Bell Tolls*: "The wine was good, tasting faintly resinous from the wineskin, but excellent, light, and clean on his tongue. Robert Jordan drank it slowly, feeling it spread warmly through his tiredness." The quality of Spanish wines has improved dramatically in recent years. Reds are now smooth, and whites vibrant.

Borsao

In 2010, *Wine Enthusiast* named Borsao its top bargain winery. The wines come from the Aragón region of northern Spain. Its red is 75 percent Garnacha and 25 percent Tempranillo; the white is 100 percent Macabeo; and the rosé is 100 percent Garnacha. *The Wine Advocate* gave the 2004 Borsao red 89 points, calling it a "delicious, hedonistic fruit bomb offering soft tannins, medium to full body, and loads of sexy blackberry and cherry fruit as well as hints of earth and spice box. The elegance, flavor depth, and richness are amazing for this price point." Jay Miller in *The Wine Advocate* wrote of the 2009 red: "Borsao has long been known for high quality value-priced wines and the current releases are no exception." I've seen Borsao on sale for $5, and it comes in a magnum that makes it an even better deal. Borsao standard bottles are generally in the $6 to $8 range.

Bodegas Borsao, a company made up of three cooperatives, also produces other wines, with Garnacha making up some 70 percent of its production. Among its other labels are Borgia and Tres Picos. The Borgia, a Garnacha, sells for about $7 and has avid fans. Tres Picos, also a Garnacha, costs about $13 to $15 and sometimes higher. Try them all. You can't go wrong.

Campos Reales

Many Spanish wineries began as cooperatives, and Campos Reales is one of them. The cooperative Nuestra Señora del Rosario, which is in La Mancha, a region of central Spain south of Madrid, owns it. The area is famous for its bush-trained vines that grow in every direction. La Mancha has more vines than the whole of Australia. Farming is usually done without irrigation, and old vines produce low yields but great flavor intensity. The winery brags about its "fantastic quality/price ratio."

Campos Reales produces red, white, and rosé wines from 4,000 hectares (9,884 acres) of vines. The reds are the standard Garnacha and Tempranillo, but the whites are international grapes like Chardonnay. Campos Reales is one of many Spanish wineries slowly giving up on their native whites in favor of ones that sell better on the world market.

Campos Reales wines are generally in the $6 to $8 range and have good distribution.

Campo Viejo

The Campo Viejo winery sits in Rioja, just outside the city of Logroño. When I visited this new winery with its clean lines and modern style, it seemed out of place, but I soon realized that it is one of many bold architectural statements Rioja wineries young and old are making these days. Together they make Rioja exciting to visit. Campo Viejo makes eight wines: one white, one rosé, four reds, and two sparkling. It exports only three to the United States. The reds are blends of Tempranillo, Garnacha, and Mazuelo grapes. They come in the standard Crianza, Reserva, and Gran Reserva. Winemaker Elena Adell says she wants the Crianza to be defined in three words: "velvety and elegant."

Prices of Campo Viejo wines start at about $6 to $8 for the Crianza, and $8 to $10 for the Reserva, which is a good price for a Reserva. The Gran Reserva starts at $15.

El Coto de Rioja

El Coto is part of the Barón de Ley Group, whose star winery is the super-premium Barón de Ley, maker of Finca Monasterio, a knockout product that sells for $40. El Coto claims to be the biggest brand in Spain, even though it released its first wine only in 1975. It was an instant hit at home, and only two years later doubled its production. The winery is fortunate to share property with Barón de Ley.

El Coto has a white made with 100 percent Viura grapes, a rosé of 50 percent Tempranillo and 50 percent Garnacha, and the Crianza, Reserva, and Gran Reserva that are all 100 percent Tempranillo.

The wine has particularly good distribution and should be easy to find in most markets. The white, rosé, and Crianza sell for $7 to $9.

Marqués de Cáceres

In a country where wineries go back centuries, Marqués de Cáceres is a newcomer, having started in 1970 and with its initial vintage in 1975. It was the first new winery in Rioja in a half century. Founder Enrique Forner hired Bordeaux's famous Émile Peynaud to help plant vineyards and build the winery. His French compatriot Michel Rolland is today a consultant. The Forner family was originally from Spain but left during the Spanish Civil War for France, where they helped restore two of Bordeaux's most famous wineries. The label gives the impression that the winery has been around for a long time, but many Spanish bottles like to hint at a royal background.

Marqués de Cáceres is strongest in red wines, but in addition has both dry and sweet whites, and a rosé for hot days.

Prices for the Crianza, the youngest wine in age, are about $8 to $10, and the same for the rosé and whites. Aged wines are more expensive, but still a good value.

Paso a Paso

Paso a Paso means "step by step," and it's a good name for a winery that makes no claims to being upmarket. Paso a Paso offers just good wine at excellent prices. The red comes from La Mancha and is 100 percent Tempranillo. The white is from Rueda in northwestern Spain and is made from Verdejo grapes, which once were used to make Sherry. Many Spanish wineries age in less-expensive American oak barrels, but Paso a Paso uses more costly French oak.

Jay Miller in *The Wine Advocate* gave the 2009 Verdejo 87 points and wrote: "The 2009 Paso a Paso Verdejo is the first Verdejo produced from La Mancha. The advantage is that it can be grown less expensively there with the question being how it compares in quality to those produced in Rueda. The answer seems to be so far, so good." Critic Stephen Tanzer gave the 2008 red 88 points.

Prices for both wines are between $7 and $9.

Red Guitar

Red Guitar is owned by America's Constellation, which gives it good distribution in the United States. In 1927, fifty-two grape growers started it as a cooperative in Lerga, a village in Navarro province. Red Guitar comes in a red, a blend of Garnacha and Tempranillo, and also a dry rosé made with 100 percent Garnacha. The two wines are made with grapes harvested from old vines. An enthusiastic blogger at the *Cork'd* website gave it 92 points and wrote: "Great smooth taste. This is a trusty, casual wine that I would buy again and again. Very good!"

The prices for both are generally between $8 and $10.

René Barbier Mediterranean

The Barbier family has been making wine for a century in the northwestern part of Spain called the Penedès, which lies between the provinces of Barcelona and Tarragona. Nothing fancy, but it's good wine at a good price. Founder Léon Barbier, whose family owned vineyards in Avignon, France, arrived first and passed it over to René, who has led a wine revolution in that area of Spain. The winery makes a line of red, white, and rosé wines plus Reservas and even a cava. René's expensive wines have won many of the biggest awards in Europe, but he also caters to the less affluent. As he told *Wine Spectator* editor Thomas Matthews, "I don't want to make wines only for rich people."

The company makes three bargain wines called simply René Barbier Mediterranean. The red is made from Tempranillo, Garnacha, and Monastrell grapes, and Mediterranean White contains 40 percent Xarel-lo, 30 percent Macabeo, and 30 percent Parellada. The Rosé is made with 100 percent Trepat, a local grape also used for cava. Prices start in the $5 to $7 range. You won't be disappointed.

Riscal 1860

Marqués de Riscal is an old and famous winery located primarily in Rioja. Its wines from there are fine, but expensive. The red Riscal 1860, which is made with grapes from the wine region of Castilla y Léon, is a bargain at about $8. The wine is a Tempranillo, and it is aged only three to five months in American oak barrels. It is smooth and fruity. *Wine Enthusiast* called it "a lot of wine for the money."

Riscal also makes an inexpensive white that comes from the Rueda wine area. This is a blend of 85 percent Verdejo grapes and 15 percent Viura. It's a nice crisp Spanish white, and usually sells in the same price range as the Riscal 1860. Both are examples of inexpensive wines coming from a famous brand but less prestigious region.

Venta Morales

Jorge Ordoñez, the importer and relentless promoter of Spanish wines in the American market, first discovered Venta Morales. It comes from La Mancha, which is particularly dry and hot. As with many bargain wines, it doesn't see any oak, but the Tempranillo grapes in that climate do well without wood. That's the only wine so far coming out of the winery. It's unusual for *The Wine Advocate* to review wineries with so few products and selling for its price, but Jay Miller wrote that its 2008 "over-delivers in a very big way." I agree.

Venta Morales Tempranillo normally sells for about $6 to $8.

Ten Washington/Oregon Bargain Brands

The Pacific Northwest, which sometimes gets lost because all the attention goes to California, turns out some excellent wines, but they tend to be a little pricey. Oregon hit the big time when vintners discovered it was a good place to make Pinot Noir. Washington, on the other hand, is best known for Riesling, but reds have been coming on strong. Both Washington and Oregon have many boutique wineries that charge premium prices, so it can be difficult to find wines under $10. Your best bet is to stick with the big brands.

Barnard Griffin

In 1983, Rob Griffin and Deborah Barnard founded Barnard Griffin at the point where the Yakima, Columbia, and Snake rivers come together in south-central Washington. Rob had been general manager and winemaker at Hogue Cellars. His reds are out of our price range, but the winery has two nice whites that make the price cut. The White Riesling lists for $10, and the Fumé Blanc goes for $9. If you check around retail stores, though, you will find them on sale for less. The Sangiovese Rosé is a good splurge wine at $12.

Castle Rock

This creative company calls itself a West Coast winery since its products come from Washington, Oregon, and California. Founder Greg Popovich, a wine veteran, started it in 1994 with the goal of "making delicious wines at great prices." Castle Rock now has nearly forty wines in a wide variety of styles. It has Cabernet Sauvignon from Columbia Valley, Washington, as well as three from California, one from Napa Valley, another from Paso Robles, and a third from Sonoma. Castle Rock also offers Pinot Noirs from both the Willamette Valley of Oregon and Sonoma.

Castle Rock sells many wines for less than $10 and has great distribution.

The *Connoisseurs' Guide to California Wine* called its 2007 Pinot Noir from Carneros in southern Napa a "Good Value," adding, "It has more than its fair share of fruit and mass to be entirely priceworthy."

Chateau Ste. Michelle

Chateau Ste. Michelle is one of the biggest American wineries. It started in 1912, but really didn't get going until the late 1960s, when Napa's legendary André Tchelistcheff became a consultant. Given his French and Napa background, it was not surprising that he gave the wines a combined Gallic and American touch.

Chateau Ste. Michelle works both sides of the mountains that cut through Washington State. All of its vineyards are located on the east side of the Cascade Mountains, where the climate is dry and sunny. The whites are made in western Washington, near Seattle. The reds, on the other hand, are vinified at the Canoe Ridge Estate winery in eastern Washington.

The winery has a complete line of wines from sparkling to dessert, with many whites and red in between. It has dry Riesling and Gewürztraminer selling for about $9, and fine Cabernets and Merlots at about $15. The Mosel's Ernst Loosen of the Dr. Loosen winery works together with Chateau Ste. Michelle to make Eroica, which some critics consider America's finest Riesling and costs abut $16.

Columbia Crest

In 2009, a Columbia Crest Cabernet Sauvignon was *Wine Spectator's* Wine of the Year. It was the first time a Washington State wine received that award. The winery was established only in 1984, and has been growing quickly ever since. It's located in the Columbia Valley of central and eastern Washington, where red wines do particularly well. The area has a long growing season and in some spots only about eight inches of rain a year.

Columbia Crest's Two Vines label offers eleven varieties, each selling at a list price of $7.99. Those include reds, whites, and rosés. The Grand Estates line sells for $12.99 and provides a step up in quality. The H3 (Horse Heaven Hills) wines are another increase to $15, but sometimes get 90 points from critics.

Covey Run

This winery in 2003 nabbed a place on the list of *Wine Spectator*'s Global Wine Values. Its wines come from vineyards in both the Columbia and Yakima valley appellations in Washington. The conditions there are desert-like, and the harvests are long and hot. The winemaker is Kate Michaud.

Bargain hunters will be interested in the Quail series of wines, which includes six whites and two reds, all the standard international varieties. Prices for Quail wines are in the $6 to $8 range, a good bargain for Washington State. The winery also produces a Sémillion Ice Wine that runs about $25.

Hogue Cellars

Located in eastern Washington's Columbia Valley, Hogue offers a strong series of inexpensive wines sold in screw cap bottles. The winery was one of the earliest and strongest supporters of that closure. It produces well over a half million cases annually and has excellent distribution. When it started in 1982, Hogue was only the eighteenth bonded winery in the state.

Hogue has three tiers of products. The Hogue line is the least expensive, with most selling for less than $10 a bottle. Gewürztraminer, Chardonnay, and Merlot lines are all big sellers. It is perhaps best known for two Rieslings, a late harvest and a regular one. The late harvest is moderately sweet, while the other is slightly sweet. It sells Sauvignon Blanc, Chenin Blanc, Pinot Grigio, and more. On the red side, in addition to Merlot, Hogue has a Cabernet Sauvignon and one called simply Red Table Wine that is a blend of Cabernet Sauvignon, Merlot, and Syrah. It sells for about $8. There are a host of other Hogue wines at about the same price.

Kirkland Signature

Seattle-based Costco is the world's largest wine retailer. If there is a Costco near you, check it out. The chain carries both famous brands such as Dom Pérignon Champagne and also a seemingly endless number of wines with the Kirkland Signature house-brand label. It operates much like any other *négociant,* buying wine in the bulk market and then bottling it and putting its name on the bottle. Prices are often very good, with many under $10. Costco often has surprising offerings of wines from unusual locations such as Central Otago, New Zealand.

Mike Veseth, founder of *The Wine Economist* blog, has closely studied the company's wine operation. "Costco buyers suspect that it must be a good value to get on the Costco shelves and know that any particular wine might not still be there next week or next month," he writes. "Better run back and buy more, if you want it."

Costco has a website (costcowineblog.com) with reviews of currently available wines.

Pacific Rim

Pacific Rim is almost exclusively a producer of Rieslings, which range from dry to very sweet. It is best known for slightly sweet ones, which have lots of fans. Most of Pacific Rim's products fall into the category of medium dry, which really means medium sweet. It also makes a sparkling Riesling. Pacific Rim does small amounts of Chenin Blanc and Gewürztraminer, but 90 percent of production is Riesling. The staff call themselves Riesling zealots. Pacific Rim also makes Vin de Glacière, a dessert Riesling that is a good value at about $18 for a half bottle, and Framboise, a sweet wine.

Pacific Rim calls the Columbia Valley home and has a winery in West Richland, Washington. Its wines generally sell in the $8 to $10 range.

Red Diamond

Winemaker Laura Sorge got it right about her craft, when she said, "I want to make wines that everyone can enjoy. Red Diamond wines aren't meant to intimidate or mystify people."

The winery has been around only since 2003 and proves that someone can succeed quickly if it offers a good wine at a good price. It is a wholly owned subsidiary of Chateau Ste. Michelle, which probably introduced these bargain wines so it wouldn't cheapen its lead brand.

Red Diamond now makes only four varieties: Merlot, Cabernet Sauvignon, Chardonnay, and Shiraz. I suspect there will be more coming along.

Retail prices range from $6 to $8, although the suggested retail price is $10. It already has excellent distribution. Red Diamond is also a big hit in restaurants because of the price even after the normal markup.

Snoqualmie

And you thought all the names of those French wineries were difficult to pronounce? This one comes from the Snoqualmie Pass, which cuts through the Cascade Range in Washington and is a favorite destination for skiers.

Started in 1984 as a boutique, premium winery, it's been a leader in biodynamic production and in 2003 introduced the Naked line of organic wines. Originally located in the foothills of the Cascade Mountains, the winery is now in Prosser, Washington, at the eastern end of the Yakima Valley.

Wine Enthusiast gave the winery a Best Buy designation, and you can do even better if you purchase the wines in retail stores rather than at the winery. Its best deals are Riesling and Sauvignon Blanc. The Whistle Stop Red, a Cabernet Sauvignon–Merlot blend, is also a good value at about $10.

My Favorite Box Wines

The least expensive way to buy wine is in a box. That does away with costly bottles, corks, capsules, labels, and excessive shipping costs. I'm sure Château Lafite-Rothschild will never be sold in a box, but there are already some solid wines packaged that way. Boxes, though, still have to outlive their bad reputation and be judged not by the type of container but by the contents. The trend is clearly moving that way, and it's only a matter of time until boxes become a fully accepted part of the wine world.

Bandit

Bandit is not technically in a box. The wine comes in one-liter and half-liter Tetra Paks from California's Three Thieves. This was the wine being served in economy class on my most recent flight to Europe. None of the passengers complained, and the stewardess said she liked it because it was easy to open and pour. That should be a requisite for any food or drink on an airline.

Joel Gott, one of the three founders of Bandit, knows his wines, so the quality is good. But this is not the best buy among boxes. The one-liter size retails for around $8, which works out to $6 for a standard bottle. The half liter is about $6, but that would be $9 for a bottle. Convenience yes, bargain not so great.

Black Box

Black Box created the three-liter box market in the United States and remains the best at it, although the category of premium boxes has become competitive (see Chapter Five, "Thinking Outside the Bottles"). All the eight Black Box varieties are good, but my favorites are Cabernet Sauvignon and the still relatively new Malbec from Argentina. The quality has held up well despite its rapid growth. Black Box wines are always fresh and the tastes bold.

The price has gone up a little since the days when founder Ryan Sproule said he wanted a customer to be able to put down a $20 bill and get some change. Prices now are closer to $22. That works out to $5.50 for a standard bottle of good wine. Not a bad deal.

Bota Box

Bota Box is the Delicato venture into the field. The company has taken a green approach in hopes of capturing a young ecologically minded audience. If you don't mind the eco-preaching, the wine inside is good. Not surprising, since Delicato is an old hand at winemaking in California's Central Valley. Bota Box comes in eight varieties. Perhaps the best is Old Vine Zinfandel. The 2008 Shiraz won a gold medal at the California State Fair.

This is a three-liter box, and the price is usually about $20. That's the equivalent of $5 per bottle. In early 2011, Bota Box introduced a half-liter Tetra Pak for $5.

Corbett Canyon

Not satisfied to dominate the less expensive part of the box wine market with its Franzia products, The Wine Group has put others in the box. Corbett Canyon launched what it called the three-liter Premium Wine Cask that sells right alongside its bottled products. The wine had already earned a good reputation as one of the Fighting Varietals, so market acceptance came easily. To my taste, the Chardonnay and Merlot are best.

The Corbett Canyon box commonly sells for about $13.

Franzia

Franzia is the giant of box wines and by now has lots of experience. Its boxes come in nearly two dozen styles, ranging from nondescript names such as Sunset Blush and Chillable Red to Chardonnay and other varieties, and finally, house favorites. The four listed as Vintner Select are the best: Chardonnay, Merlot, Cabernet Sauvignon, and Shiraz. Wine snobs look down their noses at Franzia, but you can stick with the basic varieties for your daily wine.

Franzia is available in either five-liter or three-liter boxes, with savings greater in the bigger size. Franzia is often for sale at bargain prices that are hard to believe. I found a five-liter box once in a Southern California drug-store for $6.99. That's even less than Two Buck Chuck!

Within the wine business, Franzia has a good reputation for keeping a close eye on inventory to make sure that the boxes don't spend too much time on the shelves, recalling ones that do.

French rabbit

Anyone looking for a French-style wine outside a bottle should check out French rabbit. It came on the market at the end of 2005 and offers Pinot Noir, Chardonnay, Cabernet Sauvignon, and Merlot in Tetra packages. Burgundy's Boisset family, which has its feet planted in both old- and new-world viticulture, is behind the project. In 2003, Boisset bought DeLoach Vineyards, a Pinot Noir specialist in Sonoma County. Jean-Charles Boisset, the leader of the next generation, now lives in the United States and is married to Gina Gallo. The wines for the French rabbit line come from Languedoc-Roussillon.

Prices are $7 to $8 for a liter, $5 for a half liter, and $3 for a quarter liter.

Hardys Stamp

Hardys Stamp draws on Australia's experience in inventing the wine box to produce one of the best brands on the market. Shiraz is the top grape variety from the land down under, so it's not surprising that's the best wine for Hardys Stamp. The Chardonnay, though, is also good. In fact, the whole Hardys Stamp line is fine. I sometimes worry about damage done to the bags inside the box during the long trip from Australia, but I have yet to experience any problems.

A three-liter Hardys Stamp box usually costs about $17.

Pepperwood Grove

The Sebastiani family traces its history in California wine back to Samuele Sebastiani, who in 1904 started a winery in Sonoma. The clan has had its share of squabbles and splits along the way, and one of the successor companies is Don Sebastiani & Sons, which produces some good bargain wines. Pepperwood Grove is one of its star products, offering both bottles and a three-liter Big Green Box in four varieties: Cabernet, Chile Cabernet, Chardonnay, and Zinfandel. I'm a big fan of the Chile Cab.

Peter Vella

Peter Vella is the best of Gallo's box wines. Another is Carlo Rossi, which offers a five-liter box for wines, as well as glass jugs. Peter Vella offers Cabernet Sauvignon, Chardonnay, Merlot, and White Zinfandel, as well as what it calls its table wines: Blush, Burgundy, Chablis, Delicious Red, Sangria, and White Grenache. I suggest sticking to the varietals, which are both good quality and good value.

You should have no trouble finding Peter Vella at between $8 and $10.

Wine Cube

The Wine Cube is sold only at Target stores, and only in states where wine and food can be sold in the same store. There are two sizes: liter and a half, which consists of four Tetra Paks, and three liter, which is a standard bag-in-box. They come in the standard grape varieties plus a Sangria in both red and white. Napa's Trinchero Family Estates, which also owns Sutter Home, makes Wine Cubes, which provides a strong name and lots of experience behind the product.

The price is $9.99 for the smaller size, and $17.99 for the three liter.

My Favorite Boxes by Grape Variety

Cabernet Sauvignon	Black Box
Cabernet Sauvignon Chile	Pepperwood Grove
Chablis	Peter Vella
Chardonnay	FishEye
Pinot Noir	French rabbit
Malbec	Black Box

Merlot	Corbett Canyon
Red Zinfandel	Bota Box
Riesling	Bandit
Sauvignon Blanc	Wine Cube
Shiraz	Hardys Stamp
Sweet Red	Wine Cube Sangria
White Zinfandel	Franzia

Selected Bibliography

In addition to the books and journals listed below, I also consulted the holdings of the Regional Oral History Office and the Bancroft Library, both at the University of California–Berkeley, and conducted interviews with Leon D. Adams, Maynard Amerine, John De Luca, Ernest Gallo, Louis B. Gomberg, Louis A. Petri, and Arpaxat Setrakian.

Books

Ackerman, Diane. *A Natural History of the Senses*. New York: Vintage Books, 1990.

Amerine, Maynard A., and Edward Roessler. *Wines: Their Sensory Evaluation*. New York: W. H. Freeman, 1976.

Baggese, Carl P., and the McHenry Museum. *Modesto (Images of America)*. San Francisco: Arcadia Publishing, 2009.

Bernstein, Leonard. *The Official Guide to Wine Snobbery*. Fort Lee, N.J.: Barricade Books, 2003.

Briggs, Asa. *Haut-Brion: An Illustrious Lineage*. London: Farber and Farber, 1994.

Broadbent, Michael. *Wine Tasting*. London: Mitchell Beazley, 2009.

Cass, Bruce, and Jancis Robinson, eds. *The Oxford Companion to the Wines of North America*. Oxford: Oxford University Press, 2000.

Chelminski, Rudolph. *I'll Drink to That: Beaujolais and the French Peasant Who Made It the World's Most Popular Wine*. New York: Gotham Books, 2007.

Conaway, James. *The Far Side of Eden: New Money, Old Land, and the Battle for Napa*. Boston: Houghton Mifflin, 2002.

Elias, Sol P. *Stories of Stanislaus*. Modesto: Self-published, 1924.

Englund, Steven. *Napoleon: A Political Life*. New York: Scribner, 2004.

Forrestal, Peter. *Quaff 2010: The Best Wines in Australia under $15*. Prahran: Hardi Grant Books, 2009.

Goldstein, Robin, and Alexis Herschkowitsch. *The Wine Trials: A Fearless Critic Book*. New York: Fearless Critic Media, 2008.

———. *The Wine Trials 2010*. New York: Fearless Critic Media, 2009.

Goldstein, Robin, Alexis Herschkowitsch, and Tyce Walters. *The Wine Trials 2011*. New York: Fearless Critic Media, 2010.

Hachette. *Vins de Pays: A Buyer's Guide to the Best French Country Wines*. London, Octopus Publishing Group, 2004.

Hawkes, Ellen. *Blood and Wine: The Unauthorized Story of the Gallo Wine Empire*. New York: Simon & Schuster, 1993.

Heintz, William F. *Almond Raleigh Morrow*. Healdsburg, California: Sonoma County Wine Library, 1993.

Johnson, Hugh. *Wine*. London: Thomas Nelson and Sons, 1966.

Jones, Idwal. *Vines in the Sun: A Journey through the California Vineyards*. New York: William Morrow, 1949

Kim, W. Chan, and Renée Mauborgne. *Blue Ocean Strategy: How to Create Uncontested Market Space and Make Competition Irrelevant*. Boston: Harvard Business School Press, 2005.

Mazzeo, Tilar J. *The Widow Clicquot: The Story of a Champagne Empire and the Woman Who Ruled It*. New York: Harper Business. 2008.

McGovern, Patrick E. *Uncorking the Past: The Quest for Wine, Beer, and Other Alcoholic Beverages*. Berkeley: University of California Press, 2009.

Mountstephen, Jenny. *Filippo and the Blonde from Sciara*. Richmond, Victoria: Red Nose Pty. Ltd., 2009.

Mountstephen, Nick. *In the Blink of an Eye*. ichmond, Victoria: Red Nose Pty. Ltd., 2010.

Okrent, Daniel. *Last Call: The Rise and Fall of Prohibition*. New York: Scribner, 2010.

Peynaud, Émile. *The Taste of Wine: The Art and Science of Wine Appreciation*. San Francisco: Wine Appreciation Guild, 1987.

Peyrefitte, Alan. *Quand la Chine S'Éveillera . . . le Monde Tremblera*. Paris: Fayard, 1973.

Posert, Harvey, and Paul Franson. *Spinning the Bottle: Case Histories, Tactics and Stories of Wine Public Relations*. St. Helena, CA: HPPR Press, 2004.

Robinson, Jancis. *How to Taste: A Guide to Enjoying Wine.* New York: Simon & Schuster, 1983.

———. *Oxford Campanion to Wine.* Oxford: Oxford University Press, 2006.

Safire, William. *Safire's New Political Dictionary: The Definitive Guide to the New Language of Politics.* New York: Random House, 1993.

Shaw, Thomas George. *Wine, the Vine, and the Cellar.* London: Longman, Green, & Roberts, 1864 (second edition).

Simon, André L. *Wine and Spirits: The Connoisseur's Textbook.* London: Duckworth & Co., 1919.

Steinbeck, John. *The Grapes of Wrath.* London: Penguin Classics, 2010.

Sullivan, Charles L. *A Companion to California Wine: An Encyclopedia of Wine and Winemaking from the Mission Period to the Present.* Berkeley: University of California Press, 1998.

Sun, Jim. *The Thirty Years of China's Wine Industry 1978–2008.* Beijing: China Light Industry Publishing House, 2009.

Tiger, Lionel. *The Pursuit of Pleasure.* New Brunswick: Transaction Publishers, 2000.

Tuccille, Jerome. *Gallo Be Thy Name: The Inside Story of How One Family Rose to Dominate the U.S. Wine Market.* Beverly Hills: Phoenix Books, 2009.

Vaynerchuk, Gary. *Gary Vaynerchuk's 101 Wines: Guaranteed to Inspire, Delight, and Bring Thunder to Your World.* New York: Rodale, 2008.

———. *Crush It! Why NOW Is the Time to Cash In on Your Passion.* New York: HarperStudio, 2009.

Wallace, Benjamin. *The Billionaire's Vinegar: The Mystery of the World's Most Expensive Bottle of Wine.* New York: Crown Publishing, 2008.

Journal Articles

Ali, Héla Hadj, et al. "The Impact of Gurus: Parker Grades and *en primeur* Wine Prices." *Journal of Wine Economists,* vol. 5, no. 1.

Cao, Jing and Lynne Stokes. "The Evaluation of Wine Judge Performance Through Three Characteristics: Bias, Discrimination, and Variation." *Journal of Wine Economists,* vol 5., no. 1.

Cicchetti, Domenic V. "The Paris 1976 Wine Tastings Revisited Once More: Comparing Ratings of Consistent and Inconsistent Tasters." *Journal of Wine Economists,* vol. 1, no. 2.

————. "Assessing the Reliability of Blind Wine Tasting: Differentiating Levels of Clinical and Statistical Meaningfulness." *Journal of Wine Economists*, vol. 2, no. 2.

————. "A Proposed System for Awarding Medals at a Major U.S. Wine Competition." *Journal of Wine Economists*, vol. 4, no. 2.

Goldstein, Robin, et al. "Do More Expensive Wines Taste Better? Evidence from a Large Sample of Blind Tastings." *Journal of Wine Economists*, vol. 3, no. 1.

Hodgson, Robert T. "An Examination of Judge Reliability at a Major U.S. Wine Competition." *Journal of Wine Economists*, vol. 3, no. 2.

————. "An Analysis of the Concordance Among 13 U.S. Wine Competitions." *Journal of Wine Economists*, vol. 4, no. 1.

————. "How Expert Are 'Expert' Wine Judges?" *Journal of Wine Economists*, vol. 4, no. 2.

Quandt, Richard E. "On Wine Bullshit: Some New Software?" *Journal of Wine Economists*, vol. 2, no. 2

Reuter, Jonathan. "Does Advertising Bias Product Reviews? An Analysis of Wine Ratings." *Journal of Wine Economists*, vol 4, no. 2.

Weil, Roman L. "Debunking Critics' Wine Words: Can Amateurs Distinguish the Smell of Asphalt from the Taste of Cherries?" *Journal of Wine Economists*, vol. 2, no. 2.

Acknowledgments

The immediate inspiration for this book came from my editor, Kara Watson, who first proposed the topic. After planting the idea, she then patiently nursed it along as the concept took shape, then evolved into words, and finally ended with this printed product. For all that I'd like to thank her.

The idea of a book on bargain wines appealed to me for two important reasons. First, I had long felt that too much wine writing concentrated on expensive bottles that many people could never afford. In addition, important recent developments in wine production have not been sufficiently appreciated. The most important of those is the dramatic improvement in the quality of less-expensive wines. So I set out to write a book that would correct both of those lacunae.

The book, though, would not have come together without many people in the wine fraternity who generously gave me their time, their ideas, and their contacts. Since wine is a global business, those people came from all around the world. Often one person with one idea led to another person with a new concept.

The people who play such important roles in this book were crucial. Jon Fredrikson generously shared his unique understanding of world wine developments from having been at the epicenter of the trade for nearly half a century. Jon and his wife, Eileen, opened their home and some of their bottles as we worked our way through the ups and downs of the business. Jon explained the good times and the bad and the frequent birth of new value wines.

I was lucky to have met some of the vintage iconoclasts over the years and went back to them to talk about how their ideas evolved. Tim Hanni patiently explained his revolutionary theories about how people taste. Professor Robert T. Hodgson shared with me his studies on wine judging.

Ryan Sproule patiently explained how his Black Box wines created a whole market category. Established gatekeepers such as retailer Dean Gargaro and master sommelier Doug Frost, as well as pioneers of the new media such as Robin Goldstein of *The Wine Trials* and Jeff Siegel, the Wine Curmudgeon, helped me understand their roles. The two people who have produced the most successful new wines of the past generation, Fred Franzia and John Casella, also let me inside their worlds.

French winemakers nearly a decade ago first told me about their important work in China. When I decided to investigate that wine country of the future, I contacted Dominique Renard, an old friend in Bordeaux, and asked for the name of someone laboring in those vineyards. He immediately recommended Gérard Colin, who proved to be an excellent guide. Gérard in turn introduced me to Jim Sun, the founder of China Wine Online. They were both invaluable in helping me understand Chinese wines. I brought home two bottles of Chinese Cabernet Sauvignon and served one blind to two of my most knowledgeable wine friends. They both guessed it was a five-year-old Bordeaux First Growth! The future of Chinese wine is going to be interesting.

Jack Lynch, a lawyer and Block Island friend, provided help in tracking down crucial legal documents about important cases.

This book, though, would not have been possible without the help of the strong backup team that keeps me going. The first member is my wife, Jean Taber, who supports my work steadfastly and is the first reader of anything I write. The second is my agent, Harvey Klinger, who is always prodding me to live up to his high standards. I'm also lucky that Robyn Liverant will again be helping me promote this book, as she has done so well in the past.

Index